AF652491

OF CLOWNS AND GODS, BRAHMANS AND BABUS

Humour in South Asian Literatures

SOUTH ASIA INSTITUTE, NEW DELHI BRANCH
HEIDELBERG UNIVERSITY
SOUTH ASIAN STUDIES NO. XXXII

OF CLOWNS AND GODS, BRAHMANS AND BABUS

Humour in South Asian Literatures

Edited by
CHRISTINA OESTERHELD
CLAUS PETER ZOLLER

MANOHAR
1999

First published 1999

© Christina Oesterheld and Claus Peter Zoller, 1999

All rights reserved. No part of this publication may be reproduced or transmitted, in any form or by any means, without prior permission of the editors and the publisher.

ISBN 81-7304-260-8

Published by
Ajay Kumar Jain for
Manohar Publishers & Distributors
2/6 Ansari Road, Daryaganj
New Delhi 110002

Typeset by
A J Software Publishing Co. Pvt. Ltd.
305 Durga Chambers
1333 D.B. Gupta Road
Karol Bagh, New Delhi 110005

Printed at
Rajkamal Electric Press
B 35/9 G T Karnal Road Indl Area
Delhi 110033

Contents

Note on Transliteration

The transliteration of words and expressions written in Devanāgarī—unless stated otherwise—follows the system adopted by S.R. McGregor in the *Oxford Hindi-English Dictionary*, OUP 1993. Some deviations occur in the transliteration of the nasals and in the denotation of vowel nasality.

Bengali and Kannada are transliterated in analogy with the system used for Devanāgarī.

Oral texts are transcribed according to the system used by R.L. Turner in the *Comparative Dictionary of Indo-Aryan Languages.*

The transliteration of Tamil words follows the system adopted by the Madras University *Tamil Lexicon.*

For the transliteration of Urdu words, the following system has been used:

آ	ā	ذ	ẓ	ف	f
ا	a, i, u	ر	r	ق	q
ب	b	ڑ	ṛ	ک	k
پ	p	ز	z	گ	g
ت	t	ژ	ż	ل	l
ٹ	ṭ	س	s	م	m
ث	s	ش	ś	ن	n
ج	j	ص	s̲	و	v, ū, o, au
چ	c	ض	z̲	ہ	h
ح	h̲	ط	t̤	ء	’
خ	k̲h̲	ظ	z̤	ی	ī
د	d	ع	‘	ے	y, e, ai
ڈ	ḍ	غ	ġ		

Silent final *-h* in Arabic and Persian words is omitted. The *izāfat*-construction is transliterated *-i* irrespective of the proceeding vowel or consonant. Vowel nasality expressed by *nūn-i ġunna* is marked by a tilde.

Introduction

Humour as a competence inherent in all human beings defies description. Its variety of manifestations, in contrast, whether it be on the level of physiological reactions or psychological dispositions, whether it be in the world of social interaction or in the domain of artistic creation, the countless faces and forms of humour have always engendered curiosity. For centuries they have inspired people to attempt to pinpoint the essence of humour.[1]

Of course, the contributors to this volume are somewhat more modest in their endeavours. Their topic is humour in the written and oral literatures of South Asia, a problem which they all initially approach intuitively, from their own sense of humour. However they go beyond that. First, they display a 'receptiveness to foreign phenomena', the recognition that humour as 'performance' is culture specific and therefore not always be comprehended on the spot (cf. Attardo 1994: 213; Apte 1985: 16; Siegel 1989: 200f.). And second, several authors cast their work in various theoretical frameworks, particularly theories of humour.

Humour as a universal competence is not made tangible by the numerous terms (such as joke, quip, derision, irony, satire), concepts, and definitions that crop up in an immense number of works in which the apparently obvious is illuminated. All of its manifestations, on the other hand, its multitude of cultural constructions, are invariably a product of history. So, too, is the long history, running parallel to it, of reflection on humour. The term is known to have its origin in the medieval theory of humours (body fluids). In the usage current in the present-day humanities, however, the theory encompasses a broad chronological and geographical horizon whose high points are classical Greece, the Renaissance, and the Western modern period. This chronicle begins with Plato and Aristotle and ends with Freud and Bergson. In-between are the Romans and the Middle Ages. The latter have the status of 'dark ages' 'from the point of view of humor theory' (Attardo 1994: 33). And what lies beyond this horizon?

The theoretician of humour Attardo differentiates humour theories according to the field they belong to as well as various epistemological principles on which they are based (1994: 1). Thus he distinguishes essentialist theories, which seek the fundamental 'mechanisms' of linguistic humour; teleological theories, which attempt to identify the 'purpose' of humour, that is, why jokes, etc., are told at all; and substantialist theories, which look for recurring 'elements'. The theoreticians of ancient Greece inquired into concrete psychological contents (1994: 18-26) and therefore belong principally to the last group (as do the ancient Indian theoreticians [see below]. None the less, Plato's idea that ridicule combines delight with pain represents a prototype of modern ambivalence theories, which assume the simultaneous occurrence of two different emotional states (Keith-Spiegel 1972); and his emphasis on envy, ridiculousness, and hate can be seen as a model for modern theories of aggression. Aristotle's concept of laughing at bad imitations is seen as the origin of hostility or superiority theories, and his statement that humour is 'something bad' is often compared with modern incongruity theories (Attardo 1994: 48), which will occupy us in various ways herein.

Theories of humour can also be linked to specific academic fields. A distinction is drawn between the sociologically and psychologically oriented hostility theories, centered around concepts like superiority, malice, aggression, derision, disparagement, and so forth (see Raskin 1985: 36-8) and the psychoanalytical release theories, according to which humour releases tensions or energies or lifts prohibitions. To hostility theories, laughter is a kind of war (Raskin 1985: 21), for 'in laughing, we show teeth' (Ludovici 1932: 69). The rather teleologically oriented release theories, in contrast, recognize 'that laughter provides relief for mental, nervous and/or psychic energy and thus ensures homeostasis after a struggle, tension, strain, etc.' (Raskin 1985: 38). Of course, humour and laughter are not the same thing (Kerbrat-Orecchioni 1981).

In Europe, humour seems to have traditionally been viewed somewhat negatively. Thus, Hobbes describes 'the *passion* [my italics] of laughter' as 'nothing else but sudden glory arising from sudden conception of some eminency in ourselves, by comparison with the infirmity of others . . .' and to Hegel laughter is 'an expression of self-satisfied shrewdness' (both quotes from Raskin 1985: 36). Even Freud beats this same drum when he describes the function of humour within the domain of one of his main scientific interests: 'for they [the spheres of sexuality and obscenity] can show human beings in their dependence on bodily needs (degradation) or they can reveal the physical demands lying beneath the claim of mental love (unmasking)' (cited in Siegel 1989: 10). An entirely different viewpoint from those exploiting the inferiority-superiority opposition is that of Bachtin, who celebrates 'that happy, liberating, regenerative, that creative laughter' (1990: 30), which is characterized by 'freedom' (1990: 33).[2]

With this we have reached the theories stemming from literary criticism, which are generally received by Attardo with shades of disparaging irony. Thus he says (1994: 51) that they are 'resolutely anti-theoretical, uninterested in generalizations applicable to "humor" at large' and 'seem to adopt a "polythetic" view of comedy'. Taken together, this supposedly yields a mixture of 'psychological ideas . . . with genre theory and scattered observations'.

Beside the question of whether humour is mean or liberating (or both?), many also discern a polarity between frivolity and aesthetics. Because humour tends to ban everything unambiguous, it is not an easy thing to talk about. In the end humour invariably 'unmasks' to a certain extent the one who tells the joke, even within the scope of a book on humour. There are two strategies for controlling this ambivalent situation. One is to approach the subject by playing the eccentric, thus to discuss humour humorously, or, like Attardo, to thank his/her spouse for 'marrying me in defiance of common sense' (1994: viii), or to be purposely ambiguous: 'This is the funniest book I have ever written . . .' (Raskin 1985: xiii). The other strategy is to decidedly distance oneself and follow a path of 'humorous correctness': 'The entire language of the book is hereby declared as non-sexist in intention' (op. cit.: xvii). These and similar strategies are entirely legitimate, yet they also indirectly reveal that humour means more to us all than what is officially respected, by which I mean 'purely satirical laughter' and 'entertaining laughter' (Bachtin 1990: 30). Whereas the latter is banal, the former is pedantic. Siegel remarks (1989: 65): 'The satirist excuses his hostility aesthetically by making it funny, he may excuse it morally by insisting that it serves an ethical end, that it somehow changes society for the better, that it has a corrective function.'

As opposed to the literary and linguistic approaches (the latter to be introduced later), anthropological studies of humour are not centered around texts and verbal humour in the same way. The majority of studies are of sociological or psychological bent. For example, Apte sets forth the following programme for the investigation of humour (1985: 13-14):

> It appears that three elements need to be considered: (1) sources that act as potential stimuli; (2) the cognitive and intellectual activity responsible for the perception and evaluation of these sources leading to humor experience; and (3) behavioral responses that are expressed as smiling or laughter or both.

He is quite justified when he repeatedly emphasizes that humour is culturally determined and that it is impossible to define. It is also this that distinguishes his from the linguistic theories to be described later, since, unlike them, he does not look for fundamental mechanisms, but rather interprets humour exclusively as a 'culturally shaped individual cognitive experience' (op. cit.: 261). His relativistic position thus does not permit him to make claims as to the fundamental differences between humour experience and other experiences. In contrast, some of the linguistic theories do just that, clearly distinguishing between humorous and non-humorous uses of language. The result for Apte is that he, unlike linguistic theories, cannot formulate any universals, but instead summarizes, 'I do not believe that a global anthropological theory of humor and laughter is possible until many minitheories have been developed' (1985: 265).

The concept of incongruity, important for many linguistic theories, has a long history. In the literature it is common to refer not only to Aristotle but to Kant and Schopenhauer as well (Raskin 1985: 31; Attardo 1994: 48). Schopenhauer's finding in *The World as Will and Representation* (as cited in Siegel 1989: 32) runs thus:

> In every case, laughter results from nothing but the suddenly perceived incongruity between a concept and the real objects that had just been thought through it in some relation; and laughter itself is just the expression of this incongruity. . . . All laughter is therefore occasioned by a paradoxical, and hence unexpected subsumption, it matters not whether this is expressed in words or deeds.

The incongruity theories, which have much in common with the ambivalence theories, 'are based on the mismatch between two ideas in the broadest possible sense' (Attardo 1994: 48) and therefore appear in a variety of different disciplines and theories. As we will see, they are also known in India. Two elements are obligatory: incongruity and resolution or justification (see Attardo 1994: 143). It should be noted that the second element, resolution or justification, does not refer to the dissolution of incongruity, but rather to its 'explanation' or justification, which itself often takes the form of a further incongruity.

According to the above epistemological classification, the following linguistic theories are of essentialist bent—that is, they start with positively identifiable features that produce humour—and consequently stand in opposition to the new anti-essentialist approaches, the prominent polythetic-prototypical theories (see Ferro-Luzzi 1986), which are based on Wittgenstein's 'family resemblances'. These assume that in a class of related objects, several objects will share a certain number of features but it will never be the case that even one feature is common to all the objects. Now, this would mean, in addition to the problem of the intuitive determination of what belongs to specific classes (all types of humour would share the property of being humorous, after all), that incongruity theories must permit for there to be forms of humour without the elements incongruity and resolution. As far as I can see, no convincing evidence for this has ever been offered.[3]

The linguistic theories are entirely based on text and language. They are not to be confused with the pragmatic and context-based semiotic approaches of Koestler and Eco. To the former we can trace the so-called bisociation theory which also stresses incongruity, namely, the simultaneous association of one idea with two different sets of connotations (Koestler 1964). Attardo distinguishes three models, which actually, however, represent three phases in a uniform line of thought. All three stress the importance of the elements incongruity and resolution. The first model, which is connected with the name Greimas, is called the Isotopy-Disjunction Model (Attardo 1994: 62ff.) after Greimas' theory of isotopy. However, Greimas is only peripherally interested in humour and joke, whereby he uses joke to illustrate how it 'voluntarily showcases the linguistic processes that it uses' (cited in Attardo 1994: 69). By this he means that the joke 'consciously' creates ambiguity where in normal language use isotopies (repetitions of semes) set up an unambiguous 'totality of meaning' (ibid.). This ambiguity is caused, according to Greimas and Raskin, by a disjunctor which stops the disambiguation process in speech production (Attardo 1994: 135).

The second approach, called the Semantic Script Theory of Humour (Attardo 1994: 196), is particularly defended by Raskin (1985). Its principal difference from other linguistic theories lies in the analysis of how the elements displaying incongruity are internally structured. For Raskin, too, believes that incongruity is of central importance, as his definition of the joke demonstrates (1985: 99):

> (107) A text can be characterized as a single-joke-carrying text if both of the conditions in (108) are satisfied.
> (108) (i) The text is compatible, fully or in part, with two different scripts.
> (ii) The two scripts with which the text is compatible are opposite. . . .

The term 'script' is used by Raskin in the special sense of 'large chunk of semantic information surrounding the word or evoked by it' (1985: 81). He uses this notion to build upon the semantic component analysis especially associated with the linguist Jerrold J. Katz. A simple example would be a polysemy-based pun with homonyms: the divergent semantic components of the homonyms would be broken down under semantic component analysis.

The third model is called the General Theory of Verbal Humour (Attardo 1994: 222). It attempts to compensate for the gaps and weaknesses in the second model with the modest goal 'to account . . . for any type of humorous text' (ibid.). This expansion is meant to extend the investigation of humorous texts, which in the Semantic Script Theory was principally limited to the semantic component analysis of short texts such as jokes, puns, and bon mots, to larger text corpora and also to bring in other areas of linguistics, such as text linguistics, narratology, and pragmatics (ibid.). The intention is to introduce further analytical criteria such as 'narrative strategy' (the narrative organization of, say, a short story) and 'logical mechanism' (how incongruous components are brought together) (1994: 224-6). However, this is little more than the refinement of already recognized categories.

The state of development of humour theories in India differs from that of the West in that since Bharata's *Nāṭyaśāstra* (*NS*), relatively few new theoretical advances have been made. One of the reasons may be that the comic (Sanskrit *hāsya*) has always been investigated within the scope of aesthetic (or *rasa* 'flavour, sentiment') theories and not, as in the West, in isolation as a social, psychological, or linguistic phenomenon. The *rasa* theories are 'substantialist' in the broadest sense, since the *rasa* schools have analysed the varying conditions of the emotional atmosphere at dramatic performances. In the *NS* the claim is that the *hāsya rasa* is a copy or imitation (*anukṛti*) of the *śṛṅgāra rasa*, the 'erotic sentiment', which belongs to the group of four main *rasas* (beside *raudra* 'sentiment of wrath', *vīra* 'sentiment of heroism', and *bībhatsa* 'sentiment of disgust'): *śṛṅgārānukṛtiryā tu sa hāsya iti saṁjñitaḥ* (*NS* 6.40). This makes *hāsya rasa* one of the four *uparasas* 'secondary feelings' (beside *karuṇa* 'pathetic sentiment', *adbhuta* 'sentiment of the marvellous', and *bhayānaka* 'sentiment of terror' [Prakāś 1986: 4]). Each *rasa* or *uparasa* is related to a *sthāyibhāva* 'stable emotional mode'. The *sthāyibhāva* of *hāsya rasa* is *hasa* 'laughter', which according to Bharata, is evoked by the following *vibhāvas* 'causes': 'unseemly dress and ornaments, impudence, greed, quarrel, deformity, use of irrelevant words, fault-finding nature and the like, noticed in others' (translation by Ramaratnam (1987: 18) of unnamed sources).

Specific details and the further development of Bharata's *rasa* theory are not of concern to us here. However, it is interesting that the comic is derived from the erotic sentiment, which is utterly contrary to the views of Western psychology. Moreover, Bharata assigns the colour white to the *hāsya*, although it is an imitation of the *dark* erotic sentiment: *śyāmo bhavettu śṛṅgāraḥ sito hāsyaḥ prakīrtitaḥ* (*NS* 6.42). Parallel to this disparity, the erotic sentiment is connected with Vaishnava deities, but the sentiment of humour, to *pramatha* deities, that is, to the fantastic *Śivagaṇas*: *śṛṅgāro viṣṇudaivato hāsyaḥ pramathadaivataḥ* (*NS* 6.44). Everything that is *viparīta* 'turned round' or *vikṛta* 'deformed, disfigured' is laughable (see *NS* 6.49-50). And to Abhinavagupta centuries later, laughter occurs when a *rasa* is characterized by *anaucitya* 'inappropriate-ness' (Sharma 1941: 107).

Thus we encounter incongruity here as well. And indeed, it is associated with humour again and again. Siegel makes the following comment on the 'comic incongruity' (1989: 38) in the *Karpūramañjarī* of Rājaśekhara, in which 'the whiteness of blossoms of jasmine and *sinduvāra*' is compared with 'rice pudding and strained buffalo milk'. 'The bad simile . . . causes laughter. The simile is comic because, instead of comparing the flowers to objects higher than themselves, in an aesthetic hierarchy, they are compared to something lower.' The rhetorician Rudrata means much the same thing when he observes that the greatest poetic error is wonderfully suited to the comic sentiment (Siegel 1989: 35).

Analogical to the often skeptical attitude toward humour in Europe observed by Bachtin is the claim by Bharata that the sentiment of mirth is particularly appropriate to women and people of low birth (*NS* 6.51). But since *hāsya* has its source in the gentle erotic sentiment yet is inherent in the nature of the wild *Śivagaṇas*, it is not surprising that in India humour often appears together with erotic allusions and, as we will see, even aggressive obscenity. There is no difference between 'folk' and 'classical' form with respect to this pattern.

Even today, amusing figures of ambivalent nature are a part of many festivals in rural India. It seems as if they are there to permit the simultaneous occurrence of contradictory elements: humour, holiness, and obscenity. This is not a distinguishing aspect of 'folk culture', for Bharata says (*NS* 36.34): 'Once they had mastered the Scripture of Dramatic Arts, my sons began to ridicule everyone in the universe with farces . . . and soon they performed a satire of the Divine Sages, a play full of vulgarities' (cited in Siegel 1989: 57). Sanskrit farces, then, are supposed to make fun of Brahmans, ascetics, and holy men (*NS* 18.102). However, according to Abhinavagupta's didactic explanation, it is not the reputable ones, but only the 'evil' ones, who are targeted (Ramaratnam 1987: 44). But this is not the real point: this is not pedantic satire but rather the lively 'carnivalistic world feeling' (Bachtin 1990: 49) that temporarily dissolves class distinctions, hierarchies, and rules. Siegel shares this view: 'the genre [of farces] was always traditionally popular, and . . . a vast number were written and performed throughout the history of Indian theatre . . .' (1989: 69). Now, it is plain that the genre is directed not at evil persons but at those in high places: 'Laughter does not only not exclude the exalted—it is in fact directed most particularly at the exalted. . . . Laughter builds itself a counterworld, as it were, to stand against the official world' (Bachtin 1990: 32). The official world and counterworld are incongruous; and the clown is not only foolish but also threatening.

But that is also the very reason that 'the Sanskrit satirical farces have been largely ignored. They have been censured and dismissed as meritless' (Siegel 1989: 69). Thus it was that the Indologist Georg

Bühler collected many Sanskrit farces but did not want to publish them, because he found them too obscene (Siegel, ibid.). The results: 'The puritanical scholarship of the pioneers of Indian studies created an impression that, while there was ample truth and beauty, elegance or wisdom, in Sanskrit literature, there was little humor or satire' (Siegel, op. cit., p. 465). Should we then conclude that humour and satire are principally characteristic of folk literatures? If we think so, we will forget that folk literatures are often structured similarly to classical literatures, and that farces and satires may be directed at the 'exalted of the common people', such as village elders or shamans.

Erotically coloured humour and obscenities in the world of the holy are likewise phenomena to which the opposition between folk and classical literature does not apply (for examples from Sanskrit literature, see Siegel 1989; O'Flaherty 1980; Ramaratnam 1987, with further bibliographic references). At religious festivals in western Garhwal, such as the *Buṛi Divāli* and the *Ḍaknatsaṇ*, there are always Sanskrit-reciting pundits involved. But there is also the singing of obscene songs and the performance of farces in which the boundaries between (demonic) gods, humans, and animals like monkeys, pigs, and water buffaloes more or less disappear, in order to make an exaggerated display of the 'physical' aspect they share. There appear yogis, vigorously swinging their hips, to fight over women, and women sing sad love songs about yogis who have left them. Others sing as gopīs who tell Kṛṣṇa to put his hand into their bodices—'and look what happens then'. Here life is released from its shackles, so to speak, and everyone feels its quickened pulse. Hence the widespread conviction that these festivals bring blessings and prosperity.

Apart from a few exceptions, like the astounding experiences of the Brahman *Khaṭṭar Kakā* (presented by Lothar Lutze), such vivid life experiences are as a rule no longer familiar to the humorists of modern Indian literature. Consequently, what such Hindi authors as P.J. Srivastav, Amritlal Nagar, and Kesavchandra Varma produce is not really humour (*hāsya*) but *śiṣṭ hāsya* 'decent humour' (*Hindī Sāhitya Koś, bhāg* 1, p. 967). Amritlal Nagar has also written a serious book entitled *Ye Koṭhevāliyāṁ* 'These Prostitutes' (1969), in which he draws a realistic picture of life as a prostitute. One chapter is called *Kuṭṭanīmatam* 'Teachings of a Bawd', clearly borrowed from the amusing Sanskrit work of the same name by Damodaragupta. However, what had been the ancient Indian teachings of a bawd turns into a collection of interviews with prostitutes in Nagar's book, and what had been mockery of foolish lovers turns into mere sympathy for a group living at the edge of society. Although we may find this new perspective admirable, this example shows that in India too the 'carnivalization of literature' (Bachtin 1990: 47) appears to be past its climax; it is not the case that, as is claimed in the *Hindī*

Sāhitya Koś (*bhāg* 1, p. 967), literary humour has not yet reached maturity (*aparipakva*). It would surely be interesting to investigate to what extent the modern literatures of South Asia have lost all but pedantic satire and entertaining laughter (and to what extent this can be attributed to Western influences), or whether there is still subversive humour which turns the existing order and its norms upside-down.

The shift from mockery to sympathy indicated above is also stressed by Prakash (1986: 245) as being a characteristic of the originators of the *Nayī Kahānī* (New Short Story). Their self-image, in which *nirāś aur kuṇṭhit man*, 'despairing and frustrated mind' plays a major role, is of course not compatible with too much humour. As a result, the movement itself runs the risk of becoming the target of mockery (see, for example, Gyan Chaturvedi's *Hindī sāhitya meṁ cintāvād* ' "Worryism" in Hindi literature' [1992]). Prakash's critical remarks on the *Akavitā* 'non-poetry' movement (1986: 248), which he charges with confusing humour with 'accusation' (*ārop*) and 'aggression' (*ākramaṇ*), are also illuminating. But he himself, in turn, reveals forthwith that he is caught in the dualism of triviality and intimidation, by actually claiming that humour must be 'pure' and should serve the 'happiness of the community'. He says that the racy humour of the *Akavitā* movement is simply not humour at all and for this reason is threatened with censorship.

Thus, humour in modern Hindi literature is not directly related to folk traditions, even if these are sometimes imitated (for example, by Baccan; see Prakash 1986: 246), nor to the classical humorous literature of Sanskrit, even if, as we have seen, external/formal elements are occasionally borrowed. Nowadays humour is no longer a copy of the erotic sentiment, but is viewed as the opposite of *dukh* 'sorrow'. Hence Bharatbhusan Agraval, who penned the first Hindi limericks (*tuktak*), says, 'Since my childhood suffering has been my constant companion. And just as suffering has been my constant companion, so too has laughter.' The new context for humour, then, is the Aristotelian opposition of comedy and tragedy, which has already profoundly influenced European thought.

CLAUS PETER ZOLLER

The papers presented in this volume are revised versions of contributions to a seminar titled 'Sense of Humour in South Asian Literatures', which was held at the South Asia Institute of the University of Heidelberg during winter semester 1991-2. In his introductory paper, L. Lutze outlines his conception of the term 'sense of humour' viewing it as one of the subcategories or aspects of the comic—as is the common practice in German literature on the subject. Most of the contributors to the seminar, however, adopted the use of 'humour' as the general category subsuming all varieties of the comic, as is prevalent in English and American sources. 'Humour' in their usage covers all varieties of the comic—jokes, irony, parody, satire, caricature, and humour in the narrower sense of the word as defined by L. Lutze. Interestingly, his definition to a great extent corresponds with Lee Siegel's which is based on the classical Indian categorization. Siegel remarks that the old Indian terms for laughter at oneself and laughter at another can be understood as roughly comparable to the Western categories of humour and satire (Siegel 1987: 51). Humour for him is 'laughter in spite of disease, in acceptance of old age, in surrender to death' (Siegel 1987: 5). With regard to incongruity in humour, he writes:

> In humor the incongruity exists not within the comic figure, but between that figure and an ordered, logical, reasonable world. The improprieties of the object of humor, unlike those of the object of satire, are neither intentional nor correctable and do not, therefore, demand denunciation. (Siegel 1987: 33)

Humour of this type seems to be rare in contemporary literatures of the region—one example is presented by L. Lutze himself, and some traits of a good-natured, conciliatory humour can be found in Renu's Hindi short story *The Third Vow* discussed by K. Meisig. As might be expected, however, here as anywhere else we do not find a 'pure' form but different varieties of humour overlapping.

L. Lutze's article along with two papers on oral epics and R. Snell's exposition of Bihārīlāl's verses provide cases of humour based on 'vegetative' experiences that is, indulgence in food and sex. The seventeenth-century Braj poet Bihārīlāl is shown to handle erotic and devotional themes in a comic mode. An oral ballad and various other songs of the Indian Himalayas are examined by C.P. Zoller who demonstrates how a reversal or distortion of the facts of social order generates humour. Here, too, sexuality and virility are of central importance. They are closely connected with the heroic and the funny simultaneously. Laughter and death are equally close in the Rajasthani epic presented by A. Malik, as are the divine and the comic. The clown acts as the alter ego of the god, and gluttony is transformed into a deadly feast of poison and opium; but the god always comes to the rescue of the clown. Elements of the lively and not so prudish humour of folk/popular theatre have been used in Girish Karnad's Kannada play *Hayavadana*, discussed by H. Brückner. Here, too, the indulgence in very down-to-earth forms of humour can be credited to a transgression of the limits of strictly 'modern' literature. Many of the humorous effects in the play are produced by the author's use of different sources which undergo ironic transformations in the new context. D. Mayan's observations on the lack of deviant speechplay in contemporary Hindi literature, attributed by him to a puristic undermining of the lexico-semantic order, may also be caused—in part at least—by those very factors which are responsible for the absence or scarcity of certain types of humour in modern South Asian literatures in general.

The other papers dealing with modern literatures created under the impact of Western education and produced and received/consumed by the rapidly growing middle class, on which they also focus, display more 'serious' forms of humour—often satire and parody in line with the moralizing, didactic function ascribed to literature in the course of the Indian reform movements of the nineteenth and early twentieth centuries. This fact is amply illustrated by the contributions on Urdu poetry. The parodies on Iqbal dealt with by F.M. Malik attack the blatant gap between official ideology and proclaimed ideals in Pakistan. The source of humour and enjoyment lies not only in the revelation of the all too obvious incongruity, however, but also in the amusing fall from the pathetic heights of Iqbal's diction to the banalities of everyday life brought about by slight shifts of words. Another master of word play famous for his use of English words in Urdu verses, Akbar Allahabadi, is presented by S.R. Kidwai. Akbar's often grim and bitter humour is directed at the cultural dilemma or rather tragedy he witnessed as a result of colonial rule in India at the turn of the century. In a somewhat lighter vein, the blend of indigenous and Western cultures is mirrored in the various forms of Calcutta humour analysed by W. Radice. Here, we come across a wide spectrum from the playfulness of nonsense poetry to the comic reversal of colonial master and subject in *Ulaṭ purāṇ* and social satire in literature and cartoons. G. Eichinger Ferro-Luzzi presents a general review of humour and joking in Tamil literature.

The present volume covers a wide area from Garhwal in the north to Tamil Nadu and Karnatak in the south, from the Punjab and Rajasthan in the west to Bengal and Mithila in the east. Generally, the stress is more on the description and analysis of texts from an essentialist and/or teleological perspective than on theoretical aspects. (D. Mayan's paper is exceptional insofar as it does not examine a text but the reason for the lack of a certain type of texts.) Most contributions contain material illustrating the central importance of incongruity for the production of a humorous effect—even where the term 'incongruity' may not be used. W. Radice employs the 'bisociation theory', which explains incongruity without referring to it as such. G. Eichinger Ferro-Luzzi, however, is of the opinion that incongruity is not a necessary but only a prototypical aspect of humour. Her polythetic-prototype concept of humour is discussed briefly by L. Lutze. G. Eichinger Ferro-Luzzi, R. Snell and C.P. Zoller stress the contextuality of specific varieties of humour. Some papers focus on the linguistic devices used to create humour, while others underline functional aspects of humour or combine different perspectives. Recent publications on the theory of humour are not considered by most of the authors. This is due to the fact that their papers are the result of taking stock of South Asian texts from the perspective of humour for the first time. With the exception of Tamil jokes studied by G. Eichinger Ferro-Luzzi, all of them have one characteristic in common: they deal with material that has not been explored so far in humour research. These empirical studies of South Asian texts should therefore be viewed as a first step towards a theoretical analysis of humour in South Asia. The multi-regional character of this publication shows the potentials of comparative humour research in the literatures and verbal arts of contemporary South Asia.

CHRISTINA OESTERHELD

NOTES

1. For the sake of consistency, the editors have decided that the word *humour* be spelled in the British fashion throughout this book.
2. These and the following quotations from Bachtin have been translated from German into English by this writer.
3. See the criticism of Holenstein (1985: 169-80).

REFERENCES

Agraval, Bh. 1984 (1963). *Kāgaz ke Phūl.* Delhi: Bharatiya Gyanpith Prakashan.

Apte, M.L. 1985. *Humor and Laughter. An Anthropological Approach.* London: Cornell University Press.

Attardo, S. 1994. *Linguistic Theories of Humor.* Berlin: Mouton de Gruyter.

Bachtin, M.M. 1990. *Literatur und Karneval. Zur Romantheorie und Lachkultur.* Frankfurt: Fischer Taschenbuch Verlag.

Chaturvedi, G. 1992. 'Hindī Sāhitya meṁ Cintāvād.' In: *1991 kī śreṣṭh Hāsya Vyaṅgya Racnāeṁ.* Edited by G. Agraval. Bijnaur: Hindi Sahitya Niketan, pp. 119-23.

Eco, U. 1986. 'The Comic and the Rule.' In: *Travels in Hyperreality.* New York: Harcourt Brace.

Eichinger Ferro-Luzzi, G. 1986. 'A polythetic-prototype view of Hinduism.' In: *Hinduism Reconsidered,* edited by Günther D. Sontheimer and Hermann Kulke. New Delhi: Manohar.

Ghosh, M. 1967. *The Nāṭyaśāstra ascribed to Bharata-Muni.* Calcutta: Manisha Granthalaya.

Holenstein, E. 1985. *Sprachliche Universalien. Eine Untersuchung zur Natur des menschlichen Geistes.* Bochum: Brockmeyer.

Keith-Spiegel, P. 1972. 'Early conception of humor: varieties and issues.' In: *The*

Psychology of Humor, edited by Jeffrey H. Goldstein and Paul E. McGhee. London-New York: Academic Press.

Kerbrat-Orecchioni, C. 1981. 'Les usages comiques de l'analogie.' In: *Folia Linguistica.* 15: 1-2, pp. 163-83.

Koestler, A. 1964. *The Act of Creation.* London: Hutchinson.

Ludovici, A.M. 1932. *The Secret of Laughter.* London: Constable.

Meyer, J.J. 1903. *Dāmodaragupta's Kuṭṭanimatam (Lehren einer Kupplerin).* Ins Deutsche übertragen von Johann Jacob Meyer (Altindische Schelmenbücher II). Leipzig: Lotus-Verlag.

Nagar, A. 1969. *Ye Koṭhevāliyāṁ.* Allahabad: Lokbharati Prakashan.

O'Flaherty, W. 1980. *Women, Androgynes, and other Mythical Beasts.* Chicago, London: University of Chicago.

Parsai, H. 1994. *Inspector Matadeen on the Moon. Selected Satires by Harishankar Parsai.* Translated from the Hindi by C.M. Naim. Madras: Manas.

Ramaratnam, S. 1987. *Prahasana in Sanskrit Literature.* Mysore: Kavyalaya.

Prakash, G. 1986. *Hindī ki Hāsya Vyaṅgyamayī Kavitā kā Sāṃskṛtik Vivecan.* Meerut: Anuradha Prakashan.

Raskin, V. 1985. *Semantic Mechanisms of Humor.* Dordrecht: D. Reidel.

Sharma, H.D. 1941. 'Hāsya as a Rasa in Sanskrit Rhetoric and Literature.' In: *Annals of the Bhandarkar Oriental Research Institute,* vol. 22, pp. 103-15.

Siegel, L. 1989 (1987). *Laughing Matters. Comic Tradition in India.* Delhi: Motilal Banarsidass.

Varma, Dh. *et al.* (eds.) 1985. *Hindī Sāhitya Koś, Bhag 1 [Pāribhāṣik Śabdāvalī].* Varanasi: Gyanmandal Limited.

From Dingley Dell to Darbhanga: Some Introductory Remarks on the Meaning of '(Sense of) Humour'

LOTHAR LUTZE

In memory of Heinz Wohlfahrt (1925-60),
who first made me take humour seriously

What do we mean when we say that Mr So-and-so has a sense of humour? Our attempt to answer this question will, at least initially, be determined by our own cultural background, i.e. in the case of the present author, it will be a specifically European one. There is nothing wrong about that, even within a seminar on South Asian humour, as long as we do not claim general validity for the conclusions thus reached and remain aware of the fact that the material on which they are based is bound to be as localized, both regionally and socially, as the South Asian varieties of (sense of) humour which will be presented in the forthcoming contributions. And indeed, the present seminar, like its predecessors, is meant to involve a process of learning and, as a probable consequence, a modification of ideas with regard to its subject. The following reflections, which are of an introductory nature, should therefore be seen as an attempt to provide some points of departure for this process—for a journey of the mind, as it were, from Mr Pickwick's England to Khaṭṭar Kakā's Mithila. They are meant to question and be questioned, to challenge and be challenged, until at the final stage (but only then) the seminar may want to proceed to examine the possibility of formulating universal aspects of humour as an anthropological phenomenon.

What, then, to begin with, may '(sense of) humour' mean in the European context? Even this question cannot easily be answered, in view of the abundance of regional and social variety existing in our own culture. In order to find some common denominators which could help us to lay down at least a tentative working basis for the purposes of this seminar, a random look at one or two of the numerous handbooks of literary terminology should be of some use. *A Handbook to Literature* by W.F. Thrall and A. Hibbard, e.g. juxtaposes 'wit' and 'humor' (the latter in its American spelling), 'wit' being 'primarily intellectual', while 'humor' is presented as its kindly brother, as it 'implies a sympathetic recognition of human values and deals with the foibles and incongruities of human nature, good-naturedly exhibited'. In this context, Shakespeare's Falstaff is introduced as 'an example of a subtle interweaving of wit and humour', and it is 'the easy recognition on the part of the reader . . . that the old rascal is inwardly laughing at himself, that he sees clearly the incongruities of his situation and behavior' that is an element of 'humor'. (Thrall/Hibbard 1936: 463-6).

In a German handbook, the *Metzler Literatur Lexikon*, the article on 'Humor' initially deals with the etymology of the word, with its extension and shift of meaning from 'body liquid' (Lat. 'humor') to 'temperament', 'disposition' and, first and foremost in eighteenth-century Britain, to a peculiar way of viewing and depicting the world. In this way, humour has become an aesthetic concept designating an aspect of the comic, characterized by a 'positive valuation of the discrepancy between the actual and the non-actual' (a rather insufficient attempt to render Germ. 'Eigentliches' and 'Uneigentliches'), which 'evokes the humoristic attitude towards the world' (Germ. 'humoristische Welthaltung'): 'smiling, cheerfulness, forgivingness, a serene view of human weaknesses and earthly insufficiences, strength to endure suffering and even horror'. In literature, the humoristic effect of a piece of writing will depend either on its subject-matter or its technique of presentation or both; in its most accomplished form, humour may function as the 'principle of composition' (Germ. 'Gestaltungsprinzip') of a literary work of art, where the 'discrepancy between idea and appearance constitutes the structure of meaning' (transl. L.L.) (Schweikle 1984: 202).

2

Encouraged by such statements, we may now attempt our own summary of the characteristics of a European, or—more comprehensively—Western, concept of humour. Note that no attempt will be made to define the undefinable; at this point, we agree with Gabriella Eichinger Ferro-Luzzi, whose theorizing on humour should be of particular interest to us as it operates, most of the time, on South Asian material: her 'polythetic-prototype approach stresses the indefinability of the concept humor [*sic*!]' (Eichinger Ferro Luzzi 1990: 147).

(1) As an aspect of the comic, humour functions dialectically: it deals with the incongruities and discrepancies arising from the insufficiencies and weaknesses of human nature, as they appear in dichotomies like talking *v.* doing (cf. Hi. *kathnī-karnī*), promise *v.* fulfilment, appearance *v.* reality (cf. Germ. 'Schein'-'Sein') or, in W.H. Auden's words, in a 'contradiction in the relation of the individual or the personal to the universal or the impersonal' (Auden 1975: 371).

Most humour theorists seem to agree on this point. According to

G. Eichinger Ferro-Luzzi, however, there is a group of theories which 'captures some demonstrably existing aspect of humor but goes too far in making this aspect an essential or defining feature of humor', and incongruity, in her opinion, 'is the current favorite among' such, 'presumed defining features of humor.' Even though she finds that 'incongruity is very prevalent in jokes, including Tamil jokes' and ultimately concedes that there are 'falsifiable criteria . . ., in particular surprise and incongruity', which 'remain valid as prototypical elements', she reminds us 'that incongruity is based on subjective judgement'—a subjectivity, we presume, determined by social convention. She then proceeds to dethrone incongruity by introducing what she calls 'nonincongruous humor'. One of the ways 'of amusing through congruence', she finds, is the repetition of words:

> *Q.*: How is your sleeping pill business doing?
> *A.*: It sleeps (. . .).

But on closer inspection, her example—taken from among the more than 2000 Tamil jokes examined for her study—makes us wonder whether the comic effect here is produced not so much by the 'repetition of words'—i.e. by identity or similarity of sound, which may, of course, contribute to be amusements—as by a semantic transfer and the resulting discrepancy between the literal and the figurative meaning of 'sleep'—which would make this example one in support of incongruity rather than the opposite.

If we have dealt, at quite some length, with 'the polythetic-prototype approach to humor' in the *present* context and not, in view of the South Asian material on which it is demonstrated, at a later stage, it is because it appears not to have emerged from this material but rather to have been imposed on it. G. Eichinger Ferro-Luzzi is out 'to demonstrate the inadequacy of current theories of humor'; 'Western jokes might have served just as well', and the use of Tamil jokes 'should add a slightly exotic note to humor studies based almost exclusively on Western material' (Eichinger Ferro-Luzzi 1990: 153, 154, 157). All things considered, there remains some doubt whether this is not another case of robbing Peter to pay Paul; apart from this, the use of 'humour' in the 'polythetic-prototype approach' appears to be too unrestricted to be of much help here.

(2) Unlike satire, which is aggressive and will seek to expose its object to ridicule in order to set it right or, failing to do so, even demolish it, humour does not hurt but heals; as we have seen, it is good-natured and sympathetic and indicative of a fundamentally positive view of the world.[1] In literature, apparently as an artistic consequence of this difference in attitude, satire will as a rule produce, in E.M. Forster's well-

known terminology, two-dimensional types, whereas humour tends to create three-dimensional characters.

(3) Humour, which comprises the ability to laugh at oneself, is the expression of an inner strength, of a superiority which, as it triumphs over one's own ego, is devoid of arrogance and pride. It is this attitude which in German has quite appropriately been called 'heiteres Darüberstehen' (serene superiority)[2]: it enables a person to endure suffering and face the horrible and thus makes humour, especially in its 'black' variety, an instrument of survival.[3]

If one accepts W.H. Auden's prerequisite that the comic 'does not involve the spectator or hearer in suffering or pity, which in practice means that it must not involve the actor in real suffering' (Auden 1975: 371), humour, at a certain point, transcends the comic, i.e. as it is one of its aspects, it transcends itself.

3

'Humor ist, wenn man trotzdem lacht' (Humour means laughing nevertheless): Otto Julius Bierbaum's (1865-1910) definition of humour, with all its aphoristic nonchalance, comes to one's mind here. It links up humour with laughter, that universally human activity, on which there has been much philosophizing in the West—such as in Henri Bergson's *Le rire* (1900)—as well as in India, where the *rasa* chapter of the time-honoured *Nāṭyaśāstra* deals at length with the *hāsya-rasa* and lists a whole hierarchy of laughter varieties, from a boorish guffaw to a gentle smile (6.49-61). The *Natyaśastra* is, of course, primarily concerned with stage laughter; what is universal about *natural* laughter is, first of all, its spontaneity: it cannot be forced by the individual concerned without being perverting it. The same is true for the act of crying: in the first chapter of *Flegeljahre* (Boorish Years, 1804), its author Jean Paul—famous, at least in Germany, not only as a novelist but also for one of the wittiest contributions to the aesthetics of the comic[4]—introduces a group of would-be heirs desperately trying to force themselves to cry (the one who cries first will inherit some property)—the effect is extremely comic:

> 'Ich glaube, meine verehrtesten Herren'—sagte Flachs, betrübt aufstehend und überfließend umhersehend—'ich weine'—setzte sich darauf nieder und ließ es vergnügter laufen, er war nun auf dem Trocknen . . . ('My most respected gentlemen, I believe'—said Flachs, rising sadly and looking around with overflowing eyes—'I am crying'—then sat down and let it run more happily; he was now out of the rain. . . .). (transl. L.L.) (Paul 1976: 15)

By way of contrast, the perversion of laughter has an extremely depressing effect. In one of his most powerful poems, which is remarkable for its leitmotiv-like repetition of the imperative *hāso* (laugh!),

Raghuvir Sahay, the Hindi poet (1929-90), has made commanded, i.e. perverted? laughter the key image for the poisoning of the political atmosphere in Emergency India:

Laugh don't laugh at yourself the bitterness
Will be found out and they will kill you
Laugh in such a manner as you don't appear too happy
Or else they will ask themselves whether this person knows no shame
...
Laugh but beware of jokes
They have words
Perhaps with meanings somebody gave them a hundred years ago
You had better laugh while saying something
So that nothing makes sense any longer
...

(transl. L.L.) (Raghuvir Sahay 1975: 25-6.)

In the last collection published during his lifetime, *Kuch pate kuch ciṭṭhiyā̃* (Some Addresses, Some Letters; 1989), the poet takes up this theme again, in a poem whose original title, significantly enough, is 'Emergency':

It happened in the days of the Emergency
Somewhere in a room four officers are sitting
Cracking one joke after the other
As soon as one is through the second starts
This one has not finished when the third begins
Then the fourth, fifth, sixth and seventh
The eighth etc. etc.
Their tireless laughter deepened
The hatred in them
Of all the others
...

(transl. L.L.) (Raghuvir Sahay 1989: 57)

This is laughter at its lowest, and it has little to do with Jean Paul's 'Lachen, worin noch ein Schmerz und eine Größe ist' (laughter in which there is still some pain and some greatness) and which is born out of humour (Paul: 184).

4

One of the purposes of this contribution, especially the preceding digression into the philosophy of laughter, is to supplement and counterbalance at least to some extent, the prospective predominance of an anthropological approach to the subject, which replaces the philosopher's inquiries into the universals of humour by the exploration of culture-specific details.[5] Most of the questions to be expected can probably be summarized in one: What does a certain (group of) individual(s) laugh at, and how, in a certain situation?

When do, e.g. Westerners giggle rather than laugh? According to W.H. Auden, the

> sacred is that at which we do not laugh. Now a situation arises in which the profane intrudes upon the sacred but without annulling it. If the sacred were annulled, we should laugh outright, but the sacred is still felt to be present, so that a conflict ensues between the desire to laugh and the feeling that laughter is inappropriate. A person to whom the distinction between the sacred and the profane had no meaning could never giggle.

The poet is aware that his answer is a specifically Western one, 'because we have been brought up in a culture which makes a distinction between sacred and profane love' (Auden 1975: 389-90).

Now, in the context of the present seminar, the question to be asked will be: When, if at all, do South Asians giggle?

But as this is a seminar on humour *in literature*, our attention will be focused on what makes a work of literature produce a certain kind of laughter in a certain kind of audience or reader or, more philosophically, on the functioning of the 'humoristische Welthaltung' in literature. For the present purpose, it may suffice to say, rather summarily, that the humoristic attitude shows in an author's way of viewing and depicting the world (v.s.), which he or she may delegate, as it were, to one or several of his or her characters. And, trivial as it may sound, only persons, whether real or fictional, can *have* a sense of humour; things or situations can at most *be* comical.

5

Western literatures have produced some characters which, at least within our own culture, are generally recognized as personifications of some nationally and/or socially determined variant of humour. Shakespeare's Falstaff is one, Jaroslav Hašek's good soldier Švejk another; these two warriors are joined by Charles Dickens' utterly peaceful and unsoldierly Mr Pickwick. That two out of the three characters mentioned here are English is more than a coincidence: most of us would agree with Jean Paul that it is to this 'melancholy people' that we owe the best humorists (Paul: 184).

What about Cervantes' Don Quixote? In our opinion, his is a case by itself. If the Spaniard's novel is recognized as one of the great achievements of humoristic writing, it is due not so much to its hero but to the latter's down-to-earth companion, Sancho Panza—or rather, the combination of the two, which is vaguely reminiscent of the combinations of Kṣatriya hero and Brahman *vidūṣaka* in the classical

Sanskrit play. Don Quixote is originally a comic figure, a product of satire; whatever sense of humour Cervantes may have had at his disposal, whatever sympathy he may have felt for his ridiculously chivalresque hero have entered the novel through the character of Sancho Panza. Most probably, the two represent two sides of one personality or, according to W.H. Auden, two modes of writing one person's autobiography (Auden 1975: 96).

Like Don Quixote, Mr Pickwick is introduced by Auden as one of the characters 'who are products of the mythopoeic imagination' and as such 'instantaneously recognizable by the fact that their existence is not defined by their social and historical context; transfer them to another society or another age and their characters and behaviour will remain unchanged. . . . After Cervantes, as a writer who combines literary talent and a mythopoeic imagination, comes Dickens and, of his many mythical creations, Mr Pickwick is one of the most memorable.' This is high praise from a professional colleague: what Auden claims for the hero of *The Pickwick Papers* is what more conventionally would be called timelessness. To Auden, Mr Pickwick's progress from Dingley Dell to the Fleet is no less than the story of the Fall of Man (Auden 1975: 407-8).

And indeed, whether we are ready to accept the critic's claim or not, the Dingley Dell of the novel has touches of the Garden of Eden, not only for Mr Pickwick himself:

> 'Pleasant, pleasant country,' sighed the enthusiastic gentleman, as he opened his lattice window. 'Who could live to gaze from day to day on bricks and slates, who had once felt the influence of a scene like this?. . .' (. . .) The rich, sweet smell of the hayricks rose to his chamber window; the hundred perfumes of the little flower-garden beneath scented the air around; the deep-green meadows shone in the morning dew that glistened on every leaf as it trembled in the gentle air; and the birds sang as if every sparkling drop were a fountain of inspiration to them. (Dickens 1984: 155)

The most conspicuous feature of Mr Pickwick's character is his innocence; and it is the irreconcilability of this lovable trait with the harsh reality of nineteenth-century London that provides the breeding ground for the Dickensian variety of humour:

> Mr Pickwick, it is quite unnecessary to say, was one of the most modest and delicate-minded of mortals. The very idea of exhibiting his night-cap to a lady overpowered him, but he had tied those confounded strings in a knot, and, do what he would, he couldn't get it off. The disclosure [of his involuntary presence in a middle-aged lady's bedroom, L. L.] must be made. (Dickens 1984: 391)

As a bourgeois version of 'reiner Tor' (pure simpleton), Mr Pickwick becomes a late descendant and distant relative of Parcival, even though that medieval knight's quest for the Holy Grail is in Dickens' novel inverted to Pickwick's originally unsought-for encounter with real life in the Fleet Prison. The moment his eyes are opened to human viciousness and misery there, his innocence is lost and he ceases to be a humorous character (Auden 1975: 428).

6

Our introductory remarks on the meaning of '(sense of) humour', however summary they had to be, were meant to increase our awareness of the intricacies of dealing with this subject even within the limits and limitations of our own culture and thus to create an openness in our minds for what may be in store for us when trying to discuss humour in South Asian literature. In other words, only now that we may have some idea of what we are leaving behind in Dingley Dell are we ready to depart for Drabhanga.

This openness will be required, in the first place, for the widening of our concept of literature in the context of South Asian culture. We have to realize that the very term 'literature' reduces our thinking to writing. There is no such restriction in Skt./Hi. *vāṅmaya* and *sāhitya* or, for that matter, Russ. *slovesnost.* In short, let it be understood that in what, for want of a better word, has been called 'South Asian literature(s)', oral tradition will figure prominently.

One of the characters we shall meet at our destination is Khaṭṭar Kakā, the Maithil Brahman. As the very embodiment of a sense of humour peculiar to his region and his caste, he is, not surprisingly, extremely popular not only among Maithil Brahmans: after Vidyāpati (b. c. 1360-80), there has hardly been a regional figure of identification more generally accepted by the people of Mithila than Khaṭṭar Kakā.

His peculiar sense of humour is demonstrated in a series of episodes, or somewhat one-sided dialogues, which were first collected in book form in 1946, under the title of *Khaṭṭar kakā ke taraṃg* (Uncle Khaṭṭar's outpourings) (Jha 1967). By now, Uncle Khaṭṭar's fame has spread far beyond his own region; in a special preface to the Hindi edition of 1971 (Jha 1989), his procreator, Harimohan Jha (1908-84), made a point of introducing his hero to non-Maithils:

> Khaṭṭar Kakā is a mad creature (Hi. *mast jīv*). He drinks *ṭhanḍhāī* and rains joy and amusement (Hi. *vinod).*[6] When he is in high spirits, he makes a current of *adbhuta rasa* flow (i.e., people are wonder-struck when listening to him). He is a tough reasoner. In a debate on the *śāstras* he makes no concession to anybody. As a resident of Rāmacandrajī's in-laws' home (Mithila), he considers it his birthright to be mildly sarcastic (Hi. '*mīṭhī cuṭkiyā̃ lenā*') even with God himself. . . . Like Kabīrdās, Khaṭṭar Kakā makes the Ganga flow upstream (Hi. *ulṭī Gaṃgā bahā dete haĩ,* i.e., he talks paradoxically).

'Food is Good to Laugh': this statement, quoted by G. Eichinger Ferro-Luzzi with reference to *A Tamil Comic View of Food* (Eichinger Ferro-Luzzi 1990), applies at least as much to Maithil Brahmans, some of whom are known for using a special variety of guffaw as a mechanism for expediting their digestion, so that their stomach is prepared for another helping as quickly as possible—their own culture-specific, though pardonable, 'perversion' of laughter. There was occasion to taste their meat and fish dishes: they were most delicious—a judgement which may provide a background for the following Khaṭṭar Kakā episode, entitled *Māchak mahattva* (The importance of fish) (Jha 1967: 10-14):

On that day began a learned debate on fish. What happened was that Khaṭṭar Kakā was coming from the pond after a bath there. I asked, 'Khaṭṭar Kakā, what about eating fish?'

Khaṭṭar Kakā said, 'Certainly, certainly. What fish is it? Is there some lemon, or should I bring it from the garden?'

I said, 'I have just asked as a matter of principle.'

Khaṭṭar Kakā said, 'Then you have done grievous wrong. To ask somebody at mealtime, 'What about eating curd?'! And afterwards say you just asked as a matter of principle! Is this a good thing to say? (To insist that) when the subject of fish comes up it should be discussed as a matter of principle!'

I: A Vaishnava has come . . . (whose) principle it is that nobody should eat fish.

Kh.: Then what should one eat? The bones?

I: They are considered the uneatable parts of the fish.

Kh.: Then why all this?

I: There is life in it.

Kh.: There is life in plants as well. Let's eat earth then.

. . .

I: The Vaishnava says that Man is by nature vegetarian.

Kh.: Not at all. If Man were by nature vegetarian, he would sniff like an animal at the sight of a fish and leave it.

I: Then what's your idea?

Kh.: The idea is that we don't belong to the species of sheep and goats.

. . .

Another episode, also one of the favourites, celebrates, with the same fervor, a vegetarian delicacy: *Dahī cūṛā cīnī* (Curd, rice and sugar) (Jha 1967: 1-4). Khaṭṭar Kakā is invited to a *jayvārī bhoj*, a community feast, and reacts with pleasant anticipation:

'. . . What (all) will they feast us on?'

I: Curd, rice and sugar.

Khaṭṭar: Enough, enough, enough. In the whole creation, this is the most excellent matter. In milk (Mai. Hi. *goras,* cow juice), the most auspicious thing (is) curd—among cereals, the most splendid (is) rice (in Mai., a pun: *sabhak cūṛāmaṇi cūṛā*)—among sweets, the origin of all (is) sugar. Considering the combination of all these three, this is the *Triveṇī-saṃgam* (i.e. the confluence of the rivers Gaṃgā, Yamunā and Sarasvatī). To me, there appears to be the happiness of the three worlds in this: rice—the terrestrial world! curd—the subterranean world! sugar—the celestial world!

I saw that Khaṭṭar Kakā was in high spirits (Mai./Hi. *taraṃg mẽ*) now. Whatever he said would be amazing (Mai./Hi. *adbhut*). Therefore, though there was work to be done, I sat down to listen to him. . . .

And Khaṭṭar Kakā, the resident of Mithila, Rāmacandrajī's in-laws' home, can afford to be more than mildly sarcastic with the divine hero of the *Rāmāyaṇa* when he is invited to attend the local Rāmlīlā:

Khaṭṭar Kakā asked; 'Which *līlā* (episode) is on?'

I: Sita's *vanvās* (forest exile).

Khaṭṭar: Then I'll not go.

I: Why so, Khaṭṭar Kakā? The *maryādā puruṣottam* (most exemplary of men, i.e. Rāma) has exemplified so many ideals.

Khaṭṭar Kakā said, 'Indeed, so he has. How to inflict suffering on the weaker sex. How to throw one's faithful wife out of one's home. Have some woman's nose cut. Shoot arrows at another. Come to think of it, his gallantry begins with his making a woman cry, and it ends with the same feat.'

(Jha 1967: 13)

Maithil Brahmans find this extremely funny. They laugh at it, most heartily and unabatingly. In Khaṭṭar Kakā, they recognize themselves; when they laugh at him, they are laughing at themselves. His greed and his gluttony, his indolence and his selfishness—all his human frailties are their own, and so are the principal instruments which he uses to cover them up: his brahmanic eloquence and verbosity, the sophistry which enables him to 'make the Ganga flow upstream' and to convert the *śāstras* into a reservoir of excuses for the satisfaction of the most elementary of his needs. Like Khaṭṭar Kakā, they are on intimate terms with God, and as fellow-Maithils they share with him his birthright to make fun even of Him (—Khaṭṭar's remarks on the Most Exemplary Of Men may well be read as a contribution to the discussion on what some people would call Hindu Fundamentalism). If Maithils *like* their Khaṭṭar Kakā (to say the least), along with his sense of humour, it is because he allows them to like their own humorous selves.

And we, the recent Western arrivals in Mithila—do we also find Uncle Khaṭṭar's 'outpourings' funny? Do we feel like joining the Maithils in laughing at them? If we do, should we laugh for the same reason, or would we rather giggle? And if we don't why not? Because of the otherness of their humour? Could Mr Pickwick be in our way when trying to understand his Indian counterpart? Or could he, quite on the contrary, in his own amiable manner, be helpful to us in our attempt to appreciate the Maithil's sense of humour; and is Darbhanga, after all, only a stone's throw from Dingley Dell?

NOTES

1. Cf. Auden 1975: 388: 'Satire and comedy both make use of the comic contradiction, but their aims are different. Satire would arouse in readers the desire to act so that the contradictions disappear; comedy would persuade them to accept contradictions with good humour as facts of life against which it is useless to rebel.'
2. 'Heiteres Darüberstehen' is the title of a collection of letters written by Theodor Fontane (1819-98) to members of his family (Fontane 1937).
3. According to Karin Babbit, the American comedian, humour is one of the most elementary techniques of survival. In 1992, she organized a comedy workshop with nine HIV-positive patients; a film based on this workshop is entitled 'The Last Laugh' (*Die Zeit*, Nr. 11 (6. März) 1992: 102).
4. Jean Paul, *Vorschule der Aesthetik* (Preschool of aesthetics). Hamburg: Friedrich Perthes, 1804 (first edition). He also sees the difficulty of defining what he calls 'das Lächerliche' (the ridiculous): 'Das Lächerliche wollte von jeher nicht in die Definizionen der Philosophen gehen . . .' (The ridiculous would never fit into the definitions of philosophers, transl. L.L.) (I.VI. 24: 140).
5. Cf., e.g. Pfleiderer 1986: 338-51.
6. Besides *parihās*, Hi. *vinod*, here translated by 'amusement', appears to be semantically closest to Engl. 'humour'. Characteristically enough, the primary meaning of *vinod* is 'recreation', 'entertainment' (cf. Bahri 1960: 679).

REFERENCES

W.H. Auden. 1975. *The Dyer's Hand and other essays.* 3rd edn, London: Faber and Faber.

Hardev Bahri. 1960. *Bṛhat aṃgrejī-hindī koś/ Comprehensive English-Hindi Dictionary.* Varanasi: Jnanmandal Limited.

Ch. Dickens. 1984. *The Posthumous Papers of the Pickwick Club.* Harmondsworth: Penguin Books Ltd.

Eichinger Ferro Luzzi. G. 1990a. 'Food is Good to Laugh: A Tamil Comic View of Food.' *Food and Foodways*, vol. 4 (1): 39-52.

———. 1990b. 'Tamil jokes and the polythetic-prototype approach to humor.' *Humor*, 3-2: 147-58.

F. Fontane (Hrsg.). 1937. *Heiteres Darüberstehen.* Familienbriefe. Neue Folge. Berlin.

Ha. Jha. 1989. *Khaṭṭar Kakā.* 2nd edn, New Delhi: Rajkamal Prakashan.

———. 1967. *Khaṭṭar kākā ke taraṃg.* Patna: Bharati Bhavan.

Jean Paul. 1976. *Flegeljahre.* Werke in drei Bänden, Band III. München: Carl Hanser Verlag.

———. 1804. *Vorschule der Aesthetik.* Hamburg: Friedrich Perthes.

B. Pfleiderer. 1986. 'Anlächeln und Auslachen: Zur Funktion des Lachens im kulturellen Vergleich.' In *Lachen—Gelächter—Lächeln: Reflexionen in drei*

Spiegeln, ed. by D. Kamper und Ch. Wulf, 338-51. Frankfurt a. M.: Syndikat Autoren- und Verlagsgesellschaft.

Raghuvir Sahay. 1975. *Hãso hãso jaldī hãso.* Delhi: National Publishing House.

———. 1989. *Kuch pate kuch ciṭṭhiyā̃.* New Delhi: Rajkamal Prakashan.

G.u.I. Schweikle (Hrsg.). 1984. *Metzler Literatur Lexikon.* Stuttgart: J.B. Metzlersche Verlagsbuchhandlung.

W.F. Thrall and A. Hibbard. 1936. *A Handbook to Literature.* Garden City, New York: Doubleday, Doran & Company, Inc.

'Deviant' Speechplay and Hindi Ideology: A Nexus Suggested

DIETMAR MAYAN

Reflection on the Vernacular

In cooking petits pois, or lesser peas,
Some use receipts, and some use recipes.
In spite of opposition warm,
I choose to use the former form.
In fact, though you may think me gossipy,
I plan to settle near Lake Ossipee,
And when my settlement is complete,
To change its name to Lake Osseipt.

(Ogden Nash)

Deliberate deviation from language rules is one of the outward signs of literary modernity. In German Expressionist poetry, language rules have been violated on an unprecedented scale in a bid to symbolize the ruptures and agonies of the age; about the early poems of Johannes R. Becher, which in formal respects may be said to epitomize the movement, a contemporary critic wrote that from a grammatical point of view they presented 'the sight of a blasting' (Jacob 1927: 20). To a lesser extent, the same literary device has been used in other Western literatures also, but there mainly with the objective of achieving humorous or satirical effects. It is this latter use of the instrument that justifies a comparative—and let me say at once, subjective—look at it in the course of this seminar.

To try to define or illustrate only the most common forms of calculated deviation from grammatical, semantical or orthographical norms would take volumes, so I subsume all of it undefined under the term 'deviant' *speechplay* and hope that everyone can think of instances and of authors whose work features the device in one form or the other. To English speakers it will probably suggest the names of Edward Lear and Lewis Carroll, and in more recent times perhaps of Ogden Nash, one of whose poems I have chosen as epigraph. Germans will think of Christian Morgenstern, Joachim Ringelnatz and the Dada movement, and since the late sixties also of a genial band of writers and cartoonists connected with the satirical journals *Pardon* and *Titanic*, who set standards for a new era of linguistic humour and became known, in mocking allusion to an influential school of sociological thought, as *Neue Frankfurter Schule.* In England *Private Eye,* in the self-mocking words of its editors 'the most consistently brilliant, amusing and informed periodical in the long history of journalism', has similarly served as a forum for satire and 'deviant' speechplay, exerting a like influence on the style of other publications in the country.

But deliberate deviation from language rules is a feature not only of overtly funny literature; the device has been most effectively used by writers, with whose names it is not commonly associated—for instance by Kurt Tucholsky in devastating political commentaries, or by Elias Canetti in his collection of characters, *Der Ohrenzeuge.* It is also not confined to literature that would be relished only by intellectual readers. Ever since *Heinz Meanz Beanz,* forms of 'deviant' speechplay have been common in commercial advertising. In fact, so ubiquitous is the feature in Western languages that many people have developed a mild addiction to it.

If some such 'addict' were fluent in Hindi—a remote likelihood only, unfortunately—he or she might be disappointed in finding very little of it there. At least I have not noticed it in 25 years of exposure to modern Hindi fiction, poetry and journalistic prose. I make no claims to being an expert on Hindi literature, but I think that what I have read is extensive and varied enough to count as a respectable random sample. In the field of modern Hindi poetry, I know of no experimental movements that would cultivate the instrument in the way Expressionism and Dada did during the first decades of this century in Europe. I have also not seen specimens of genuine nonsense poetry. Short onomatopoetical poems of Raghuvir Sahay[1] come to my mind, but they achieve their mildly surrealistic quality without any violation of grammatical or semantic rules. These are rigidly adhered to also in humorous and satirical prose writings, the bulk of which are in the form of contributions to regular columns in Hindi journals and newspapers. (There are, as far as I know, no independent humorous or satirical periodicals of any standing, and only a small number of books in this line.) What is offered in these sections of the print media is, by and large, a very conventional sort of humour, with little or no linguistic joking and intellectual wordplay. Figuring prominently in these pages are anecdotes about the wit and wisdom of culture heroes, political leaders and film stars, of a kind which reminds me of the 'constructive' or 'positive' humour in yesteryear's *Readers' Digest.* The situation is not different with respect to the most popular forum for verbal humour in India, the *Hāsya Ras Kavi Sammelan.* As far as the typical setting, the style of presentation and the audiences' reactions are concerned, these poetry sessions have features in common with carnival functions in southern Germany, but apart from their not being confined to a particular season and from their lasting considerably longer—sessions of seven or eight hours are no exception—the participating *vinodī* poets cherish more literary ambitions. To expect them to indulge at least occasionally in some form of 'deviant' speechplay is therefore not entirely unreasonable, but apart from a certain amount of punning, this feature is absent in their productions also.[2]

I do not deduce a lack of humour in Hindi literature from these observations. I refer to them only in order to ask why a particular device, which is widely and imaginatively used by Western writers, is so much less or not at all, if my impression is correct, explored by modern Hindi authors. There is no obvious explanation for it. Structurally there is nothing that sets Hindi, a member of the Indo-European family of languages, apart from familiar languages here. Attempts to argue with differences in syntactical, morphological, or semantic structure would not lead far. Neither would social and attitudinal factors convincingly explain the observation. On the contrary—in view of a remarkable indigenous tradition of verbal play in classical Sanskrit literature and a keen responsiveness to Western literary fashions in modern times, it seems to be all the more puzzling.

Let me suggest a nexus, far-fetched though it may seem, between the non-use of the device and language ideology. My hypothesis is that purism has undermined the lexico-semantic order to such an extent that fundamental prerequisites of 'deviant' speechplay are no longer met. Speechplay in general, but especially the 'deviating' kind, depends on a far-reaching consensus among speakers with regard to, among other things, rules of wordbuilding, the denotative and connotative meaning of words, collocational restrictions, etc. If misapplying or overextending patterns of wordbuilding, or ignoring collocational restrictions and style levels has a calculable effect on competent speakers, it is because of the existence of subtle, but generally accepted and recognized rules. They guarantee that, though wrong in a grammatical or semantical sense, the message of intentionally deviant language is nevertheless perfectly well understood, and its effect on competent speakers almost as predictable as that of correctly formed speech. Where, on the other hand, lexical standards are yet to become established, or where they are not clearly recognizable from among a multiplicity of choices and usages, the reaction to 'deviant' speechplay is far less predictable; in such a situation the listeners to or readers of an intentionally deviant word or phrase might not even notice anything deviant about it.

The arguement adumbrated

Here I can only give a sketchy account of how, as I see it, efforts to resanskritize Hindi have destabilized its lexico-semantic order. Central to the argument is my understanding of resanskritization as puristically motivated endeavour. 'Purism' is not a very clear term to designate what I mean, but there is also no better one at hand. *Webster's Ninth New Collegiate Dictionary* (1988) defines it as 'an example of rigid adherence to or insistence on nicety esp. in the use of words', placing the underlying attitude second in the order of senses. Only the definition of the subsequent entry 'purist' introduces the aspect which I have in mind: 'one preoccupied with the purity of a language *and its protection from the use of foreign or altered forms*'. Thinking here primarily of the attitude and the resultant practice, I use the word for a systematic effort to substitute established lexical elements of a language for other than functional reasons, notably for the reason of their not having a particular origin. By this definition, I think, one is dealing with an exceptionally clear case of purism, and one on a very large—maybe unparalleled—scale at that.

Amazingly, it is not generally recognized as such. So far, neither the Shuddh Hindi-ideology nor its practical consequences have received the attention which they deserve. Foreign scholars have also shied away from the subject, sensing perhaps that it is still an emotional issue and likely to land them in tedious discussions. (They may also not be familiar enough with socio-linguistic theory and with linguistic realities in modern India, or as original Sanskritists be predisposed to agree with the arguments of Shuddh Hindi-ideologists.) It is, therefore, important to stress that the all-out resanskritization of Hindi is *not* a requirement of consistent language planning, however plausible the stated objectives—such as a richer choice of derivational patterns, greater uniformity in the matter of technical terms and ultimately a technical and scientific vocabulary common to all modern Indian languages—may look at a first glance. Nor is the underlying premise, i.e. that of Sanskrit being still present in the heads of modern Indians as a dormant language, waiting to be reactivated, a realistic assumption. It is not possible here to discuss the logic of resanskritization from a language planning point of view, but it is clear that the movement is inspired largely by extralinguistic motives, one of them being chauvinism. (For once I use the word; there is no way around calling a spade.) What occupies the minds of many Shuddh Hindi-ideologues more than the provision of a uniform 'higher vocabulary' is the purging of the language of supposedly un-Indian (un-Hindu) elements. It is, although much older, the spirit of Ayodhya set upon obliterating lexical 'symbols of humiliation'—with scant regard for considerations of practicality.

Not only 'Urdu words', i.e. words of mainly Persian and Arabic origin, are sought to be replaced. There is a strong intralingual strand of purism as well, which prompts enthusiasts to write *X se pūrv* instead of *X se pahle*, and *vṛkṣ* instead of *peṛ*. Countless *tadbhavas*, as elements of compounds but also as independent words, are sought to be restored to their *tatsama*-forms in what amounts to a reversal of centuries of sound change: *ghar* > *gṛha*; *gānv* > *grām*; *byāh* > *vivāha*; *bikrī* > *vikraya*; *ūncā* > *ucca*; *nangā* > *nagna*, etc. In many cases both a Perso-Arabic word and a corresponding *tadbhava*-item are rejected in favour of a Sanskrit form; *baras* 'year', for instance, is hardly more acceptable to Shuddh Hindi-ideologists than Persian *sāl*; both are commonly replaced by *varṣ*.

How large a percentage of the vocabulary is thus affected is difficult to say in the absence of reliable lexicostatistical data, but it would be no exaggeration to say that there are now puristic substitutes for between half to three quarters of the basic vocabulary,[3] adding up to several thousand lexical items. The situation is confusing not only for sheer numbers but also because one is not dealing with simple one-to-one relations. Many of the words of which purists want to rid the language have more than one substitute. For instance *kośiś* ('effort', 'attempt') may be replaced by *āyās, prayās, yatna, prayatna* and *ceṣṭā*; in place of *garīb* ('poor') one commonly meets with *nirdhan* and *daridra*; for *maśhūr* ('famous') there are at least *prasiddh* and *vikhyāt*; for the conjunction *aur* ('and')—an indigenous word (Skt. *apara*) but one that looks or sounds Arabic to many—there is the choice of *evam*, *va* and *tathā*, and so on. This asymmetry is the result of equating the lexicon of modern Hindi unreservedly with that of its 'mother', which encourages those who can use a dictionary to draw liberally on the cornucopia ('*asim śabdarāśi*') of classical Sanskrit vocabulary. In absolute numbers there are now considerably more substitutes than substituends.

In spite (or because) of the fact that there is no dearth of puristic substitutes and that a century has passed since efforts to promote them were taken up in earnest in the 1890s, the older, naturally evolved words have nowhere been supplanted. Very little, in fact none of the vocabulary deemed un-Indian or in need of refinement has become obsolete or shows signs of gradually getting out of use. Its continued presence in the spoken language is not surprising in view of widespread illiteracy, but it is hardly less alive in written Hindi. A look at any commercially viable newspaper or journal will show the resilience of what to purists is Urdu and even High Urdu vocabulary.

Linguistic theory does not envisage a situation like this. Theory demands that of two words with identical function one will give way eventually to the other, or that dissimilation/specialization gives both words a right to exist. Neither appears to be happening. The introduction of puristic substitutes has not, generally speaking, led to a revision of conceptual boundaries within lexical fields.[4] When we look at written Hindi as it presents itself in the overwhelming majority of publications—in German one would call it *die real existierende Schriftsprache*—we find most of the older words and their puristic substitutes coexisting without stateable differences in meaning and function. Often they are used alternately in the same text by the same author. If there is a difference, it is chiefly a difference of acceptance among the community of Hindi speakers at large; so far, puristic substitutes are known only to a literate and, in addition to that, ideologically motivated minority.

There is thus, on the level of the written language, an overabundance of lexical items. It is commonly hailed as an asset, a reservoir to draw upon for subtle semantic distinctions, but without these actually being made, it is only a dysfunctional surplus. One disadvantage of this condition—not the most serious though—is that it does not allow speechplay of the 'deviating' kind. A situation in which the choice of words is to a large extent arbitrary is the exact opposite of a situation conducive to it.

The tendency of foreign observers to look at modern Hindi with the model of their own languages in mind makes them ignore the pathological aspect and come up with Europocentric explanations for a highly unusual lexical situation. A widespread misconception with regard to the sphere of utilization of the two categories of vocabulary can thus in part be attributed to a wish to make sense of it. But while it is correct to speak of a marked dichotomy between spoken and written Hindi, it is certainly a mistake to equate, as it is often done, these two systems of linguistic expression with the two categories of vocabulary. That puristic substitutes hardly ever occur in uncontrived conversation does not mean that non-puristic and 'Urdu' vocabulary, conversely, has no place in the written language. It is, as everyone can see, very much present there. Only a small number of rather extreme works manage to avoid it.

Average texts in Hindi, literary ones as much as others, are more like a *khicṛī* when analysed from the point of view of lexical homogeneity. Given the general disregard for consistency, I do not see in which sense one can conceive of normal—by which I here mean non-puristic—words and their puristic substitutes as *style synonyms*. When speaking of the Hindi-Urdu style dichotomy, one had better not speak of styles but of standards, as it is altogether different standards (ultimately languages), not different styles of a single standard, which are sought to be created by contrived lexical homogeneity. Under these circumstances it is also not logical to ascribe a *stylistic meaning* to isolated lexical items, if by this one understands that a word spontaneously suggests a particular style-level. It seems impossible to rank isolated normal words and their puristic substitutes hierarchically on a scale and label them 'informal', 'neutral', 'formal', 'elevated', 'poetical', etc., in the way in which this can be done with much of the vocabulary of European languages. The difference between, e.g. *ghar* and *āvās*, or between, *kharīdnā* and *kray karnā*, is therefore not really comparable to that between 'home' and 'residence' or 'buy' and 'purchase'. In the context of the present argument this means that Hindi writers can hardly hope to achieve *subtly* humorous or satiric effects through contrived stylistic incongruity; efforts in this direction are likely to go unnoticed. What is one of the most useful and common forms of intentional deviancy elsewhere would turn out to be a rather ineffectual means in modern Hindi.

A closely related misconception, which also in a way serves to explain the unusual lexical situation, exists with regard to *connotational meaning*. It is often believed that normal words and puristic substitutes have specialized somewhere in the area of non-conceptual meaning, and that it is possible to differentiate between them, as also between competing purisms, in much the same way as between English synonyms. But such connotational differences are more readily imagined than actually proved to exist in the linguistic subconscious of Hindi speakers.[5] They may perhaps be observed in the idiolect of a particular author, but it should be difficult to prove, through informant testing or through adducing textual evidence, that they are recognized by a critical percentage of the speech community so that it would be justified to regard them as features of the (synchronic) system. My personal impression is that at the present stage one cannot even point with certainty to instances of connotational differences in the process of becoming established. In practice it is often extrasemantic factors that determine the choice, e.g. the wish to avoid repetition, considerations of euphony, or typographical constraints. (Thus shortage of space often dictates the use of the non-puristic alternative in headlines, as it is usually the shorter one.)

There is of course a marked difference in *emotive meaning* between non-puristic and puristic vocabulary. But especially with the latter, this is not so much a feature of the individual lexical item, distinct and different with each, as rather the uniform property of the whole category. It is thus more or less the same for all puristic substitutes; it might roughly be translated as 'vocabulary item to be preferred by conscious Hindus to a corresponding vocabulary item X which is Muslim language', with the implication that the 'Muslim word' has been forced into the language by invaders and ought to be thrown out.[6] In that puristic substitutes thus carry an inbuilt affective bias and generally serve to underline the separate sense of political and cultural identity on the Hindu side, they are symbols of communal antagonism. But, though doubtlessly real, this emotive meaning is hardly more exploitable for 'deviant' speechplay than are the largely imaginary (or merely idiolectal) differences of connotational meaning. It is restricted, together with the use itself of puristic substitutes, to the section of the speech community that approves of the underlying ideology. It is by no means valid for all speakers of the language, in fact not even for all who consider themselves Hindus. For Muslim speakers of Hindi, it is obviously not acceptable; to them it might even be positively offensive. When they make use of Shuddh Hindi vocabulary, as they increasingly must nowadays for want of alternatives, they do not choose it in conscious opposition to 'Urdu words', and do not attach this emotive meaning to it.

Considering the dimensions of the puristic endeavour, the disparate multiplicity of proposed changes and the almost complete lack of authoritative guidance—I think this alone is enough to confound and disorientate literate speakers. But the situation is further complicated by a large number of neologisms which fill lacunae in the lexical system that have come to be felt with the advent of modern institutions and industrial civilization. I am not speaking of technical terms, but of words occurring in non-specialist everyday communication. Many have come about as rather mechanical loan translations, and not all are really needed.[7] What distinguishes these neologisms from the category of puristic substitutes is mainly the difference in motivation. Although they are not meant to supplant existing vocabulary, they may also be said to be puristic for the reason that only very rarely an attempt is made to coin needed vocabulary with the help of ordinary base forms or through extending the meaning of existing words, as, e.g. in *panḍubbī* 'submarine (boat)' and *baiṭhak* 'session (of parliament etc.)'. Generally, without exploring these possibilities, direct recourse is taken to investing Sanskrit words with English meanings: *sāhitya* 'literature'; *samskṛti* 'culture'; *sampādak* 'editor'; *vikās* 'development'; *udyog* 'industry', etc.

It need hardly be said that such neologisms, especially the more abstract and semantically complex ones, can be properly understood and used only by speakers who are familiar with the models. As practically all who communicate meaningfully through the medium of written Hindi know English (certainly all professional journalists, writers, etc. do), one might think that at least this minority feels no difficulty. But even this would seem to be too optimistic. The problem is that neologisms of this kind rarely respond to only one single model. So accustomed have all become to thinking and articulating in the mould of English phrases, and to decoding Hindi texts with reference to them, that an extremely variable use can now be made of many or most of these neologisms.[8] In consequence they are difficult to handle even for bilingual speakers. A major source of confusion is the common failure to distinguish between the direct and figuratively extended senses of the models.[9] Doubtful usages abound and are easy to spot even for outside observers like me, but I think that pointing out such cases and branding them as mistakes is better left to native speakers, up to whom it is to sanction or reject usages, and whose judgement is perhaps also for other reasons more readily acceptable.[10] Here I only wish to remark that the conceptual variability of this category of neologisms is something different from normal polysemy, that it results from their assuming different meanings after different English models in different syntactical contexts, and that this characteristic precludes their being used in any 'deviating' kind of speechplay.

All in all, I think, there has been too much lexical innovation within too short a period of time, as a result of which the lexicon of written Hindi may now be said to be unsettled—in the double sense that something which had a recognizable structure previously has lost it, and that something new has not become settled yet.

The vast majority of those who, in one form or the other, make written use of the language adopt an imitative approach to the problem, using ready-made phrases and memorizing whatever is needed to reproduce it on occasion. Creative writers are more at ease with the idiom, no doubt, but in a less evident manner they are also affected by the high rate of flux and the lack of authoritative guidelines.[11] It is illusory to think that their case was altogether different from that of ordinary literates. Hindi scholars like to assume an undefined category of 'educated speech' and, as its producers, a section of native speakers in full command of the sanskritized style, but I am afraid this is another apologetic notion. That it is a fiction becomes apparent as soon as one tries to identify individuals or classes of professionals with this assumed body of competents. Should, for instance, writers and journalists be counted among them, but schoolteachers and clerical staff not? Which educational qualifications should mark the criterial line? One would immediately face the difficulty of accounting for literally *lakhs* of educated or, as is now fashionable to say, 'highly educated' speakers, even holders of degrees in the subject, whose command of the written style is palpably less than complete. What one has to accept—as a matter of logic, I think—is that no individual or group can have a full command of a standard which has yet to emerge and be codified in detail. Not even an elite of creative writers. With respect to the innovating areas of the language they too can be *competent speakers*, in the technical sense of this term, only to a degree.

If that were not the case, they would probably be more actively engaged in a crusade against stereotyped language and clichés. They also would—this is my argument, at least—be experimenting with linguistic structure and discover this both as a theme and as a source of poetical inspiration. They would at least occasionally use its openness as a door to leave well-worn grooves of expression and break the linguistic expectation of readers. In short, they would play with their tool, and in the process create also for Hindi the type of abstract, language-inspired poetry which does not so much strive to make sense in its relation to the real world, but is meaningful mainly with reference to itself. (This must not necessarily be humorously intended or nonsense poetry.)

Social constraints

Of course social and attitudinal factors may also play a role, though I think they are of less consequence here. A restraining influence could be the reverential, with some people overreverential, attitude towards Sanskrit[12] which extends to Hindi when the *baṛī beṭī* assumes the form of Neo- or Pseudosanskrit. Authors may also feel shy to take what could easily be seen as liberties with a language for whose national status many people have fought and made personal sacrifices, and which has been credited with the very highest qualities, thus making a kind of fetish of it. Still I am convinced that if Hindi writers were more sure of their own and their readers' understanding of the precise semantic and grammatical properties of lexical innovations and their exact place in the overall lexical system, they would lose whatever inhibitions they may have and start playing also with the *rāṣṭrabhāṣā*. After all, it is only in their dealing with this language that a relaxed and playful attitude is rare. Otherwise it exists and shows where writers feel more at ease with linguistic rules. Much of the phenomenon of code-mixing, so uninhibitedly and ingeniously indulged in Indian English journalism, can only be explained, I think, by a natural fondness for playing with words and language.

In support of my argument let me briefly add two observations which I think are symptomatic of an unsettled state of lexical affairs: (1) Faulty use of the *rāṣṭrabhāṣā*, by people who are expected to have a full grasp of it, is rarely an object of ridicule; mistakes are also not regarded as a potential source of amusement. (2) There are, to my knowledge, no literary parodies.

Since Ramchandra Varma first hinted at the massive occurrence of mistakes, instances of faulty use of the language have not only increased in number and variety, they have also become more visible and audible with the growth of the mass media. But no-one seems to take notice of them, whereas the public use of English is a concern of many. Mistakes are certainly not yet regarded as a source of amusement. While in our part of the world slips of tongue, 'spoonerisms', meaningful printing mistakes, awkwardly phrased advertisements and newsreports, unwitting nonsense in official correspondences, errors from composition books of schoolchildren, etc., are all eagerly registered and reproduced for the entertainment of readers in humorous collections or in the very periodicals from whose pages the mistakes have been culled, such sources of unintentional humour lie untapped as far as the public use of Hindi is concerned. One would expect that at least howlers from the mouths of politicians were ridiculed as part of the fun which in other respects is made of the utterings and posturings of public figures, but this is very rarely done. Except for the occasional mention of leaders stumbling over the articulation of oaths of office in Hindi, hardly any notice is taken of their performance in the *rāṣṭrabhāṣā*. The general attitude seems to be that, since the correct use of the language is beyond the capacity of everyone anyhow, lampooning instances of a common inability would not be very funny.

I don't think that a culture-related reserve with regard to open and ad-personam critique comes in as a factor here. This is no longer a problem today,[13] and even if it were, criticism of faulty usages and undesirable trends in the development of the language could always be expressed through fictional characters. But in my reading I have also not encountered figures like Fielding's Mrs Slip-slop or Sheridan's Mrs Malaprop—bywords in English for the pretentiously incompetent use of 'superior' vocabulary. The linguistic joking which I have witnessed on the stage and the screen was at the expense either of wholly illiterates, or of dialect speakers, or of Bengalis and 'Madrasis' talking Hindi. The 'funny accent' was usually enough to provoke hilarity; only in exceptional cases was chance homonymity or a conflict with grammatical norms of the standard exploited for a comical effect.[14]

With regard to parodies, I mean the lack of those that are intended as comment on the style of an author, as an artistic form of literary criticism. Parodies of this kind 'shoot for a writer with the weapon of his own style', as Robert Neumann, a leading exponent and theorist of the art in German literature, has defined the genre which began to flourish only after the turn of this century.[15] What was understood by parody earlier was generally a less subtle affair, mere imitations or changes in the function of stock rhetorical forms that were put to grotesque or untypical uses.

Parodies in Hindi are still exclusively parodies of the older type,[16] although there is ample occasion for literary ones. A good many works of twentieth-century Hindi literature, by the pen of some of the most respected authors, appear to an amateur like me to be both clichéd and vacuous contentwise and stylistically mannered to such a degree that I cannot help thinking that, if comparable works by authors of comparable standing were to appear in a Western literary milieu, they would attract the attention of parodists. But as far as I know, no Hindi author has ever been subjected to parody. I wonder even whether the idea as such—of parodies as an intelligent and legitimate, in the present situation even necessary form of critique—has occurred to independently-minded writers, and whether sketches in this line would find appreciative readers. The general tendency is more to 'honour' authors than to question their literary credentials. The fact that some of those canonized by the Hindi world have few or no natural readers perpetuates their status as icons; authors who are not read, except by students who cram a few of their lines together with an interpretation, can only be idolized or forgotten. There is the additional problem that not a few stalwarts of Hindi literature have gained their position as much in recognition of their role in politics as on account of literary merits. If their creative output was subjected to a parodistic treatment, it would probably be seen as an act of disloyalty towards the cause and meet with strong disapproval from the entire community.

In book reviews, a critical evaluation of style is rarely attempted, although *ālocanā*, i.e. literary criticism, has traditionally been the backbone of Hindi Studies in the region itself. Literary works are often discussed at length with regard to their theme and message in the social context, but they are seldom criticized on properly stylistic grounds. Accordingly not many words are available for making unfavourable judgements. There are practically no translation equivalents for the wealth of uncomplimentary adjectives available in English, each expressive of a particular demand on good style. If one wanted to describe a text as 'verbose' or 'woolly', a phrase as 'trite' or 'hackneyed', or a style as 'precious', 'stilted', 'highflown', 'pompous', etc., one could only try to do this in a roundabout way. One of the few words is *kliṣṭ*—a clearly negative, but rather unspecific comment.[17]

Conclusion

I have argued on the assumption that the incidence of 'deviant' speechplay says something about the degree of standardization of a language, in particular the consensus among its speakers with regard to lexico-semantic norms. The ubiquity and variety of 'deviant' speechplay in the literatures of modern European languages would thus be indicative of a high degree of standardization, a final stage perhaps, beyond which standardization will not go, as languages keep changing. This does not, of course, allow us to argue in reverse and to conclude from the non-occurrence of 'deviant' speechplay that a language will not be standardized. But the conspicuous absence of the feature in the works of Hindi authors, who in other respects show that they are well aware of international trends in literature, may point to an uncompleted process of standardization or a setback owing to interference with the naturally evolved system of the kind I have tried to describe here. To me it suggests that written Hindi has still to adjust to the massive dose of innovation administered to it largely on ideological grounds, and that it may take sometime before a restructured and wider system of lexico-semantic norms has become sufficiently stabilized for writers to feel free to play with it.

NOTES

1. See, e.g. *Agar kahīn main totā hotā* or *Prabhu kī dayā*, in: *Sīṛhiyon par dhūp men*, an early collection of poems, short stories, and essays (Bharatiya Jnanpith, Kasi 1960).
2. Readers who have no personal experience of these functions and find it difficult to follow cassette recordings available in the market, can get an impression from the printed works of Ḳaka Hathrasi (Prabhulal Garg), who is eulogized in commentaries as *hāsya ṛṣi* and *hindi ke ādhunik hāsya-vyangya-sāhitya men sarvocca sthān kā adhikārī*. See *Kākā Hāthrasī Hāsya Racanāvalī*.
3. This estimate agrees with a remark which Raghupatisahay 'Firaq Gorakhpuri' is reported to have made during the Hindi-Urdu Symposium on the occasion of Sir Teg Bahadur Sapru's death anniversary in Delhi in 1977, that if a taperecorder were running for a whole day in a typical household it would be found that *ham log apnī bolcāl men pachattar phīsadī urdū śabdon kā istemāl karte hain*. The ideological factor stands in the way of a satisfactory definition of 'basic vocabulary'. Here it loosely means vocabulary used by urban speakers in everyday communication, disregarding slang and regional and social dialects.
4. The opportunity to stabilize conceptual differences is often not seized or recognized. There would, e.g. have been a case for *divas* in the sense of 'special day'—*hindī divas* 'Hindi Day'; *bāl divas* 'Day of the Child', etc.—but this development is counteracted by coinages like *do-divasīy* 'lasting two (normal) days', which make it just another word for *din*.
5. An elaborate attempt in this direction was made by Kali Charan Bahl, who in a dictionary-type study of synonymous conjunct verbs with *karnā* comes up with an amazing range of connotational differences between the nominal elements of such constructions. But though these are said to derive from the appended evidence, they are in most cases difficult to reconcile with the facts of actual language use. The discrepancy shows already in the very first group of synonyms (*prayog/ upayog / vyavahār / istemāl karnā*) discriminated by Bahl. While one may agree, or at least think it desirable, that *vyavahār* 'stresses customary, habitual use', one hesitates to accept that *upayog* 'refers to the use of an object for a purpose other than that for which it is primarily meant', or that *prayog* 'implies suitability' (of the thing used, one supposes), or that *istemāl* 'indicates nothing more than the idea of use' and therefore occurs 'in careful writings in contexts where the distinctions indicated by *prayog, upayog* and *vyavahār* are to be definitely avoided'. The study gives the impression of an imaginative attempt to construct for Hindi something which corresponds to the neat synonymies in the Merriam Webster dictionaries. Bahl's distinctions were tested in another study in connection with the question as to whether they could perhaps explain the many vocabulary changes which Mohan Rakesh has made in subsequent editions of his short stories. It is concluded that they cannot. Both in this study and in Bahl's, purism has been completely ignored as a factor. Cf. Kali Charan

Bahl, *Studies in the Semantic Structure of Hindi.* (2 vols.; I have not yet come across an advertised third volume.) Theo Damsteegt, *Mohan Rakeś and Literary Hindi* (104-5).

6. The emotive meaning of *tatsama*-forms consciously substituted for *tadbhavas* is something like 'word of greater purity hence superior quality', 'more refined word', 'word signaling education on the part of the user'.
7. Take, e.g. *śāsak*, a word that I have always considered redundant. Though it can be regarded as a kind of superordinate term for the group of lexemes comprising *rājā, mahārājā, navāb, nizām, jāmsāhib, gāyakvāṛ*, etc., probably nobody would have thought of it but for the English word 'ruler'.
8. The conceptual variability of neologisms can be compounded by an undefined dual membership in two grammatical classes, for which also only bilinguals will have an explanation. For instance *nāgarik* may take the meaning of English 1. civil 2. civilian a. 3. civic 4. civilian n. 5. citizen (townsman) 6. citizen (national n.); *sahāyak* can mean 1. helper/assistant 2. assistant (a grade among government employees) 3. orderly n. (milit.) 4. [political] aide 5. assisting/assistant 6. subsidiary [tax] 7. auxiliary [verb] 8. secondary [literature] 9. tributary [river] 10. supporting [role] 11. ancillary [industry] 12. helpful, useful (*kām men ānevālā*). It is by no means rare that a neologism corresponds in this form to a dozen and more conceptually distinct English models, which a reader must be able to recognize if he is to decode a text the way it is intended.
9. This particular problem may be illustrated with *samvedanśīl*, an adjective for sometime on the rise. Coined to mean 'feeling', 'compassionate' (akin to *hamdard*), it has become so much identified with E 'sensitive', that it is now met in sentences like *śahar ke sabhī samvedanśīl muhallon men baṛī tādād men pulis bal taināt kar diyā gayā hai* 'In all sensitive quarters of the town police forces have been deployed in large numbers' (*Janasattā* 9.10.92: 10), or *nyāyamūrti ne kahā ki kisī mahatvapūṛn aur samvedanśīl kṣetra men kisī ek vyakti ko adhikār denā, bhale hī vah vyakti ucca pad par kyon na ho, buddhimānī nahīn hogī* 'The judge said it would be unwise to empower a single person to deal with matters in an important and sensitive field, even if that person was holding a high office.' (*Hindustān* 31.12.81: 4)
10. The most persistent and outspoken critic until now has been Ramchandra Varma, who, as one of the editors of the *Hindī Śabdasāgar*, later freely admitted to the great number of errors in that work ('*saikṛon prakār ke hazāron bhūlen*'), and already in the 1940s lashed out at the blind imitation of English ('*chāyā kaluṣit bhāṣā*'). Recently, a polemic by linguist Anvita Abbi on the 'esoteric Sanskritized hot-house Hindi' of official application forms complained about 'poorly attempted Sanskrit translations (generally incorrect and inappropriate) of various English words', noticing in this context also the phenomenon of semantical variance. Cf. *Will the 'preshak' affix a 'mudraank*? (*The Sunday Times of India*, 12.7.92). Incidentally, though Abbi observes that '. . . we have created a whole new vocabulary even in areas where we already had a perfectly serviceable one', she does not wonder about the motives of it and nowhere uses the word 'purism'.

11. Here I should add that the more popular or successful authors are seldom nowadays partisans of Shuddh Hindi. They generally pursue a moderate line. If they at times adopt a sanskritizing diction this must not necessarily be attributed to a chauvinistic bent of mind.
12. An idea of this attitude can be had from Lee Siegel's book *Laughing Matters* (New Delhi 1989), especially a passage in which the author recounts a conversation with a museum administrator on the subject of Sanskrit comedy. An extract: 'Sanskrit is a lofty language, too lofty to accomodate such a trivial thing as a joke. Sanskrit is not a funny language.' And, a little further, 'Of course it is true that there is always laughter among the lower classes. And it is true that one can joke in the lower languages. But not in Sanskrit. That is why the *vidūṣak* speaks Prakrit—how could he amuse us in Sanskrit, the perfect language, the sacred language, the language spoken by the gods, the language from which all other languages have descended?' (p. 440). The opinion expressed in these sentences is doubtlessly very common, although the opposite view, that of Sanskrit being eminently suited for funny literature and richly endowed with it, is also encountered. In the same chapter, Siegel forms an interesting theory which he later rejects; namely that '. . . social conventions for joking and public outlets for the comic are difficult in India because of the sacrality of the hierarchy, the power with which it pervades all experiences and interactions' (456f.).
13. Ramchandra Varma must still have felt this inhibition, for in the *bhūmikā* to the first edition of *acchī hindī* (1944) he assures readers that he is not mentioning his sources respectively the names of those who had provided him with mistakes, as his intentions were far from ridiculing anyone.
14. A typical *nāṭak* in this respect is Amrit Nahata's *kissā kursī ka* (the play underlying the film that fell victim to the Emergency), in which a bunch of corrupt politicians at the head of the state show every sign of depravity and stupidity, but appear to have no difficulty with intricacies of the sanskritizing style. Only a Marwari tycoon, terrified by the rotters' threat to *proclaim samājvād,* provides for laughter with his dialect. (Rajpal & Sons, Delhi, 1977, 2nd edn).
15. 'Parodie schießt auf einen Mann mit der Waffe seiner eigenen Form' (Zur Ästhetik der Parodie). Neumann maintains that both outstanding and substandard authors[1] works are by definition beyond the reach of parody. The only way to deal with the latter was the 'revealing quotation'.
16. See the second volume of Kaka Hathrasi's *Collected Works* (op. cit.) which contains *philmī pairoḍiyān,* humorous poems written in the metre of well-known film songs and singable to the familiar tunes, but in no way intended as a critique of this type of lyric. The short publisher's note illustrates the current understanding of *pairoḍi.*
17. Whatever technical meaning it has in Hindi rhetorics, in normal usage it is simply an antonym of *saral.* It covers the range from 'difficult to understand' to 'incomprehensible' and implies no specific cause. A text may be said to be *kliṣṭ* for being crowded, for containing hard words or for other reasons. Once characterized with this attribute, there seems to be no need to ask whether it is grammatical in the first place.

REFERENCES

Bahl, Kali Charan. 1974/1979. *Studies in the Semantic Structure of Hindi* (Synonymous Nouns and Adjectives with *karanā*), vol. I, Delhi: Motilal Banarsidass; vol. II, Delhi: Manohar.

Damsteegt, Theo. 1982. *Mohan Rakeś and Literary Hindi*. In: Studien zur Indologie und Iranistik. Heft 8/9. Reintek: Verlag für Orinetalistische Fachpublikationen.

Kaka Hathrasi. 1982. *Kākā Hāthrasī Hāsya Racanāvalī* (Complete Works of Kaka Hathrasi), 5 vols. Delhi: Prabhat Prakashan.

Jacob, Heinrich Eduard (ed.). 2nd edn, 1927. *Verse der Lebenden*. Deutsche Lyrik seit 1910. Berlin.

Nahata, Amrit. 2nd edn, 1977. *Kissā kursī kā*. Delhi: Rajpal & Sons.

Raghuvir Sahay. 1960. *Sīṛhiyon par dhūp men*. Kasi: Bharatiya Jnanpith.

Siegel, Lee. 1989. *Laughing Matters*. Chicago: University of Chicago Press.

Carter and Courtesan—The Ox and the Tigress: Humour in Phanishwarnath Renu's Hindi Story 'The Third Vow'

KONRAD MEISIG

Introdcution

Humour, to which a category of its own, viz., the *hāsya-rasa*, had already been dedicated even in old Indian aesthetics, has produced a special genre, the satire (*vyaṅgya, hāsya-vyaṅgya*), in Hindi literature, as well.[1] Prominent Hindi satirists after World War II include Harishankar Parsai, Shrilal Shukla and Ramesh Bakshi. Premchand (1880-1936), the founder of modern realistic Hindi prose, had already written a number of short stories (*kahānī*) which could be described more accurately as satires, e.g. the series of stories making fun of the Brahman charlatan Moteramji Shastri, such as 'Nimantraṇ' (The invitation, 1926),[2] 'Gurumantra' (The initiation spell, November 1926 or earlier[3]), or 'Moṭar ke chī̃te' (Splashing from a car, before[4] 1936?). The so-called New Narrators (*naye kahānīkār*) of the fifties and the beginning of the sixties wrote, among other works, satirical stories (*vyaṅgyātmak kahānī*) as well. I refer to Kamleshvar's *Jārj pañcam kī nāk*[5] (The nose of George V, 1963) and *Sā̃p*[6] (The serpent, 1963) or to Mohan Rakesh' *Paramātmā kā kuttā*[7] (The dog of the lord, 1958).

The story which I am going to present in this paper as an example for humour in Hindi literature, viz., 'Tisri qasam' (The third vow) came from the quill of an author who himself was one of the New Story writers: Phanishwarnath 'Renu' (4 March 1921-11 April 1977).[8] Renu is the most prominent representative of those modern Hindi writers who take their subject-matter and characters from their own rural surroundings. He is regarded as the founder of the socially critical 'regional literature' (*ā̃calik-sāhitya*), which has also been called 'regional realism'.[9] 'Tisri qasam',[10] first published in 1956,[11] is probably Renu's most renowned story and may be considered a modern classic. It has been repeatedly anthologized[12] and has been translated into English twice.[13] In the mid-sixties it was made into an award-winning film, the dialogues of which was written by Renu himself, with Raj Kapoor acting as Hiraman in the title role.[14] The story is set in Renu's native country, near and in the city of Fārbisgañj (Forbesganj) in north-eastern Bihar (near Biratnagar in Nepal). Renu attended the elementary school in Forbesganj; he was intimately familiar with the countryside and the people of this region. This may suffice as an introduction. I now turn to the story itself and begin with a concise summary.

Summary of 'Tisri qasam'

Hiraman, a bullock carter from a village near Forbesganj, has sworn two vows: after smuggling goods across the Nepalese border, where he escaped a customs raid by the skin of his teeth, he will never again carry illegal goods; and having speared a horse and carriage with bamboo sticks jutting out in front of his cart and having been beaten up by the coachman, he will never again transport a load of bamboo. But otherwise he is regarded as one of the most able and bravest carters around, especially since he last year was able to induce his two oxen to transport the tiger of a travelling circus, thus saving the reputation of his whole guild by their boldness.

This time, again, he has to carry a very special load of freight for a travelling company, freight of a kind which had never before been found under the awning of his bullock cart: an actress, Hirabai, who has been engaged as a singer and dancer at the fair (*melā*) in Forbesganj. Hiraman, a child widower and since then a bachelor, has the greatest respect for women—of his sister-in-law, for instance, he is almost a bit afraid. At first the woman who had been loaded onto his cart at midnight gives Hiraman the creeps: might he be transporting a *rāksanī* (p. 121, Skt. *rākṣasī*), a demoness? Soon, however, the two begin chatting and get to know each other; Hiraman sings folk songs of his native country to Hirabai; and, before fully realizing it, he is head over heels in love with his passenger. Actresses are regarded as women with questionable reputations and loose manners; but such matters are far beyond innocent Hiraman's horizon. Hirabai, for her part, feels that she has found in this Hiraman a genuine *hīrā*, a diamond. Having reached the fair, she provides her carter, who has looked after her so touchingly, also and four of his colleagues with free tickets (*pās* 'pass', p. 131). For ten days the carters are present at each of her performances, watching her jealously, shielding her from importunate admirers, even fighting her offenders with their bullwhips. On the eleventh day Hirabai's engagement is finished. Hiraman is called to the station to collect his purse, which the actress has kept for him in a safe place. 'The company woman is on her way back to her company' (*kampanī kī aurat kampanī mẽ jā rahī hai,* p. 129), by train. And Hiraman, to whom the bullock cart behind him feels empty and hollow, returns to his village. His lips are moving: perhaps he is swearing the third vow.

Sense of humour

Phanishwarnath Renu's 'Tisri qasam' is one of the most outstanding New Stories. It captivates by its intensity and suggestivity, its imagery and complexity, and especially by its humour.

Renu achieves humorous effects by the combination of various narrative techniques, frequently involving the use of metaphors. Metaphors used as leitmotifs, being inspired by the close connection between human being and animal, play an important role in 'Tisri qasam'.

The carter as an ox

To begin with the ox: it is nothing but a metaphor for Hiraman, the simple man from the country. Hiraman thinks of himself and his two oxen as the 'three beings' (*tīnõ prāṇī,* p. 107) or the 'three creatures' (*tīnõ jan,* ibid.). His heart is 'yoked', just like an ox, by Hirabai's friendliness (*Hiraman kā jī juṛā gayā,* p. 118). Hiraman loves his oxen, to which he talks, and which even understand his speech (*bail samajh gaye unhẽ kyā karnā hai,* p. 106).

'Hoonk-hoonk.' His oxen, one after the other, said something. Hiraman, who was just leaving, turned and remarked: 'Yes, yes, we are all thirsty. I'll be back soon to feed you some grass; don't be naughty!'—The oxen waggled their ears.

(*uske bailõ ne bārī-bārī se 'hūk-hūk' karke kuch kahā. Hiraman ne jāte-jāte ulaṭkar kahā: 'hā̃, hā̃, pyās sabhī ko lagī hai. lautkar ātā hū̃ to ghās dū̃gā, badmāśī mat karo!'—bailõ ne kān hilāye,* p. 117).

Hiraman's closeness to his bullocks is repeated as a leitmotif throughout the story. He addresses them as 'brothers' (*bhaiyan,* pp. 106, 108, 123), an expression adopted by Hirabai:

Hirabai, who was already leaving, stopped. Addressing Hiraman's oxen, she said: 'All right, I'll be right back, brothers!'—At the word 'brother' the oxen waggled their ears.

(*Hirabai jāte-jāte ruk gayī. Hiraman ke bailõ ko saṃbodhit karke bolī: 'acchā, māi calī bhaiyan!'—bailõ ne, bhaiyā, śabda par kān hilāye,* p. 129).

At the end, as the three of them drive alongside the railway, the oxen stare longingly in the direction of the rails (p. 141), just as Hiraman had gazed at the train with the departing actress at the railway station shortly before (p. 140). The adjectives 'robust' (*haṭṭā-kaṭṭā*), 'rural' (*dehātī*), and 'guileless' (*niśchal*), used by Renu to characterize his protagonist Hiraman, would all be suited to his oxen.

The simple bullock carter Hiraman is of a nature which cannot fail to remind us of the two oxen in Premchand's 'The Tale of the Two Oxen'[15] (*Do bailõ ki kathā,* October 1931), one of which was named *Hīrā,* 'diamond' too. Hirabai's opinion: *Hiraman sacmuc hīrā hai* (p. 111), 'Hiraman really is a *hīrā*,' must be understood in this sense, as well—namely not only as 'Hiraman is a diamond' (the literal translation), but also as the author's allusion to Premchand's short story, so that Hiraman has to be equated with Hira, the ox. In the shape of his two oxen, Hira and Moti, 'Diamond' and 'Pearl', Premchand had left a monument to the simple man from the country as Renu did with the character of Hiraman. And there is yet another allusion to Premchand's 'Tale of the Two Oxen' in Renu's 'Third Vow', it is said that Hiraman personally was not afraid of imprisonment, but it was only for the sake of his oxen that he had to flee from the customs patrol lest they would have to 'lie for so many days without fodder and water in the public pen'[16] or in the *kā̃jīhaus*, the 'congee-house' (cattle-pound), as fate would have it in the case of Premchand's two oxen.[17]

Premchand's key word, his expression for the central trait of the simple man from the country, had been *sīdhāpan*, 'straightness', 'simpleness', that is in the positive sense of unspoilt 'simplicity'. This simplicity of the country folks manifests itself at times as simple-mindedness, or rather naivety. 'Village fool' (*dehātī bhucca*, p. 120) is what Hiraman shouts after his carter colleagues because he now feels like a cosmopolite, for he drives a lady from town around. Hiraman's naivety is shown in that scene when he enters the circus tent together with his colleagues. Marvelling at the depictions of the *Rāmāyaṇa* on the stage curtain, Hiraman asks his friends whether those pictures are 'moving' or if they are 'still' (*chāpī sabhī khaṛe hãi yā cal rahe hãi?* p. 134). His friend Lalmohar is so enthused by Hirabai's singing and dancing performance that he incessantly laughs, uncontrollably: 'over each line of Hirabai's song he laughs, pointlessly' (*Hirabai ke gīt ke har pad par vah hãstā hai, bevajah,* p. 135).

Renu spices up his story with funny words from the provincial dialect which he has picked up from the simple folks from the village. Hiraman feels that Hirabai has a *fenūgilāsī bolī*, a 'gramophone' voice, *fenūgilās* for English 'phonograph'.[18] *Pākiṭkāṭ log* is a folk etymology interpreting English 'pickpocket' as 'pocket-cutter' or 'pocket-slitter'. *Kapaṛ-ghar*, 'cloth-house', is used for 'tent' (p. 134). *Patpaṭāṅga*, 'one after the other, in quick succession', is an expression which even Hirabai does not understand and which must be explained to her by Hiraman upon inquiry by her (p. 114). *Lātfārm* makes the pronunciation of English 'platform' easier (p. 139). A *mahābhakuā* is a 'giant ass' (p. 107), and a *bhucca* is a 'dopey one' (p. 120).

To the extent that Renu's sense of humour is directed at Hiraman's simplicity, it is essentially expressed in the *alternation of shyness and boasting*. Both—two sides of the same coin—are triggered and intensified by Hiraman's being in love. Because he does not know how to deal with women, because he is even a bit afraid of them, he tries to make up for his bashfulness by good-natured bragging, hiding his feelings of inferiority behind vainglory. Hiraman himself actually never knows the whole time what is happening to him. The reader, however, who effortlessly recognizes the state of affairs, can take delight in Hiraman's foolishness, but not at the expense of the courting carter: who would not know the symptoms from his own experience! By means of the rigorous one-person perspective—the whole story is consistently told from Hiraman's viewpoint—the reader comes into very close contact with him, and can even share the carter's feelings. By the choice of the consistent character perspective, alternating only between internal and external viewpoint, Renu makes it difficult, if not impossible, for himself and his readers to dissociate themselves, let alone to consider themselves superior. The laughter remains good-natured. Hiraman can share the joke.

Hiraman's past, which is communicated to the reader through flashbacks in his memory, is already moulded by the continual alternation of feelings of inferiority and self-importance. Being caught smuggling, Hiraman was scared by the inspector's 'demonic laughter' (*piśācī hā̃sī* p. 106). On the other hand, he was not afraid of jail (*Hiraman kā jel kā ḍar nahī̃*, p. 106), but did fear the wrath of his elder brother and sister-in-law, in case he should lose his oxen in the customs raid (p. 106). It is true that Hiraman succeeded in escaping from the customs officers, but afterwards he was so worn out that he 'lay unconscious for two days' (*do din tak besudh paṛā rahā̃ Hiraman,* p. 107) and then made his first vow. Thereafter Hiraman feels a regular dread of illegal goods: 'Black market goods? Heaven forbid!' (*corbāzārī kā māl? tobā, tobā*! p. 107).

Prior to his second vow Hiraman fared badly without it being his own fault. The incident with the bamboo sticks occurred not in the country, but in town, an environment which seems a bit dubious to Hiraman anyway:

> An incident such as they happen in town! Moreover the contractor's super-idiotic servant, who was walking in front guiding the protruding bamboo, began staring at the girls' school.
>
> (*śaharvālī bāt! tispar bā̃s kā aguā pakaṛkar calnevālā bhāṛedār kā mahābhakuā naukar laṛkī-skūl kī or dekhne lagā,* p. 107).

When they speared the horse and carriage at the next corner, of course it was Hiraman who got the coachman's curses and whip-beating.

But then Hiraman was highly praised for transporting the tiger on his bullock-cart. On that occasion, when all other bullocks ran away, it was more *himself* than his oxen that Hiraman had to encourage:

> Hey! Why be afraid of a caged tiger? You've already seen the [wild] tigers

roaring in the foot-hills of [the Himālayas near] Morang. Besides, I'm right here behind you.

(*are, pĩjre mẽ band bāgh kā kyā ḍar? Moraṅg kī tarāī mẽ dahāṛte hue bāghõ ko dekh cuke ho. phir pīṭh par māi to hũ,* p. 108).

The ox on the right hand, being yoked in front of the tiger, did have to 'urinate profusely' (*ḍher-sā peśāb kiyā,* p. 108), but by their courage the three of them saved the honour of their whole guild and, on top of everything, even earned the one hundred rupees urgently wanted for purchasing their own cart.

Both of Hiraman's traits, his uncertainty as well as his propensity for innocent self-importance, are really let loose when he falls in love with Hirabai without clearly seeing the implications. From this moment onwards he behaves completely like a courting fool. Hirabai, for instance, simply asks his name and his reaction is as follows: 'Each hair on Hiraman's body tingled. He was speech-less' (*Hiraman ke rom-rom baj uthe. mũh se bolī nahī̃ niklī,* p. 110). When in the midday heat Hirabai takes a bath in the river, Hiraman sneaks to her bed under the awning of the cart, props his elbow on her pillow, feels and smells it:

What a fragrance! Hiraman felt as though he had just smoked five pipefuls of ganja (marihuana) at once.

(*itnī sugandh! Hiraman ko lagā, ek sāth pā̃c cilam gā̃jā phū̃kkar vah uṭhā hai,* p. 117).

He then looks at his face in her pocket mirror, and it surprises him that his eyes are so red. When, shortly before their arrival in Forbesganj, Hirabai places her hand on his shoulder for a short while, the tears of amorous emotion well up in Hiraman's eyes (p. 124), so that it seems to him that the lights of the town shine like sunflowers. The sunflower (*sūrajmukhī phūl*) had already been used (p. 113) earlier as a metaphor for his 'goddess'. Now, having reached the destination of their journey, Hiraman sees nothing but sunflowers; he is blinded with amorous sentimentality.

Several folksongs or quotations from religious eulogies (*bandanā gīt,* p. 115) in Hindi and Maithili are closely intertwined with the portrayals of the characters in the main story. When they pass through the village of Tegachiya, the children sing a mocking song, observing that the cart is veiled:

In a bright red marriage cart
Sits a blushing bride
Eating betel leaves . . . (translation by Roadarmel)

(*lālī-lālī ḍoliyā mẽ*
lālī re dulhiniyā
pān khāye . . . ! p. 119)

And Hiraman, the forty-year-old bachelor, does not hesitate to apply the song to his present situation:

Hiraman smiled . . . A bride . . . a bright red marriage cart. The bride chews betel and wipes her mouth on the bridegroom's turban. [. . .] A long-standing ambition had been fulfilled for Hiraman. Many a time he'd seen dreams like this. He was returning with his bride. [. . .] The bride had pushed the curtain aside slightly and was watching. And so many other dreams. . . . (translation by Roadarmel).

(*Hiraman hãsā . . . dulhiniyā . . . lālī-lālī ḍoliyā! dulhiniyā pān khāti hai, dulhā kī pagṛī mẽ mũh pōchtī hai.* [. . .] *kitne dinõ kā hauslā pūrā huā hai Hiraman kā! aise kitne sapne dekhe hãi usne! vah apnī dulhin ko lekar lauṭ rahā hai.* [. . .] *uskī dulhin ḍolī kā pardā thoṛā sarkākar dekhtī hai. aur bhī kitne sapne* . . ., p. 119).

The Courtesan as a Tigress

Whereas the carter is represented by his oxen, the woman sitting behind him on the cart seems to him to be at the same time tigress, jasmine flower, and goddess.

The woman as a tigress: the tigress becomes a metaphor for the courtesan. When Hiraman's colleague Palatdas, looking inquisitively under the awning of Hiraman's bullock cart, catches sight of the dancing girl, he steps back 'as though he had spotted a tiger' (*mānõ bāgh par nazar paṛ gayī*, p. 125). Another carter cannot stop himself from observing:

'Iss! You're quite a man, Hiraman! That year it was the company tiger, this time the company woman.' (Roadarmel, p. 58)

(*iss! tum bhī xūb ho, Hiraman! us sāl kampanī kā bāgh, is bār kampanī kī zanānī!*, p. 126).

Hiraman, too, quite spontaneously connects the two, Hirabai and the tiger, when he plans to persuade Hirabai to work in a circus instead of for the theatre company:

Why doesn't she work in a circus? When she dances in front of everyone, Hiraman's heart burns continuously, crackling. In a circus company she would make the tiger dance. Nobody would have the courage to go near the tiger!

(*sarkas kampanī mẽ kyõ nahī̃ kām kartī? sabke sāmne nāctī hai, Hiraman kā kalejā dap-dap jaltā rahtā hai us samay. sarkas kampanī mẽ bāgh ko nacāyegī.*[19] *bāgh ke pās jāne kī himmat kaun karegā!* p. 138).

Both, woman and tiger, are to be recognized by their smell. The predatory smell of the tiger contrasts with Hirabai's jasmine and rose scent. Because of the 'tiger stench' (*bāghāin gandh*), Hiraman, while transporting the beast of prey, had been forced to put a piece of cloth before his nose (p. 108). This time he smells of Hirabai's perfume himself. This fragrance, which is passed on to Hiraman, is used by Renu as a leitmotif and is to be understood as a symbol for Hiraman's being in love:

The fragrance of rose perfume exudes from Hiraman's body. Hiraman is an ox of a man! At that time the tiger stench had not left his body for months.

(*Hiraman kī deh se atar-gulāb kī xuśbū nikaltī hai. Hiraman karamsā̃ṛ hai! us bār mahīnõ tak uskī deh se baghāin gandh nahī̃ gayī,* p. 126).

Lalmohar sniffed at Hiraman's towel—'Oh ha!'

(*Lālmohar ne Hiraman kī gamchī sū̃gh lī—e-ha!*).

Lalmohar whispered in Hiraman's ear, 'Your body reeks of perfume. It's true!'

(*Lālmohar ne Hiraman ke kān mẽ phusphusākar kahā, 'tumhārī deh mah-mah mahaktī hai. sac!'* p. 127).

Shortly after that, Hiraman makes Lalmohar sniff at his shoulder where Hirabai had rested her hand while they traversed the river:

'All that fragrance from just a touch of her hand! See?'

(*zarā-sā hāth rakhne par itnī xuśbu! samjhe?* p. 128).

Again and again, the fragrant jasmine flower appears as a metaphor for Hirabai:

Today a jasmine flower keeps blooming in his cart. [. . .] Is it a woman or a jasmine flower, when the cart smells and smells!

(*āj rah-rahkar uskī gāṛī mẽ campā kā phūl mahak uṭhtā hai.* [. . .] *aurat hai yā campā kā phūl! jab se gāṛī mah-mah mahak rahā hai,* pp. 108f).

There is fragrance even in Hirabai's smile (*muskarāhaṭ mẽ xuśbu hai,* p. 110).

Another metaphor for Hirabai is the goddess who appears repeatedly as a witch, a fairy, and mother goddess and is identified by Hiraman, the naive believer, with 'his' Hirabai. In the beginning he still fears his passenger might be a witch: 'It's not that she is a witch or a demoness?' (*kahī̃ ḍākin-piśācin to nahī?* p. 110).

But very soon Hirabai seems like a fairy or even like the Great Goddess incarnate to Hiraman:

'Oh god! This is a fairy!' The fairy's eyes opened.

(*'are bāp! ī to parī hai!' parī kī ā̃khẽ khul gayī̃,* p. 110).

The jasmine flower bloomed again in his cart. In its flower sits a fairy. . . . Hail to the goddess!

(*uskī gāṛī mẽ phir campā kā phūl khilā. us phūl mẽ ek parī baiṭhī hai . . . jai bhagvatī!* p. 111).

A woman of divine family travels on his cart. After all, a goddess is a goddess!

(*uskī gāṛī par devkul kī aurat savār hai. devtā āxir devta hai*! p. 114).

Blessings, blessings! Hiraman watched the mother goddess (=Hirabai!) offering the food-sacrifice [herself].

(*dhanna hai, dhanna hai*! *Hiraman ne dekhā, bhagvatī maiyā bhog lagā rahī hai*, p. 118).

Palatdas, too, takes Hirabai to be 'Siyā Sukumārī', i.e. Sītā, the bride of the god Rām, as he is familiar with her from the Rāmlīlā. In pious worship he touches the feet of Hirabai, who is sleeping in Hiraman's cart, whereupon the 'goddess', manifesting herself in her dreadful aspect, frightens him off immediately: 'Hey, are you crazy or something? Get away. Beat it!'[20] (*are, pāgal hai kyā? jāo, bhāgo*!, p. 128). Indeed, a scene from Rām's exile in the woods (*Rām-ban-gaman*, p. 134) can be seen on the theatre curtain in Hirabai's circus tent. Pious Palatdas recognizes Rām, 'Siyā Sukumārī', and 'Lakhanlāl' (Skt. *Lakṣmaṇa*) on the spot and, bowing to them respectfully, he is on the verge of tears of sheer reference.

The mother goddess is also directly connected with the tiger:

The mother goddess may bless it, the tiger of that circus company.

(*devī maiyā bhalā karẽ us sarkas-kampanī ke bāgh kā*, p. 108)

In general, religious motifs occur in *Tisri qasam* exclusively with a humorous undertone; one may infer that Renu does not take the gods seriously. Suffering from lovesickness after Hirabai has left him, what Hiraman would like to do most would be to renounce the world and go on a pilgrimage to 'Jagarnāth' (Jagannāth) in Puri (p. 140), chanting hymns.

Further humorous devices

Puns are of course one means to enriching a story with humour. For instance, Hiraman, who has not seen much of the world except his native province, laughs out loud when he hears that Hirabai was born in Kanpur:

'Good heavens, Kanpur (Ear Town). Then there must be a Nakpur (Nose Town) as well?' And when Hirabai told him that there is indeed a Nakpur, he doubled up laughing.

('*vāh re Kānpur*! *tab to Nākpur bhī hogā?*' *aur jab Hirabai ne kahā ki Nākpur bhī hai, to vah hãste-hãste duhrā ho gayā*, p. 112).

The name Palatdas is suitable for punning, too: *Palaṭdās to phir palaṭkar āyā hī nahī̃ hai abhī tak* ('Palatdas has not yet returned [*palaṭkar*]'), one of the carters informs his colleagues.

Likewise, proverbial sayings are suitable to create humorous effects. Hiraman as well as his colleagues, the other carters from the same village, first have their doubts about watching the theatre performance in town. They are afraid the villagers at home might mock them with: 'Native chicken, English acting' (*deśī murgī vilāytī cāl,* p. 127, another metaphor).

Finally, Renu's predilection for onomatopoetic expressions must be mentioned. The joker 'had shrieked grinding his teeth' (*dā̃t kiṭkiṭākar kikiyāne lagā thā,* p. 115) like a monkey. Hiraman does not like the songs booming *bhoṃpū-bhoṃpū* nowadays from the loudspeakers (*bhõpā,* p. 115).

Conclusion

Let me finally sum up Renu's techniques of humour. We found the following aspects: The principal technique is a rich imagery, especially those metaphors which are inspired by a close relationship between man and animal, or, more generally, by familiarity of man with nature: the carter as an ox, the courtesan as a tigress—or as a jasmine flower. At the same time, these metaphors serve as leitmotifs (e.g. the woman as witch, fairy, and mother goddess), of which the reader is kept aware by continual repetition. Such amassment increases the narrative denseness and thereby the suggestivity. Complexity and variety of sense has been achieved in 'Tisri qasam' by the paralleling and intertwining of secondary tales or songs with the main story. As to the portrayal of Hiraman's character, we ascertained above that the contrast of shyness and vainglory form an underlying humorous structure. By means of the consistent one-person character perspective, by the unification of narrator and protagonist (clearly recognizable not least by the choice of words and manner of speaking), the description of Hiraman's simplicity or even naivety is guided by a good-natured, empathizing sense of humour which does not degenerate into arrogant derision. Puns and especially onomatopoetic expressions appear in large numbers.

I have hoped with the quoted example—if only in a very insufficient manner—to convey an impression of Renu's inimitable skill. They were supposed to give an idea of how Renu on the highest level of narrative techniques—yet without sacrificing understandability for an uneducated audience—lets the rich sense of humour of the village folks of Bihar come to life.

NOTES

1. See Desai, *Hindī vyaṅgya vidhā: śāstra aur itithās* and the extensive bibliography of sources and criticism therein (pp. 280-92). On satirical novels see R. Varma.

2. Premchand, *Mānsarovar,* vol. 5, pp. 14-35. Publication dates of Premchand's works according to Goyanka, *Premchand viśvakoś.*
3. Premchand, *Mānsarovar,* vol. 3, pp. 217-19. English translation 'A lesson in the holy life' by D. Rubin in *The World of Premchand,* pp. 121-3.
4. Premchand, *Mānsarovar,* vol. 2, pp. 76-80. English translation 'A car-splashing' by D. Rubin in *The World of Premchand,* pp. 95-9. 'Splashes from a motor car' in Premchand, *Twenty-four Stories by Premchand.* German translation 'Autospritzer' in Premchand, *Die Schachspieler. Erzählungen,* pp. 16-21.
5. Kamleshwar: *Khoyī huī diśāẽ,* pp. 60-6.
6. *Khoyī huī diśāẽ,* 1963, pp. 109-18. English translation 'The serpent' by R.S. Yadav in Kamleshwar, *Summer Days,* pp. 80-9. See also Ansari, *Indian Social Reality of the Early 1960s as Reflected in Hindi New Short Story,* esp. pp. 296f.
7. Rakesh, *Paramātmā kā kuttā.* In: Mohan Rakesh, *Jānvar aur jānvar.* Reprinted in: Mohan Rakesh, *Mohan Rakeś kī sampūrṇa kahānīyā̃,* pp. 322-6. German translation 'Gottes Hund' by K. Meisig in Mohan Rakesh, *Großstadtgeschichten,* pp. 27-36.
8. For the author's biography, see Lötzke, 'Das indische Dorf im Spiegel der modernen Hindi-Literatur, Menschen- und Gesellschaftsbild in ausgewählten Hindi-Romanen nach 1947', pp. 229-35; and Roadarmel, *A Death in Delhi—Modern Hindi Short Stories,* p. 208.
9. See Pandey, *Regionalism in Hindi novels,* p. 1.
10. Renu, 'Tisri qasam, arthāt [urfa] māre gae Gulfām' (The third vow or slain was Gulfām the lover). Quotations according to Phanishwarnath Renu: *Ṭhumrī,* pp. 105-41. As to the subtitle cf. text on p. 137 and the *Bṛhat Hindī koś,* ed. Kalika Prasad, s.v. *Gulfām: Indar-sabhā kī kahānī mẽ Sabza parī kā prempātra* ('the beloved of the fairy Sabza in the story about 'Indra's court') and ibid., s.v. *Sabza-parī: Amānat' likhit Indra- (Indar) sabhā kī nāyikā jo Gulfām par āśiq huī thī* ('the female protagonist, who was in love with Gulfām, in [the musical drama] "Indra's court" written by Amānat [Āghā Hasan Amānat, 1815-58, court poet in Lakhnaū]'). See also Rothen-Dubs, *Allahs indischer Garten. Ein Lesebuch der Urdu-Literatur,* p. 553, s.v. Amānat. Literature: Simha, *Ādhuniktā aur Hindī kahānī,* pp. 110 (*bhāṣā*), 119 (*bolī*). Raina, *Kahānīkar Phaṇīśvarnath Reṇu.*
11. It appeared in the first number of the journal *Aparampārā,* according to Bharat Yayavar (ed.): *Phanisvarnath Renu: Cunī huī racnāẽ,* vol. I, pp. xiv, 106.
12. Yadav, *Ek duniyā: samānāntar. svatantratā ke bād kī sarvaśreṣṭh kahānīyā̃,* pp. 200-23. Phaniswarnath Renu, *Merī priy kahānīyā̃,* pp. 22-53. Varma (ed.), *Hindī kī pragatiśīl kahānīya,* pp. 62-90. Renu, *Cunī huī racnāẽ,* pp. 79-106.
13. 'The Third Vow', in Gordon C. Roadarmel, *A Death in Delhi,* pp. 38-71. 'The Third Vow' in Phanishwarnath Renu, *The Third Vow and Other Stories* (trans. Kathryn G. Hansen), pp. 49-88.
14. The film *Teesrī Kasam,* produced by Shailendra, was awarded the Rashtrapati Swarna padak (the president's gold medal), see H. Lötzke, 'Das indische Dorf', p. 233. Renu's reminiscences of the shootings in 1964 in Bombay,

Dadar Station, are to be found in: "Tisri qasam" ke set par tīn din', in: Renu: *Cunī huī racnāẽ* , 1990, II, pp. 198-205.

15. Premchand, *Mānsarovār,* vol. 2, pp. 153-66. English translation 'A Tale of Two Oxen' by Nandini Nopany and P. Lal in Premchand, *Twenty-four Stories by Premchand,* 1980, pp. 123-9. German translation 'Die Geschichte von den beiden Ochsen' by K. Meisig in Premchand, *Die Schachspieler. Erzählungen,* 1989, pp. 118-34.
16. *Na jāne kitne dinõ tak binā cārā-pānī ke sarkārī phāṭak mẽ paṛe rahẽge,* p. 106.
17. *Do bailõ kī kathā,* p. 161.
18. Pp. 109, 110, 131. There is a scene in the film *Teesri Kasam* with Raj Kapoor in which Hiraman uses the word *fenūgilās* in his conversation with Hirabai. She does not understand and asks the meaning. He makes rapid turning motions with his hand, whereupon she exclaims, 'Ah, gramophone!'
19. Add *nacāyegī* in the text of *Ṭhumrī,* in accordance with Rajendra Yadav: *Ek duniyā,* p. 222, and Renu: *Merī priy kahāniyā̃,* p. 51.
20. Translation by Roadarmel.

REFERENCES

Ansari, Dagmar. 1974. 'Indian Social Reality of the Early 1960s as Reflected in Hindi New Short Story.' In: *Archiv orientalni,* vol. 42: 289-99.

Desai, Bapurao Dhondu. 1990. *Hindī vyaṅgya vidhā: śāstra aur itihās.* Kanpur: Chintan Prakashan.

Goyanka, Kamalkishor. 1981. *Premchand viśvakoś,* vol. I: Jīvnī; vol. II: Sahitya. Delhi: Prabhat Prakashan.

Kamleshwar. 1977. *Summer Days.* New Delhi: Himalaya Books.

———. 1986, 2nd edn. *Khoyī huī diśāẽ.* Delhi: Shabdakar. (Kasi 1963, 1st edn).

Lötzke, Hannelore. 1986. 'Das indische Dorf im Spiegel der modernen Hindi-Literatur. Menschen- und Gesellschaftsbild in ausgewählten Hindi-Romanen nach 1947.' Dissertation, Humboldt-Universität, Berlin.

Pandey, Indu Prakash. 1974. *Regionalism in Hindi novels.* Beiträge zur Südasienforschung, vol. 3. Wiesbaden: Franz Steiner.

Prasad, Kalika (ed.). 2009 [=1953]. *Bṛhat Hindī Koś.* Banaras.

Premchand. 1980. *Mānsarovar.* 8 vols. Allahabad: Sarasvati Press.

———. 1980. *Twenty-four Stories by Premchand.* Translated by Nandini Nopany and P. Lal. New Delhi: Vikas Publishing House.

———. 1989. *Die Schachspieler. Erzählungen.* Aus dem Hindi übersetzt von Konrad Meisig in Zusammenarbeit mit Petra Christophersen, Wiesbaden: Otto Harrassowitz (Sammlung Harrassowitz).

Raina, Raj. 1978. *Kahānīkār Phaṇīśvarnāth Reṇu.* Simanta Prakashan.

Rakesh, Mohan. 1958. *Jānvar aur jānvar.* Delhi: Rajkamal Prakashan.

———. 1984. *Mohan Rakeś kī saṃpūrṇa kahāniyā̃.* Delhi: Rajpal & Sons.

———. 1990. *Großstadtgeschichten.* Ausgewählt, aus dem Hindi übersetzt und mit einem Nachwort versehen von Konrad Meisig. Wiesbaden: Otto Harrassowitz.

Renu, Phanishwarnath. 1985 (1st printed 1973). *Merī priy kahāniyā̃.* Delhi: Rajpal & Sons.

Renu, Phanishwarnath. 1986. *The Third Vow and Other Stories.* Translated into English by Kathryn G. Hansen. Delhi: Chanakya Publications.

———. 1981[6] (1959[1]). *Ṭhumrī.* New Delhi: Rajkamal Prakashan.

———. 1990. *Cunī huī racnāẽ*, pp. 79-106. See Yayavar.

Roadarmel, Gordon C. 1972. *A Death in Delhi—Modern Hindi Short Stories.* Translated and edited by G.C. Roadarmel, Berkeley, Los Angeles, London: University of California Press.

Rothen-Dubs, Ursula (ed.). 1989. *Allahs indischer Garten. Ein Lesebuch der Urdu-Literatur.* Neue Indische Bibliothek, vol. 18. Frauenfeld: Waldgut.

Rubin, David. 1969. *The World of Premchand.* Selected stories of Premchand transl. by D. Rubin. London: George Allen and Unwin Ltd.

Sinha, Jagan. 1980. *Ādhuniktā aur Hindī kahānī.* Delhi: Prasangik Prakashan.

Varma, Dhananjay (ed.). 1986. *Hindī kī pragatiśīl kahāniyā̃.* New Delhi: Radhakrishan Prakashan.

Varma, Radheshyam. 1990. *Hindī vyaṅgya upanyās.* Delhi: Nirman Prakashan.

Yadav, Rajendra (ed.). 1968. *Ek duniyā: samānāntar. svatantratā ke bād kī sarvaśreṣṭh kahāniyā̃.* New Delhi: Akshar Prakashan.

Yayavar, Bharat (ed.). 1990. *Phanisvarnath Renu: Cunī huī racnāẽ.* 3 vols. New Delhi: Vani Prakashan.

Humour in the *Satsaī* of Bihārīlāl

RUPERT SNELL

Bihārīlāl was a Hindi court poet of the seventeenth century, born in about the year 1600 in the Gwalior district of what is now Madhya Pradesh (McGregor 1984: 173). The common view of Bihārī's fame is that 'almost any schoolboy in northern India, and certainly any adult who has been to school, will be able to recite from memory a verse or two from the *Satsaī*' (Holland 1969: 3); but according to the experience of my own recent research in India this is far from the truth, and even the guides to the Amber fort at Jaipur in Rajasthan, where Bihārīlāl himself lived and composed his verse, needed to be convinced that the poet 'Bihārī' and the Bihārī dialect are actually two separate and distinct items.

Bihārī received patronage from Mirza Raja Jaisingh of Amber (1617-67); Bihārī's praise-poems to Jaisingh are included in his sole composition, or rather anthology. The so-called '*Bihārī satsaī*' is a (nominal) 'seven centuries' of independent couplets on assorted themes, with love predominant; it is a true poetic masterpiece, standing head and shoulders above its many imitators.

The poet's meagre biography is eked out by legends, such as one which describes how Bihārī alone was able to restore to his king a sense of royal duty: Jaisingh was so besotted with the charms of a new young wife or concubine that he totally neglected his kingdom until Bihārī concealed this couplet amongst the rose petals of his bedchamber:[1]

नहि परागु नहि मधुर मधु नहिं विकास इहिं काल।
अली कली ही तें बँध्यो आगे कौन हवाल॥

630
No pollen yet, nor nectar sweet, no blooms with fatal power;
What of the fated bee, my friend, when fragrance fills the flower?

Though Bihārī was born in Madhya Pradesh, and his literary career developed in Rajasthan, the dialect of Braj was the automatic choice of dialect for any 'Hindi' poet in the seventeenth century. This is because Braj, or Braj Bhāṣā, the language spoken to the south of Delhi where Kṛṣṇa is said to have lived his earthly life, had been associated with Kṛṣṇa devotionalism since the fifteenth century, and this association had shot the regional dialect into orbit as *the* pre-eminent vehicle for literary composition. (As a poetic language, Braj is described as having a 'sweetness' lacking in Khaṛī Bolī Hindi; certainly it maintains a true vernacular quality which Sanskritization has stolen from the modern standard language, and the extremely compact composition of Bihārī's chosen poetic metres could hardly be maintained in modern Khaṛī Bolī, whose verb composition relies so heavily on the use of syllable-greedy auxiliary verbs.)

In terms of content and genre, Bihārī's *Satsaī* looks back to a Prakrit *Satsaī* convention established in the second century AD by Hāla—though this specific connexion has yet to be fully analysed and falls beyond the scope of this paper.[2] A second element in Bihārī's literary inheritance was the complex of Kṛṣṇa mythology deriving from the tenth-century (?) *Bhāgavata Purāṇa*, and augmented by such texts as Jayadeva's twelfth-century Sanskrit poem *Gītagovinda* which provided Kṛṣṇa with a consort in the form of Rādhā. The rich language of those devotional texts, oozing with that lush and sensual imagery which took earthly love as a metaphor to express the otherwise ineffable nature of the soul's relationship with God, was part of the stock-in-trade of poets generally during Bihārī's time; and it could express either devotional or profane love with equal effectiveness. The two types share much in idea and idiom: a bittersweet sense of loss, and an imagery that relies heavily on metaphors to do with light and lustre. Many verses such as the following seem to have no particular devotional content, but are often interpreted as applying to Kṛṣṇa's consort Rādhā:

कहा कुसुम कह कौमुदी कितक आरसी जोति।
जाकी उजराई लखे आँख ऊजरी होति।।

519
What is a flower, a moonlit night, the brightness of a glass?
The lustre of her loveliness doth all these things surpass.

Other couplets, by contrast, are explicit in describing Kṛṣṇa and Rādhā as hero and heroine respectively. There is little discontinuity of mood between the straightforwardly worldly context of the previous verse and the devotional context of the next one, which romanticizes the groves where 'Hari and Rādhikā' sported as containing the essence of Prayāga, the *thīrtharāja* or 'king of pilgrimage places'. The blithe, soft-focus and sensual pleasurableness that characterized the romantic couplet above applies equally to a devotional one:

तज तीरथ हरि राधिका तन दुति कर अनुराग।
जिहिं ब्रज केलि निकुंज मग पग पग होत प्रयाग॥

682
Forget the pilgrim's path and tread
Brindabans arbour lanes

Where ev'ry step along the way
a pilgrimage contains.

Alongside the devotional and other poems are others on *nīti* or 'polity', equally characteristic of many a Sanskrit anthology and yet here given a new lease of life by their applicability to contemporary situations in seventeenth-century Rajasthan; for one of the qualities of Bihārī's poetry is a sense of relevance to the common experience of actual life. It is easy to imagine that a verse such as the following may have been a wry comment on some event witnessed in the company of Jaisingh's entourage:

जो सिर धरि महिमा मही लहियत राजा राउ।
प्रगटत जडता आपनी मुकुट सु पहिरत पाउ॥

614
A crown will lend a king some grace, when on his head he wears it;
but he, not it, meets infamy, if on a foot he bears it.

While listing themes is one way of classifying the content of the text, the more usual mode of categorization is that of classical Indian aesthetics. Sanskrit *rasa*-theory provides a sophisticated matrix against which the various narrative situations and sentiments invented or adapted by Bihārī can be assessed. The romantic-erotic sentiment *śṛṅgāra rasa* predominates, while comic *hāsya* is also formally admitted—although in a rather small number of verses. The closely related conventions of *nāyaka-nāyikā bheda* supply yet another system of critical assessment for the text.

The *rasa*-based taxonomy isolates a range of conventional conceits and narrative situations which have been dear to Indian poets over many centuries. The commentaries tend towards the dogmatic in classifying a verse as, for example, either 'devotional' *or* 'humorous'; but it is precisely in the allusiveness of the verses, and the applicability of their imagery across a range of possible contexts, that makes their poetry work. Because 'humour' or 'comedy' are here codified within the formalistic category of *hāsya*, many humorous or comic elements in the poetry are not discussed in these terms at all. (For the most part, the commentators do not concern themselves with the detail of the ancillary sentiments of *rasa*-theory.) The attitude of the commentators seems to be, perhaps unsurprisingly, to regard 'humour' as a specialist and separately prescribed function with its own set of contexts and parameters—a function carried by the *vidūṣaka* in classical drama, for example, or by one of Johnnie Walker's characters in the Bombay cinema.

Standing aside from traditional aesthetic codes, one could describe Bihārīlāl's poetic world in terms of the three complementary functions of context, theme and mode: courtly, domestic or religious contexts predominate, with erotic themes described in a comic mode. The terms should perhaps be widened a little: for 'religious' read also 'devotional'; for 'erotic' read also 'romantic' and 'sentimental'; for 'comic' read also 'humorous'. It is at the level of 'mode' that our own modern interpretations are most suspect, because the definition of humour changes so much over both space and time.

References in Bihārī's text to specific features of Rajasthan life and society, such as the Mainā bandit caste or the celebration of the *tīj* festival, locate the poetry in a distinctive regional setting; and in linguistic terms the poetic creativity of the text depends upon a characteristic vernacular blending of *tatsama, tadbhava* and Perso-Arabic vocabulary. In source, content and mood the text is a blend of convention, adaptation and invention. The short title *Satsaī* gives no clue to the content of the text, beyond alluding to the tradition of Prakrit *Satsaī* composition; if the norms of text-titling in seventeenth-century India had shared the extended glosses found in European book-titles of the same period, the *Satsaī* might have been described in terms similar to that of George Gascoigne's *A hundreth sundrie flowres,* published in London in 1572 (just a few years before Bihārī's birth):

A hundreth sun-
drie Flowres bounde
vp in one small Poesie.
Gathered partely (by transla-
tion) in the fyne outlandish Gardins
of Euripides, Quid, Petrarke, Aristo,
and others: and partly by invention,
out of our owne fruitefull Or-
chardes in Englande:

Yielding sundrie svveete sauours of Tra-
gical, Comical and Morall Discour-
ses, both pleasant and profitable to the
well smelling noses of lear-
ned Readers.

Bihārī's flowers are likewise 'gathered partely (by translation) in the fyne outlandish Gardins'—here applying to Sanskrit literature; but 'our owne fruitefull Orchardes' also make a substantial contribution—both those of Rajasthan, where the poems were written, and also those of Braj, where the seed of Hindi poetry found its most fertile ground. Gascoigne's category of the 'tragical' can hardly be read across to the Indian cultural context, the concept of the 'tragical, comical and moral discourses' all being relished in terms of 'svveete sauours' is very much of a piece with Indian aesthetics, and there is a close parallel between

Gascoigne's 'well-smelling noses of learned Readers' and the Indian concept of the *sahṛdaya* or *rasik*, the literary connoisseur who is alone able to appreciate poetic art.

After suggesting some correspondence between the Indian and the English traditions, the impossibility of translating the language-bound wit of Bihārī's poems has to be admitted. (The lack of an appropriate English couplet metre[3] adds to the problem.) Only rarely can one hit upon a parallel between the two very different vocabularies of Hindi and English; more usually, word-play in the original has to be suggested by a new device in the target language, with limited correspondence to the original. In either case the translations attempted in this paper necessarily stray some way from the literal. In the following *dohā* the character of Youth is personified as a young prince, setting up two separate contexts of meaning: on the one hand that of the royal court, in which the 'Prince Youth' rewards his courtiers for their loyalty; and on the other a physiological one, in which the onset of maturity is marked by the sudden 'filling out' of the young female body, seen as Youth's realm.

अपने अँग के जानि कै, जोबन नृपति प्रवीन।
स्तन मन नयन नितंब कौ बडौ इजाफा कीन॥

20
A budding monarch, Youth by name,
on courtly members doted;
So bosoms, buttocks, breasts and hearts
he gen'rously promoted.

Prince Youth recognizes *stana mana nayana nitamba* or 'breasts, hearts, eyes and hips' to be *apane ãga ke* —'his own parts', whether physically or in the court metaphor as 'faithful retainers'—and rewards them by giving them an 'increase'. A translation possibility lies in the *double entendre* of English 'member'; but one might get closer to the spirit of the original by trying a military metaphor:

King Youth, who knew his interests lay
with *flanks* which *(k)nightly* war did,
Through *General Emoluments*
his *privates* well rewarded.

Or, still in pursuit of that elusive play on the word *aṅga*, we could base a translation on the representation of the court as a bureaucratic institution rather than a military one:

Rewarding body corporate,
His Highness Youth gives rise
To bosoms, hearts—to buttocks too—
and last, not least, to eyes.

But this too lacks the tight construction of the original, in which the poet formalizes the little list of four items *stana mana nayana* and *nitamba* by linking them with *n* alliteration and by isolating them structurally in one quarter of the couplet. (Greater licence in the translation would allow a bolder vulgarity of idiom but might stretch the tolerance of an academic readership.) Such examples show the extreme compression of Bihārī's couplet construction; and though flippant in their triteness, the English renderings do at least serve to underline, by their very shortcomings, the skilful complexity of the originals.

The compression of the couplet is particularly striking in those narrative poems where the two short lines tell a complete and autonomous narrative, especially a humorous one. The poetic art of suggestion allows the barest skeleton of a narrative 'plot' to serve as the basis for a self-contained story-telling. In an example of 'couplet as anecdote', an astrologer (*joyasī, Sanskrit jyotiṣī*) whose wife has just given birth casts a horoscope for the newborn son. The husband is horrified when the stars predict that the boy will one day kill his own father but his dread turns to delight as the horoscope then shows the child to be illegitimate, revealing the biological father to be the mother's paramour:

चित पितु-घातक जोग लखि भयौ भये सुत सोग।
फिर हुलस्यौ जिय जोयसी, समढौ जारज जोग॥

653
An omen of a patricide
implied a grievous birth;
Then 'bastard' stars, revealing truth,
restored the father's mirth!

This couplet, cited as an example of *hāsya rasa* by the *Lālcandrikā* commentary (Pandey 1977: 356), is totally self-contained in terms of its narrative structure: it includes no external reference, and every necessary element of the narrative is present in the two lines. But the humour of the couplet lies at least partly in that part of the overall picture which is left unexpressed: the reader's imagination plays over that original act of infidelity, conducted perhaps as the astrologer was preoccupied with his books and almanacs; then there is the cuckold's detailed and expert application of astrology as a kind of medieval forensic science; and the anticipation of the death which will bring the philanderer his ultimate reward. Within the miniature verse a problem is introduced and immediately resolved: a secret lover is discovered and dispatched within a handful of syllables. The couplet allows no space for a narrative run-up: there is only the jump itself. The significance of the anecdote is held over until the very end: the words *jāraja joga* designating the paramour's part in the affair are the punchline of the story.

The compression of narrative in this couplet relies on a cultural stereotype in the character of the wily (even if cuckolded) astrologer: brain beats brawn, and the little guy with the wire-framed glasses gets his own back on the sexual predator. But the characters are 'fictional', in the sense of being simply a product of the poet's imagination, augmented by the reader's. Other verses are based on a genre known to the Bombay cinema as the existing 'mythologicals'—pre-existing stories borrowed from the Purāṇas or other public-domain sources. In Bihārī's case it is the huge resources of Kṛṣṇa/Viṣṇu myths, which provide the greatest stock of narrative improvisations—a fact which encourages the misleading representation of the text as being inherently devotional. By and large, it is the myth as anecdote, rather than as a source of potent devotional feeling, that comes across in Bihārī's adaptations of Purāṇic stories. In the following couplet, Bihārī takes that most archetypal of Kṛṣṇa stories, in which Kṛṣṇa heroically picks up Govardhan hill and holds it as an umbrella to protect the Braj people from Indra's storm; but the story is here invested with an atmosphere far removed in spirit from its pious Purāṇic origins:

डिगत पानि डिगलात गिरि लखि सब ब्रज बेहाल।
कंप किसोरी दरस कै खरे लजाने लाल॥

661
His shaking hand the mountain shakes—
the sight makes Braj afraid;
Young Lal's abashed at trembling so
on seeing his sweet maid!

The humour here derives from incongruity, a universal amongst comic strategies: in this decadent re-telling the supposed 'hero' is reduced to trembling by the sight of his beloved, and Kṛṣṇa the mountain-holder nearly becomes the mountain-dropper, with the folk of Braj anxiously standing underneath. Kṛṣṇa is here designated not by the expected heroic epithet 'Giridhārī', but by the mockingly *un*heroic epithet of 'Lāl', 'the dear one'. The verse depends upon the fact that the audience is familiar with the original story, which brings a ready-made scenario to their minds when the mountain is mentioned; the heroic aspect of Kṛṣṇa's mountain-holding is a 'given' (and the *Lālcandrikā* commentary solemnly heads this couplet *Bhayānak-rasa varṇan*!) but is not stated, and depends on the audience's familiarity with Purāṇic stories; thus the humour is facilitated by a kind of intertextuality in which the source 'text' is a common reservoir of familiar mythology.

Another example of this process alludes to another mythological episode, the story of Bali and Vāmana, and again the *new* context of the verse is a romantic one:

छूवै छिगुनी पहुँचौ गिलत, अति दीनता दिखाय।
बलि बामन कौ ब्यौंत सुनि को बल तुम्हैं पत्याय॥

225
You touch her little finger, feigning humility, then swallow the wrist;
Hearing the tale of Bali and the dwarf, who, pray, would give you her trust?

The couplet can be understood only by reference to the *trivikrama* myth: Viṣṇu in the form of Vāmana, the dwarf, begs the demonic King Bali for as much land as he can cover in three strides, and when the boon is disdainfully granted as a mere trifle, Vāmana assumes his universal form which allows him to cover the three worlds in his three steps. In the parallel context of courtship, the suitor's modest approach to the girl as he touches her little finger is seen as concealing a similar threat of later territorial expansionism; and the worldly image of the lustful lover is leant humour by its juxtaposition to the prime myth of Vaiṣṇavism.

Such a contrast is exploited in other couplets which make a straightforward reference to the superiority of happiness in this world over spiritual benefit in the next. The 'given' element here is the commonplace religious teaching that the pleasures of the flesh are to be passed over in the quest for salvation. One poem stands this pious thought on its head:

चमक तमक हाँसी सिसक मसक झपट लपटानि।
ए जिहिं रति सो रति मुकति और मुकति अति हानि॥

545
Glitter, titter, passion, sobbing,
hugging, pinching, squeezing;
Salvation lies in such a love—
no other kind's so pleasing.

A similar commitment to the pleasures of this world can be affirmed without the 'salvation' context rather less baldly stated:

तंत्री नाद कबित्त रस सरस राग रति रंग।
अनबूडे बूडे तरे जे बूडे सब अंग॥

10
Viol's note, and poesy, sweet song in passion tossed—
he who drowns in these is saved, and who escapes is lost.

A celebration of *this* world continues with the next couplet, which includes word-plays of the kind that make the foreign reader smile twice: once for the joke itself, a second time for the triumphant pleasure of understanding it. The first line has a playful rhythmic variation in the vowel lengths of *nāhī, nāhī̃, nāhī̃* ('no!')[4] in which Bihārī skilfully exploits the absence of standardized spelling in Braj Bhāṣā: the distinction between the three forms of the same word is emphasized by the fact that each occupies a separate metrical foot in the quarter-verse. A translation cannot vary the English spellings, and has to borrow some EC loanwords instead. In a second word-play in the second line, the syllables of *hā̃sī* 'laughter' reappear with the sense of 'like a "yes"' (*hā̃-sī*, plus emphatic suffix), giving the meaning 'her eyebrows filled with laughter confirm a "yes"-like answer':

जदपि नाहिं नाहीं नहीं बदन लगी जक जाति।
तदपि भौंह हाँसी भरिनु हाँसीयै ठहराति॥

720
Although her lips reiterate
a constant 'Non! Nein! No!',
She smiles with playful eyebrows,
so *she's miles* from meaning so.

The English here attempts to recreate the *hā̃sī/ hā̃sī* play with 'She smiles/she's miles'. The attempt fails because the initial 's' in 'smiles' is realized as /s/ whereas the apostrophe 's' is realized as /z/: thus the correspondence has validity in spelling only. This failure points up a feature of Indo-Aryan languages, whose syllabic structure is so much more productive of correspondences of sound and spelling than English.

Erotic contexts have a universal charm and humour, especially in the 'will she?/won't she?' territory on the borders of sexual and social propriety. Here again the possibility of reading Kṛṣṇa and Rādhā into the roles of the nameless lover and beloved is ever-present, and is usually taken up by the commentators. The sublimely sensual depictions of the grove in the *Gītagovinda* and its late medieval Hindi derivatives are precisely appropriate for the world of Bihārī's lovers, who are aided and abetted in their trysts and assignations by a team of willing *sakhī* confidantes. Specifc devotional context, however, is far from present, and the burden of any intended piety in these verses would surely have sat lightly on the shoulders of Bihārī's royal audience in the Amber court.

Though the poet's world of sexual fantasy is very obviously male-orientated (the *Satsaī* being not exactly a feminist document) the female of the species is at least able to gain the upper hand, as it were, in bed. Bihari is quick to exploit the rhetorical possibilities of *viparīta rati* or 'inverted lovemaking', one of those risqué items for which un-amused European lexicographers of the previous century took refuge in definitions safely encoded in Latin. The heroine in our next example is the mature and knowing lover, the amazon in love's war; and however conventional or even hackneyed the description of *viparīta-rati* or 'inverted love'—with the woman on top of the man—may be, it is lent a novelty by an explicitly graphic (or rather 'sonic') conceit. The ever-vigilant *sakhī* companions come to know that during the love-making the female has moved to the 'superior' position from the fact that the sound of waistbells (*kiṃkinī*) has replaced that of anklets (*maṃjīra*).[5] A moment's thought confirms the accuracy of the image, at least in theory. The brazenness of the portrayal, with its reference to a non-too-subtle wrestler's throw in *paryau jora,* is lent a delicacy by carefully balanced alliteration and the refinement of the couplet's phonetic structure. A clarity of image is ensured by the caesura's clear division of the second line into two distinct clauses, throwing the *kiṃkinī* and the *maṃjīra* into a formal opposition; and this is further reinforced by the contrasted alliteration between clattering *k*'s in the first half line and muted *m*'s in the second:[6]

परयौ जोर विपरीत रति रुपी सुरत रनधीर।
करत कोलाहल किंकिनी गह्यौ मौन मंजीर॥

207
She's gained the top position,
having thrown him on the ground:
Her waist-bells are a-jingle
and her anklets make no sound!

In a further variation, the sexual role-reversal of *viparīta rati* is conflated with a sartorial one in the 'exchange of clothes' conceit, where Rādhā and Hari dress as each other. The situation here becomes more complicated: the two role-reversals cancel each other out, with female Rādhā dressed in male clothes in the upper position, making love to male Kṛṣṇa, dressed in female clothes, underneath:

राधा हरि हरि राधिका बनि आये संकेत।
दंपति रति बिपरीति सुख सहज सुरतहू लेत॥

245
She as he and he as she
came clothed for the tryst;
Though lying in inverted roles,
in 'normal mode' they kissed.

A humorous element is often seen in exaggerated narratives and descriptions whose content is essentially serious. The striking quality of hyperbole lends new life to old metaphors; and though not intended to be inherently or primarily comical, these almost surreal images and metaphors have an incongruity which cannot help but bring a smile to the face of the reader. The comic and the deadpan are perhaps not in conflict here: this is seriously funny verse. Most narrative contexts are, unsurprisingly, romantic or erotic, and the extremes of lovesickness constitute a favourite theme. An excess of *viraha* emaciates the heroine so much that Death, her only salvation from grief, cannot find her even if he wears spectacles:

करी बिरह ऐसी तउ गैल न छाँडतु नीच।
दीनेहू चसमा चखन चाहै लखै न मीच॥

424
The pain of love won't leave her,
whichever way she goes:
So thin that Death can't see her, e'en
with glasses on his nose!

The beloved's emaciated state is so extreme that it not only makes her invisible to Death, it also puts her in danger of the raging storm of her own deep sighing, which buffets her around out of control:

इत आवति चलि जाति उत चली छ सातिक हाथ।
चढी हिँडोरे से रहै लगी उसासनि साथ॥

418
Six cubits here, and seven there,
this way and that she flies;
As though a swing transported her,
propelled by gusting sighs.

In a further image of almost macabre physicality, the poet describes the *nāyikā*'s neck as being fair to the extent of translucence:

खरी लसति गोरे गरै धसति पान की पीक।
मनौ गुलूबँद लाल की लाल लाल दुति लाक॥

492
The betel juice she's swallowing
glows through her throat so fair
As though a ruby'd collar,
red as red, were lying there.

The great and hyperbolic beauty of the *nāyikā*, whether mundane or otherwise, is often to be explained only by reference to divine inspiration. In Bihārī's world the roving eyes of the *nāyak* are commonly portrayed as wayfarers travelling the various lanes, inclines and valleys of the beloved's body. The Creator (*bidhi*), is here described as intent on protecting the *nāyikā*'s pure lustre from the trampling 'feet' of the hero's eyes, and makes her ornaments as a doormat on which they will wipe themselves before moving on to the body itself. Here a comic effect is yielded by the deliberate incongruity between the lofty context of divine will on the one hand, and a down-to-earth domesticity on the other:

मानहु बिधि तन अच्छ छबि स्वच्छ राखिबै काज।
दृग पग पोंछन कौ किये भूखन पायंदाज॥

515
Lest her body bright be sullied
by the tread of wandering eyes,
The Creator made a doormat
in her ornaments' disguise.

A similar cross-reference between the physical and the metaphysical is made in verses describing the extreme slenderness of the heroine's waist, so slight as to have no physical existence at all and to be, like God himself, an entirely abstract phenomenon. The speculative, metaphysical tone of this couplet suggests that something of Emily Dickinson's poetic diction and punctuation might serve in translation:

बुधि अनुमान प्रमान स्त्रुति किये नीठि ठहराइ।
सूछम कटि[7]परब्रह्म की अलख लखी नहि जाइ॥

680
Her waist—and God
are both inferred—
a matter of surmise;
both said to have existence—both
invisible—to eyes.

A variation on this theme has the tongue more firmly in the cheek. Here, in a conceit whose formulaic quality does little to diminish its appeal, Brahmā's role in the creating of the miniscule waist is described:

लगी अनलगी सी जु कटि करी खरी बिधि छीन।
किये मनौ वाही कसरि कुच नितंब अति पीन॥

505
So slender God has made her waist,
its being is in doubt;
He's made up the deficiency
with bust and hips filled out.

The delicacy of the *nāyikā*'s hands too calls for a description combining grace with wit. Here Bihārī conflates a conventional description of female beauty with a satirical jibe at the (equally conventional) character of the father-in-law. This householder is anxious to make savings in the domestic charity budget by entrusting the family alms-giving to the young bride; he thinks her dainty hands will dole out grain in very limited quantities to the mendicants and beggars who come to his door. But the plan backfires when that very 'daintyness of hand' proves to be a crowd-pulling attraction:

कन देबौ सौंप्यौ ससुर बहू थुरहथी जानि।
रूप रहचटे लगि लग्यौ माँगन सब जग आनि।।

651
Her tiny hands seemed perfect
for patriarchal alms,
But now the world's a-begging
for a chance to see her charms.

This couplet is another miniature anecdote, dealing with caricatures who are instantly recognizable from a stock of 'sitcom' types; yet the injection of wit, based on the double application of *thurahathī* 'meagre-handed' gives the *dohā* its poetic quality. As in the couplet describing the cuckolded astrologer's initial shock and subsequent mirth at reading his son's stars, the comic reference of the verse derives also from a reversal of expectations contained within the tiny space of the couplet, with an opposition clearly set up between the two successive lines. So concentrated is the narrative that the full detail cannot be carried by the necessarily wordier English translation. The outcome of the narrative comes in the last quarter of the couplet, *m̃āgana saba jaga āni*, following a pattern which again we have seen earlier in the 'astrologer' couplet (*samajhau jāraja joga*). This last quarter-verse again constitutes a narrative punchline, supplying the key which unlocks the whole story of the miniature anecdote.

Because poetry of this kind abounds with suggestion and non-explicit allusion, it is difficult to know how far to stretch the interpretation of certain verses; many poems have a primary literal context which yields an adequate meaning, but which seem also to hint at a further level of interpretation. Some descriptive couplets in particular are taken by the commentators to be elliptical. At face value the following verse is quite straightforward in context and content:

सोहत संग समान सौं, यहै कहैं सब लोग।
पान पीक ओठनि बनै, नैननि काजर जोग॥

366
'Like looks well with like'—it's true,
and cannot be denied;
Lips look best with betel-juice,
and eyes with kohl applied.

Some commentators read couplets of this type as alluding wryly to the disarray which follows love-making; this so-called *suratānta chabi* or 'post-coital splendour', in which the make-up, jewellery and clothes are in a state which gives away the activities of the previous night, is itself a common and explicit theme in the *Satsaī*. The verse is taken as implying that the black kohl-marks and red betel-stains are misplaced on the lover's face.

Implicit reference or allusion of this kind is a common feature of Bihārī's style; just as his sequestered heroines must communicate their feelings by allusion and an angled glance, so too does Bihārī limit himself to painting in a few narrative details whose general background has to be understood as 'given' from the stock of conventional situations, augmented by the reader's imagination. The unstated context of the following couplet is that the various crops which have provided cover for the beloved's illicit trysts are one by one being harvested, and that there will soon be no safe arbour-like meeting place where she can meet her lover safely hidden from prying eyes; but she is to take courage from the fact that the late-harvested *arhar* (pulse) crop is still standing:

सन सूक्यौ बीत्यौ बनौ ऊखौ लई उखारि।
हरि हरी अरहर अजौं धर धरहर हिय नारि॥

97
The flax is dried, the cotton gone,
the sugarcane unseen;
But do not yet lose heart, my dear—
the *arhar* still stands green.

Verses such as this ride upon a dry humour, gently mocking the eternal and all-too predictable patterns of human behaviour. By contrast with the allusive and suggestive nature of such human comedy, the category of *hāsya rasa* in the *Lālcandrikā* commentary is mostly concerned with situations in which the characters within the poem are themselves struck by mirth. In such a category the verses are *about* comic situations, are often much less comical in overall effect than others where the comedy is more subtly integrated with the narrative; the humour here is usually the protagonists', and is at one remove from the experience of the reader. This is admittedly a dangerous distinction, because humour may vary so across time and space. The rhetoric of sixteenth-century English poets like Bihārī's exact contemporary Crashaw, with his famous description of Mary Magdelene's eyes as 'Two walking baths; two weeping motions; Portable and compendious oceans' seems to us comic in its extravagant hyperbole, but was clearly intended as serious; so it is hard to be sure what intentions Bihārī himself may have had in describing the lovesick pangs of a figure such as the *virahiṇī*, whose grief is after all not so far removed from Mary Magdelene's. Such is the glow of ardour from heart of the love-sick lady (perhaps Rādhā?) that the heat output generated is enough to turn a cold winter's night into a blazing summer day, proving at least that the *virahiṇī* has not yet died of love-pangs:

सुनत पथिक मुँह माह निसि लुऐं चलति उहिं गाम।
बिन बूढे बिनहीं सुने जियति बिचारी बाम॥

435
Unasked, a traveller told me,
'A hot wind yonder blows!'
And so I know, this winter's night
my poor love's ardour glows.

or
Reports of wintry heatwaves
in the far and lonely night
Have proved to me beyond all doubt
my dear one's heart's alight.

Such extreme symptoms of the effects of love inevitably betray the emotions of the beloved. The fair beauty of the beloved's face does not just put the moon to shame—as in the standard conceit—but it fills the night sky, making it impossible to determine the phase of the moon:

पत्राही तिथि पाइये वा घर के चहुँ पास।
नितप्रति पून्यौई रहै आनन ओप उजास॥

489
Only from the almanac
we know the lunar phase
where stealing full-moon's brilliance
my darling's face does blaze.

or
'Consult the calendar!' perplexed
astrologers opine
where all around with full-moon's light
her radiant face doth shine.

Despite the humour and wit which seems to the modern reader to bubble out of the *Satsaī*, the commentators are not, for the most part, very funny fellows. The plodding seriousness of the stolid *Ratnākarī* commentary, which has come to be regarded as the standard interpretation of the text, strikes many an unwittingly humorous note in its solemnly pedantic judgements on the verses. The commentary to the following *dohā*, a hauntingly bittersweet poem about the nostalgia of days gone by, is a case in point:

इहीं आस अटक्यौ रहै अलि गुलाब के मूल।
ह्वैहैं फेरि बसंत रितु इनि डारनि वे फूल॥

632
In this one hope the bumble bee
around the rose-root stays:
that flowers will once more come to bloom
with Spring's returning days.

Ratnakar's straight-faced comment here is a solemn 'Bees do not linger around the roots of rose-trees. This is the poet's fanciful conceit' (Das 'Ratnakar' 1969: 180).

This paper has tried to show how comedy is a leavening ingredient in Bihārī's poetry, bringing lightness of touch to many a conventional or hackneyed theme. One could debate almost endlessly the intentionality behind such verses; are they 'funny' or not? A spiritual and devotional tradition in which God steals butter and nearly drops mountains on his devotees, and in which demons have to be awoken from their post-prandial slumbers by having trumpets blown down their ears, seems well-equipped to make light of the transition between the sublimely serious and the sublimely humorous; and this perhaps underlies the delightfully light comic references which run through Bihārī's poetry and contributes very substantially to making them 'both pleasant and profitable to the well smelling noses of learned Readers'.

NOTES

1. The edition used here is Sudhakar Pandey, ed., *Bihārī-Satsaī* (based on the Fort William edition of Lallulal with introduction by G.A. Grierson), Varanasi 1977.
2. For a recent translation of selections from the Prakrit text see Arvind Krishna Mehrotra, *The absent traveller: Prākrit love poetry from the Gāthāsaptaśatī of Sātavāhana Hāla*, Delhi 1991.
3. Modern Hindi poetry, which has abandoned the *dohā* (perhaps because of the prolixity of the modern Hindi verb system) shares his problem.
4. Cf. the use of Upanishadic *neti neti* in this 'No! No!' context in a devotional—but surely also humorous—reference from the sixteenth-century Rādhāvallabhī text *Caurāsī pada* (Snell 1991: 171).
5. The model for this conceit is perhaps the following verse from the *Subhāṣitaratnakoṣa*: 'When the anklet has grown still/the girdle's sound is heard./ It's ever when the lover tires,/ the mistress plays the man' (Ingalls 1968: 158).
6. The Ratnakara commentary points out, rather superfluously, that the feminine and masculine genders of *kiṃkinī* and *maṃjīra* respectively further buttress the distinction between the ascendancy of female over male during *viparīta rati*.
7. Reading cited variant *rati* for textual *gati*.

REFERENCES

Das, Jagannath 'Ratnakar'. 1969. *Bihārī-ratnākar*, 5th edn, Varanasi.

Holland, Baron. 1969. *The Satsaī of Bihārī: Hindi poetry of the early Rīti period*, Ph.D. Dissertation, University of California.

Ingalls, Daniel H.H. (trans.). 1968. *Sanskrit Poetry from Vidyākara's 'Treasury'*, Cambridge Massachusetts.

McGregor, R.S. 1984. *Hindi Literature from its Beginnings to the Nineteenth Century*, Harrassowitz Wiesbaden.

Mehrotra, Arvind Krishna. 1991. *The Absent traveller: Prākrit love poetry from the Gāthāsaptaśatī of Sātavāhana Hāla*, Delhi.

Pandey, Sudhakar (ed.). 1977. *Bihārī-Satsaī (based on the Fort William edition of Lallūlāl with introduction by G.A. Grierson)*, Varanasi: Nagari Pracarini Sabha.

Snell, R. 1991. *The Eighty-four Hymns of Hita Harivaṃśa*, Delhi: Motilal Banarsidass.

Poet who Laughed in Pain: Akbar Ilahabadi

SADIQ-UR-RAHMAN KIDWAI

Urdu language and literature had bloomed when the Mughal empire was on its last legs. It was natural that the intellectual and emotional despair resulting from the tragedy of the break-up of the empire, internal dissensions and foreign intervention should have crept into literature. Despite the popular opinion about Urdu being mainly lyrical and love-lorn, history shows that it has been most sensitive to the happenings in the external world, especially at the centres of political power, which were incidentally located in the heartland of Urdu. Poets of the eighteenth and nineteenth centuries like Sauda, Meer, Nazeer and Insha had lived through the days when Delhi—their homeland—was being invaded by outsiders. Loot, murder and plunder were the order of the day. These people had suffered a lot and had to migrate from Delhi during the attacks of Nadir Shah and Ahmed Shah Abdali. Ghalib was witness to the upheavals of 1857, and also became a victim because of his association with the poet-king Bahadur Shah Zafar, the last ruler of the Mughal dynasty. Even the *ġazal* of this period—a genre reserved for the lyrical style—is known to depict the underlying turbulence of pain and sorrow, both personal and social.

Tragic happenings 'left to themselves' would have destroyed human civilization long ago, but for the sense of humour which came to its rescue. In fact, it is during tragic circumstances that comic aspects of life emerge most effectively in contrast. Humour, apart from being a balancing force and a momentary relief, gives depth to the meaning of what tragedy had brought in its wake.

The process of the change over from the decadent Mughal period to an oppressive colonial rule by the British provided enough incentive to the humorist and satirist underlying every sensitive personality. Along with the *ġazal* there were other genres best suited to humour and satire such as *hajv*[1] and *śahr āśob*[2] which flourished during these times. In one such poem, Sauda (1707-81) described the wedding procession of a young handsome soldier of the king's army. Here, the bridegroom rode a starving horse which moved very slowly. Passers-by pitied the bridegroom and offered suggestions like putting the sail of a ship on the back of the horse or wheels under the hooves to improve the speed. When the procession ultimately reached the bride's house, the soldier bridegroom had grown too old to remain eligible for marriage (Hasan 1985: 182-5). Similarly, Ghalib (1797-1869), whose letters are among the classics of Urdu prose and masterpieces of humour and satire, made fun of the laws of succession in one of his letters to the Maharaja of a neighbouring state of Delhi. According to him, the Maharaja was due to reach maturity and quality for the age when he could be handed over the reigns of his ancestral state by the East India Company. This power, Ghalib said, would be the same as the one granted by God to man on this earth (Anjum 1985: 537).

Such were the times! Utter helplessness! The poet was not just the distant observer of the tragedy, he was himself a part of the crumbling edifice and caught in a dilemma: should he accept the change or cling to his former loyalties. By accepting the change he had to face the challenge of adapting himself to the new situation. And there was a very thin line of demarcation between adaptation and submission, learning from one's own failures or imitating the new conquerors who were alien in many ways from the point of view of religion, ethnicity, language, etc. The expression of various responses to such a change in the national scenario could take the form of both tragedy and comedy, and in Urdu we find literary masterpieces in both genres. But humour stands out in the whole gamut of Urdu literature at the end of nineteenth and beginning of the twentieth century. The heights Urdu humour reached in that period is still unsurpassed. *Fasāna-i-Āzād*, the famous prose work of Ratan Nath Sarshar (1845-1903) in four bulky volumes caricatured Lucknow's decadent aristocracy, and the poetry of Akbar Ilahabadi 1846-1921)[3] encompassed the totality of colonial culture flourishing in the nineteenth and early twentieth century in all its facets.

As an employee in the judicial department of the colonial regime, Akbar had the opportunity of seeing the new emerging culture from close quarters. He had intimately observed the life of Englishmen and the Indian career-seekers surrounding their masters. And it was this strata of society which was the target of Akbar's humour. Whatever promotion one could attain in the service of the government, Indians would never become the equals of the British. For example:

بَنے بَندَر سے ہَم اِنسَان تَرَقّی اِس کو کَہتے ہَیں
تَرَقّی پَر بھِی نیٹِو ، بَدنَصِیبِی اِس کو کَہتے ہَیں

(Kidwai 1982: 115)

From ape we progressed and became human.
But despite progress we still remain natives, what a misfortune!*[4]

He made the distinction between a s̱āẖib and a bābū. S̱āẖib was the

English officer, even if low in hierarchy, and Bābū an Indian, even if not very low (though very few Indians could reach any position of importance during Akbar's time). Besides, however high and mighty an Indian pretended to be, he remained a 'native'. Akbar was very fond of this word. It included all loyalists and imitators whether they were members of the Viceroy's Council or *bābūs* in any obscure part of the country. These so-called natives tried to out-do each other in aping the way of life of the *s̱āẖib* in mannerisms, dress, behaviour, etc. About them Akbar says:

بھلا کیا پوچھنا ہے شانِ اکبر کا زمانے میں
کہ وہ نیٹو بھی ہے ہندوستانی بھی مسلماں بھی

Why ask what Akbar's standing is these days.
First, 'native'; second, Indian; third, Muslim.
(Russell 1974: 16)

چار دن کی زندگی ہے کوفت سے کیا فائدہ
کھا ڈبل روٹی کلرکی کر خوشی سے پھول جا

Life is short. Best not to worry over much.
Eat English bread, and push your pen, and swell with happiness.
(Russell 1974: 29)

پارک میں اُن کے دیا کرتا ہے اسپیچِ وفا
زاغ ہو جائے گا اِک دِن آنریری عندلیب

Perched in their park the crow makes loyal speeches.
One day they'll make him honorary nightingale.
(Russell 1974: 37)

But Akbar was also conscious of the fact that he was far behind the times and whatever little of the past was left was not destined to survive for long. And on occasions it was a sense of tragic despair, mixed with humour that dominated his mood.

مذہب کی کہوں تو دِل لگی میں اُڑ جائے
مطلب کی کہوں تو پالِسی میں اُڑ جائے

باقی سرِ قوم میں ابھی ہے کچھ ہوش
غالِب ہے کہ یہ بھی اِس صدی میں اُڑ جائے

Religious truths? They make a joke of them.
Sound sense? Oh no! That is not policy.
The nation still has *some* sense in its head.
That too may not outlast this century.
(Russell 1974: 40)

Akbar was fully aware of the pace of change and tried to hold his ground but at the same time he was amused at his own perseverance. Hidden behind this laughter was the sorrow at the apathy of those who did not realize the depth of their degradation. By laughing at himself he cleverly disarms his adversaries, and at the same time shows them their own caricatures. For instance:

تاکیدِ عبادت پہ یہ اب کہتے ہیں لڑکے
پیری میں بھی اکبر کی ظرافت نہیں جاتی

(Kidwai 1982: 69)

When he appeals to the young boys to go to the prayers, they say 'Look at this man! Even at such an old age, Akbar has not ceased to be humorous.'*

Or on being invited to address the students of a college built on the British model, he said:

یہ اُن کا کورس کیا کم ہے کہ میں بھی کچھ کہوں اُن سے
مری جانب سے بس کالج کے لڑکوں کو دعا کہیے

(Kidwai 1982: 68)

Poor boys—already overburdened by their courses! How can they suffer one more lecture.
It is enough for them to know that I pray for them all the time.*

When Akbar laughed at himself this laughter was underlaid by the defeat of a person who had lost the cause, but at the same time had not lost faith and felt that the seemingly successful adversaries were destined to face a worse defeat. It was a defeat of both parties, a total defeat of the Indian people, but some of them took this defeat as their triumph because they were not sensitive to their own grievous loss of face. They had totally subjugated themselves to their masters, therefore even in the hour of their humiliation they would not share their sense of shame with others because of their false pride:

ہم کیا کہیں احباب کیا کارِ نمایاں کر گئے
بی اے ہوئے نوکر ہوئے پنشن ملی پھر مر گئے

What words of mine can tell the deeds of men like these,
our nation's pride?
They got their B.A., took employment, drew their pensions
and then died.

(Russell 1974: 29)

To laugh at oneself instead of laughing at others, is perhaps the most honest of all laughters. Here one accepts the reality of being out of tune with one's surroundings. In such situations a person laughs at everyone including himself. Akbar's laughter at his own cost was the most serious statement about those times when socio-political forces were not keeping pace with the aspirations of large sections of the Indian intelligentsia. The impact of colonialism on various aspects of life cannot be over-emphasized. One aspect which most stirred the sensitivities of Akbar was the gradual acceptance of a subservient, slave-like existence by a considerable section of people, especially the newly educated class who thought that they had found the solution to the malaise. The perpetuation of colonial culture under which servile intellects could pretend to represent the future hope of the nation was the most tragic consequence of the educational system brought in by the British. Dressing up like Englishmen, twisting and distorting their own language and accent to imitate the rulers, and showing off, as it were, an attitude reminiscent of a superior level of existence by action and gesture had become the distinctive mark of the graduates aspiring to become civil servants. In common parlance it came to be known as 'toadyism' or '*bābū* culture', expressions which stressed the contempt of ordinary Indians towards the loyal servants of the empire. This contempt aroused comic responses, of which Akbar's verses were the most representative.

قَتل سے پَہلے ہَے کلورَافَارم
شُکر ہَے اُن کی مِہربَانِی کَا

Before they murder us they chloroform us.
We ought to render thanks that they are kind.
(Russell 1974: 11)

تَعلِیم جو دِی جَاتِی ہَے ہَمیں وَہ کیَا ہَے فَقط بَازَارِی ہَے
جو عَقل سِکھَائِی جَاتِی ہَے وَہ کیَا ہَے فَقَط سَرکَارِی ہَے

They give us learning—just enough for us to sell our services.
And understanding—just enough for governmental purposes.
(Russell 1974: 12)

But Akbar was wise enough to see the direction in which the world was moving. After all, the demands of material comfort, good jobs and secure future could be attained only by coming closer to the ruling power. And to fulfil its requirements many had to do things which were not to their own liking. Akbar himself had started as an ordinary clerk and rose to the position of a judge. But he used this opportunity to laugh louder, where others of similar status were either shy or afraid of opening their mouths. To focus on the funny aspects of his subject and to highlight the imbalance of forces in a particular situation he exaggerated as caricaturists and cartoonists usually did. This made his tilt towards conservatism more pronounced. But he was writing in the context of the impact of the colonial assault on religion, education and science and was not prepared to equate modernization with imitation of the British. Ralph Russel and Khursheedul Islam have therefore rightly emphasized that 'He is not the wooden, unimaginative, unthinking, obstinate conservative that some have made him out to be' (1974: 57).

Imagine the Indian situation during the freedom struggle when a sharp and effective speech, article or poem used to become the talk of the town the next day. Such humour was the most refined of all tactics to attack against the loyalists. And the subtlety of laughing at oneself made humour more attractive and effective. In the Urdu-Hindi belt the oral tradition is so strongly rooted that it often lends appeal to the written word. Printed poetry, by sheer force of tradition, spreads by word of mouth instantaneously. Poetry recited at the *muśā'iras* from the stage is automatically popular both because of the musical rhyme and metre and because of its topicality and immediate appeal of the subject to the social environment. It may be good or bad poetry, but undoubtedly it moves and touches the inner core of the heart at that particular moment even though it may not survive as great poetry. Akbar's poetry survived because of its poetic quality, and also, as Russell and Islam say, because of its increasing relevance to the times, as people were becoming more and more conscious of the consequences of imperial rule on their culture (1974: 55).

The poets of Urdu have been traditionally sensitive about using words of common speech in poetry. It is not that they are against the use of ordinary speech in poetry, but its usage must be according to the accepted aesthetic standards. Even the so-called standard language of Delhi and Lucknow must be used according to the literary taste of the sophisticated literary community of Urdu, or eyebrows would be raised at the writings of even the most prominent literary figures. So with the increasing impact of English on the Indian languages, large numbers of words and phrases were adapted in day-to-day speech and the process has been increasing. Even today more and more words are being borrowed not only from English but from other European languages as well. However, these English words tended not to be used by poets. Akbar was the first important poet who used a large number of English words in his poetry. Apart from reflecting his liberal creative attitude toward language it was also one of his tactics to generate humour. Using English words in poetry always amused him because of its strangeness and its sheer contrast with the age-old tradition which Akbar loved to highlight. Akbar's use of English words was ingenious in making the *bābūs* and their culture the butt of jokes and ridicule. But often he used English words just because he wanted to attract attention and also because this was the language which was more and more used and understood by the younger generation. For example:

زِندَگی اَور قِیامَت میں رِلیشن سَمجھو
اِس کو کالِج اَور اُسے کانووکیشن سَمجھو

Life and the Last Day bear the same relation—
(Mark this)—as college does to Convocation.
(Russell 1974: 24)

There is nothing amusing in the idea as such, but the use of the English words 'relation, convocation' and weaving them into the rhyming system of Urdu verse makes for interesting verse. Also the new educational system that came with the advent of British rule was symbolized by words like 'college', 'convocation', 'speech', 'dinner', 'leader', etc.

Akbar is critical of the stress on material comfort, and this is the root cause of his pain. He says:

شِکَم ہوتَا تو مَیں اِس عَہد میں پھُولَا ہُوءَا رَہتَا
سَرَاپَا دِل بَنَا ہُوں اِس سَبَب سے کَشتَۂ غَم ہُوں

(Kidwai 1982: 67)

If I had only a tummy I would have been full and satisfied.
But I have a heart too and that makes me sad.*

The evils of colonial rule and its consequences as visualized by Akbar had occupied his mind throughout and to reinforce his argument he did not spare anything which was associated with the rulers. In his search for fresh metaphors of humour he explored even their religious faith and scientific discoveries. His apprehension of a Hindu-Muslim split due to the well-known British policy of 'Divide and Rule' carried his imagination into the arena of the Christian belief in the Trinity:

یُورَپ وَالے جو چَاہیں دِل میں بھَر دیں
جِس کے سَر پَر جو چَاہیں تُہمَت دھَر دیں
بَچتے رَہو اُن کے تیزِیوں سے اَکبَر
تُم کیَا ہو خُدَا کے تِین ٹُکڑے کَر دیں

The Englishman can slander whom he will
And fill your head with anything he pleases.
He wields sharp weapons, Akbar. Best stand clear!
He cuts up god himself into three pieces.
(Russell 1974: 18)

The India of Akbar's time stands divided into three nations today! To express his unhappiness over the gradual destruction of time-honoured social values and the re-emergence of the animal in humans Akbar went as far as Darwin's theory. He found evolution in the reverse in the Indian context where aping of the British had come to be respected:

ہَم تو اِنسَان سے بَنے جَاتے ہَیں بَندَر اے حُضُور
آپ خُوش قِسمَت تھے بَندَر سے جو اِنسَان ہو گئے

Fate favoured you, kind sir: *you* grew from monkeyhood to manhood
See *our* ill luck: once men, we grow more monkey-like each day.
(Russell 1974: 34)

More than seventy years have passed since Akbar breathed his last. The socio-political fabric of the Indian subcontinent has undergone an enormous change. So has its ethos. However, Akbar's poetry laden with biting sarcasm and tremendous wit has not lost its appeal. Wherever Urdu is spoken, Akbar's couplets still crop up in the everyday conversation of the people. Thus, even today, though the contexts might have changed the concerns of Akbar Ilahabadi have not lost their relevance. This is best exemplified in the poem which he wrote on the Delhi Durbar of 1911, which was the greatest show of pomp and grandeur put up by the British Empire (Kidwai 1982: 77-80). Here, Akbar describes the whole show in such a light vein that it brings out the inherent irony in the whole exercise and thus exposes it to great ridicule.

It is a telling comment that today what is remembered is Akbar's poem rather than the event itself.

سر میں شوق کا سودا دیکھا   دہلی کو ہم نے بھی جا دیکھا
جو کچھ دیکھا اچھا دیکھا   کیا بتلائیں کیا کیا دیکھا

I saw minds maddened by excitement
I too went and saw what Delhi was about
I got a good look at whatever I saw
How do I recount all that I saw.
. . .

جمنا جی کے پاٹ کو دیکھا   اچھے ستھرے گھاٹ کو دیکھا
سب سے اونچے لاٹ کو دیکھا   حضرت ڈیوک کناٹ کو دیکھا

I saw the expanse of Jamunaji
As also her nice and clean ghats.
I saw the highest pillar of all
And also the honourable Duke of Connaught.
. . .

پلٹن اور رسالے دیکھے   گورے دیکھے کالے دیکھے
سنگینیں اور بھالے دیکھے   بینڈ بجانے والے دیکھے

I saw platoons and cavalry
White faces and black
I saw swords and shields
And those who played the band.
. . .

اچھے اچھوں کو بھٹکا دیکھا   بھیڑ میں کھاتے جھٹکا دیکھا
منہ کو اگرچہ لٹکا دیکھا   دل دربار سے اٹکا دیکھا

I saw the high, wandering,
being jostled in the crowd
Even if their faces hung, long
Their hearts were caught in the darbar.
. . .

اوج برٹش راج کا دیکھا   پرتو تخت و تاج کا دیکھا
رنگِ زمانہ آج کا دیکھا   رخ کرزن مہراج کا دیکھا

I saw the height of the British raj
the splendour of the thrown and crown

I saw the ways of todays world
and the face of the emperor Curzon.

. . .

پہنچے پھاند کے سات سمندر تحت میں ان کے بیسوں بندر
حکمت و دانش ان کے اندر اپنی جگہ ہر ایک سکندر

They jumped the seven seas to get there
among them a score of baboons
All with wisdom and knowledge within them
Each, a world conqueror, according to himself.

. . .

جشنِ عظیم اس سال ہوا ہے شاہی فورٹ میں بال ہوا ہے
روشن ہر اک ہال ہوا ہے قصۂ ماضی حال ہوا ہے

What a great event this one
A ball in the royal fort
Every hall illuminated
The tales of the past come alive.[5]

NOTES

1. *hajv*: Poems with the object of making fun of someone.
2. *śahr āśob*: Poems which focused on the general deterioration of life at a particular time.
3. Sayyid Akbar Husain *Akbar* was born at Barah (Allahabad) on 16 November 1846. After completing his education in Arabic, Persian, Theology, etc., according to the convention of those days, he learnt English on his own. Starting with smaller jobs he got a breakthrough in the Judicial Department of the government after passing an examination in law. He rose to the post of the Session Judge, and retired due to ill health. Like others from the aristocratic stock, he lived a carefree life during his younger day, wrote amorous *gazals*, but matured with changing times. He died on 9 September 1921.
4. This author gratefully acknowledges his debt to Ralph Russell and Khursheedul Islam from whose exhaustive paper entitled 'The Satirical Verse of Akbar Ilāhābādī' (1974), most of the English renderings of *Akbar*'s verses have been borrowed. Translations attempted by the author have been marked with asterisks.
5. Translation by Saleem Kidwai, the author is thankful to him.

REFERENCES

Anjum, Khāliq (ed.), 1985. *Gālib ke khutūt,* vol. 2. New Delhi: Ghalib Institute.

Hasan, Muhammad (ed.), 1985. *Kulliyāt-i-Saudā,* vol. 1. New Delhi: Tariqqi-i-Urdu Bureau.

Qidvā'ī, Sadīqu-'r-Rahman (ed.), 1982. *Intikhāb-i-Akbar Ilāhābādī.* New Delhi: Maktaba Jamia Ltd.

Russel, Ralph and Khursheedul Islam. 1974. 'The Satirical Verse of Akbar Ilahabadi (1846-1941).' *Modern Asian Studies* 8, 1: 1-58.

Iqbal Inspired Humour: A Note on Parodies by Selected Urdu Poets

FATEH MUHAMMAD MALIK

Allama Muhammad Iqbal (1877-1938) continues to be a favourite target of Urdu humorous poets in Pakistan. The use of the art and form of literary comedy is popular among these poets. There are two good reasons for this: First, the immense popularity of Iqbal's poetry and the second, his position and prestige as the spiritual father of Pakistan.

Iqbal's name and fame had crossed the boundaries of South Asia in the initial phase of his poetic career, i.e. during the first decade of the twentieth century and increased ever since. As far as the Muslim world is concerned, Iqbal lives in the hearts and minds of common folk. Prof. Reinhold Loeffler tells us that during the course of anthropological fieldwork in a remote Iranian village, he has encountered semi-literate peasants striving to live up to the ideals enunciated in Iqbal's poetry (1988: 79).

In Pakistan Iqbal is universally quoted, day in and day out from the highest to the lowest. His poetry is recited from the cradle to the corridors of power, from the elementary school to the parliament house. But those who take pride in quoting him are seldom ashamed of doing exactly the opposite things. Their deeds belie their words. Iqbal is being used in Pakistan in the same fashion as one of his most favourite poets, Goethe, was used in the Weimar Republic. It was aptly observed on the centenary of Goethe's death that: 'Official Germany celebrates Goethe not as poet and prophet but above all as opium' (Karl von Ossietzky as quoted by Peter Gay 1968: 193)

Such is the fate of Iqbal in Pakistan. His ideal of the creation of a Universal Community based on the liberal, egalitarian and humanistic values of Islam is so far an unrealized dream, a mere poetic vision. Everyone in the ruling class quotes him but no one follows him. Hypocricy has become an accepted norm with the Pakistani elite. This moral degeneration provides an excellent occasion for the comic poet to speak the whole truth.

Humour in Urdu has always had serious consequences. From Sauda (1713-80), Ghalib (1797-1869), Akbar (1846-1921) and Iqbal to the most noted contemporary writer, Mushtaq Ahmed Yousafi, we find Urdu humorists passionately engaged in an attempt to arrest the tide of social degeneration and moral decay. They attack each and every departure from the social ideals in which they firmly believe with the weapons and skills of a humorist. They begin with mockery, joking, and pleasant fiction but end on a sad note. An acute awareness of the widespread evils of their day is the mainspring of their humour. This gives their comic compositions a significant tragic sense.

While enjoying their humour one feels that the keynotes are of a deep personal sadness. These melancholy shades of laughter have given our humour a distinct character. Urdu humour gives such rare insights into our cultural history that it can be read as a historical document without undermining its artistic achievements. Parody is no exception to this rule.

Iqbal himself composed several memorable *ẓarīfāna* (humorous) poems during the formative phase of his poetic personality. Later on he abandoned humorous verse in favour of serious and philosophical poetry. But his rich sense of humour forms an undertone to his poetry. Occasionally the humorous spirit becomes so dominant that the poem is transformed into an excellent piece of ironic verse. His poem *Mullā aur bahiśt* (Paradise and the Priest) will serve as an example:

مَیں بھی حَاضِر تھا وَہاں ضَبطِ سُخَن نَه کَر سَکا
حَق سے جَب حَضرَتِ مُلّا کو مِلَا حُکمِ بِہشت
عَرض کی مَیں نے اِلٰہی مِرِی تَقصِیر مُعَاف
خُوش نَه آئیں گے اِسے حُور و شَرَاب و لَبِ کَشت
نَہیں فِردَوس مَقَامِ جَدَلِ قَال و اَقُول
بَحث و تَکرَار اِس اَللہ کے بَندے کی سَرِشت
ہَے بَد آمُوزِیٔ اَقوَام و مِلَل کَام اِس کَا
اَور جَنَّت میں نَه مَسجِد نَه کَلِیسَا نَه کُنِشت

(Iqbal 1990a: 445)

I was present there and could not hold my tongue; when God ordained the Mulla to Paradise,
Submissively I uttered: 'Forgive me, He will not care for houri, wine and verdant fields.
Paradise is not the place to bicker, argue and quarrel,
And quibbling and wrangling form the very nature of this man
Throwing mud at people and faiths is his vocation,
And in Paradise there is no mosque, no church, no temple.'

The following quatrain in Persian is one of the best illustrations of his wit and humour:

زِ مَن بر صُوفی و مُلّا سَلامے
کہ پیغامِ خُدا گُفتند مَا رَا
وَلے تاویلِ شَان دَر حَیرت اَنداخت
خُدا و جِبرَئیل و مُصطفٰے رَا

(Iqbal 1990b: 816)

My greetings to Sufi and to Mulla,
For they interpreted to us God's message,
But their commentaries have bewildered
Even God, Gabriel and Mustafa!

It is ironic to note that we, in Pakistan, have left Sufi and Mulla far behind with our misinterpretation and distortions of the message of Iqbal. This ideological betrayal has been assailed by many a humorist poet. Syed Zamir Jafery's (b. 1917)[1] poem *Iqbāl aur Ham* (Iqbal and We) brings the gap between our ideal and our practice into sharp focus:

اِقبال کَا پَیَامِ اُخُوّت کَا تَرجُمَان
مِلّت کو دیکھیے کِہ ہَے آپس میں ہَم نَبَرد
دَاعِی وَہ فَقر کَا تَھَا پَیَمبَر خُودِی کَا تَھَا
تَن پَر ہَمَارے قَرض کی پوشَاکِ لَاجَوَرد
کَہتَا تَھَا شَالاَمَار میں کَل ایک بَرگِ زَرد
بُلبُل چِہ گُفت، گُل چِہ شُنِید و صَبَا چِہ کَرد

(Jafery 1978: 57)

Iqbal gave us the message of unity,
But the nation is involved in internal strife.
That prophet of self-reliance took pride in poverty,
But we are proud of colorful garments of borrowed luxury.
Yesterday in the Shalamar Gardens, a dry leaf said:
The nightingale said one thing, the rose understood another and the
Zephyr acted in a totally different manner.

The same conflict between the ideal and the reality inspires Mirza Mahmud Sarhadi (d. 1968)[2] to burst out in satire:

ہَم نے اِقبَال کَا کَہَا مَانَا
اَور فَاقوں کے ہَاتھوں مَرتے رَہے

جھُکنے وَالوں نے رِفعَتیں پَائِیں
ہَم خُودِی کو بُلَند کَرتے رَہے

(Sarhadi 1967: 80)

Our commitment to the ideals of Iqbal has brought us to the brink of death through starvation.
Those who could stoop low acquired the heights of progress while we struggled hard to preserve our *khudī*.

Khudī (selfhood) is one of the key concepts of Iqbal. The term *khudi* has been variously translated as ego, personality and selfhood, meaning the independence, self-determination and self-reliance of the human ego. No attempt has been made to bring this concept into play in the spaco-temporal life. The shameless disregard of Iqbal's concept of *khudī* in individual as well as collective life is the recurrent theme in our humorous poetry. Iqbal had said:

خُودِی کو کَر بُلَند اِتنا کِہ ہَر تَقدِیر سے پہلے
خُدَا بَندے سے خُود پُوچھے بَتَا تیرِی رِضا کیَا ہَے؟

Exalt your selfhood so high that
Before every decision of fate
God will ask of man
Tell me: 'What is your will?'

Majeed Lahori (1916-57) and Syed Muhammad Jafery (1905-76) have reflected in a lighter vein on how we have made a mockery of this concept in the following lines respectively:

خُودِی کو کَر بُلَند اِتنَا کِہ ہَر اِک فِیسٹ سے پہلے
خُدَا بَندے سے خُود پُوچھے بَتَا تیرِی غِذَا کیَا ہَے؟

(Lahori 1990)

Exalt your selfhood so high that
Before every decision of feast
God will ask of man
Tell me: 'What will you eat?

خُودِی جو خُود کَا مُؤَنّث ہَے گھَر میں رَہتِی ہے

(Sarhadi 1967)

Since *khudī* is the feminine gender of *khud*
she lives within the four walls of the house.

During the first decades of Pakistan's emergence as a nation new opportunities in the promised land were seized by a ruthless coterie of politicians with a shocking want of character. After grabbing positions of profit and power this small group of individuals saw to it that nothing essential changed. The revolutionary ideas highlighted during the movement for Pakistan were thus turned into conformist ideas within a very short span of time. In order to check the spreading disenchantment the humorist poet responded with an overriding impulse for reform. Parodies of Iqbal's tremendously popular poems became the main weapon to combat political opportunism and moral bankruptcy.

Parody appeared on the horizon of Urdu literature with the advent of humour itself. In picking up Iqbal's poetry as the prime target of their parodies, Pakistani poets were inspired by the continuing tradition of literary parody. From Ratan Nath Sarshar (1845-1903) to the contemporary humorist Inam ul Haq Javed (b. 1949), many a gifted writer has contributed to the prestige and popularity of parody as a medium of humorous verse. These poets targeted Iqbal not only because of his popularity as a poet who has elevated poetry to prophecy but also because of his exalted position as the patron saint of Pakistan. Iqbal symbolizes great human ideals that are in sharp contrast with the ugly realities of the state and society that he had envisioned.

Syed Muhammad Jafery and Majeed Lahori are the most gifted parodists among the Urdu humorist poets who have tried their hands on parodies of Iqbal's poems.

Syed Muhammad Jafery was born to a family of educational reformers in Bharatpur. The family moved to Lahore in 1911 when his father became the founder principal of the Islamia College. He took his masters in English literature from Government College and secured a diploma in drawing and calligraphy from the National College of Arts. His skill at calligraphy brought him close to Iqbal. The Jaferis lived in the neighbourhood of Iqbal and his father visited Iqbal frequently. Sometimes Muhammad Jafery used to accompany his father. He was asked by Iqbal to write down his latest verse during the poet's last illness when his eyesight had almost vanished. After teaching at a number of institutions he joined the Press Information Department of the government and attained the highest bureaucratic position before retirement in 1966. Jafery started composing while still a student and made his mark during the early forties. The collection of his humorous verse, *Śokhī-i-taḫrīr*, appeared posthumously in 1985.

Jafery has written a number of parodies including *Tarāna-i-Dihlī, Vazīrõ kī namāz* and *Election kā sāqī nāma.* His *Tarāna-i-Dihlī* (Song of Dehli) is the parody of Iqbal's widely popular poem *Tarāna-i-hindī* (Song of Indian Children), which according to Rajmohan Gandhi, is the unofficial national anthem of India (1988: 50). Iqbal Singh regards this poem as 'the best patriotic poem written by any poet in modern times. It comes nearest to truly non-communal, national anthem for India' (1951: 24).

Vazīrõ kī namāz (Ministerial Prayers) is a parody of Iqbal's popular poem *Śikvah,* which in the words of Wilfred Cantwell Smith is a 'superlatively significant' long poem. Smith identifies 'certain values of ethical orientation' embodied in this poem as the values that 'constitute the essence of Islam. Iqbal considered these values as crucial both to the survival and development of mankind' (Smith 1957: 54). Jafery's *Vazīrõ kī namāz* highlights the betrayal of these values. The following three stanzas will serve as an illustration:[3]

عِید اُلَضحٰی کی نَماز اَور وَہ اَنبوۂِ کَثِیر
جَبکِہ اَللہ کے دَربَار میں تھے پَاک وَزِیر
وَہ مُصَلّوں پَہ مُسَلَّط تھے بَہ حُسنِ تقدِیر
تھے رِیزَرو اُن کے مُصَلّے، یَہ مُسَاوَاتِ کَبِیر

آج کَل یَہ ہَے نَمَاز اَور کَبھِی وَہ تھِی نَماز
ایک ہِی صَف میں کھَڑے ہو گَئے مَحُمود و اَیَاز

عِطر میں ریشمِی رُومَال بَسَایا ہَم نے
سَاتھ لَائے تھے مُصَلّٰے وَہ بِچھَایَا ہَم نے
دُور سے چِہرَہ وَزِیروں کو دِکھَایَا ہَم نے
ہَر بَڑے شَخص کو سِینے سے لَگَایَا ہَم نے

«پھِر بھِی ہَم سے یَہ گِلَّہ ہَے کِہ وَفَادَار نَہِیں»
کَون کَہتَا ہَے کِہ ہَم لَائِقِ دَربَار نَہِیں

ذِکر خُطبے میں وَزِیروں کَا جو پَایَا ہَم نے
آسمَانوں کو زَمِینوں سے مِلَایَا ہَم نے
کَعبَۂِ دِل کو صَنَم خَانَہ بَنَایَا ہَم نے
نَقشِ تَوحِید جَبِینوں سے مِٹَایَا ہَم نے

خوگرِ پیکرِ محسوس ہے اِنسان کی نَظر
مَان لیتا کوئی آن دیکھے خُدا کو کیونکر

لوگ مَصرُوف تھے بَاتوں میں تو خُطبے میں اِمَام
اَور مُشکِل تھا وَزیروں پہ قِیَام اَور خِرَام
توڑ کر اَپنی صَفوں اَور قِطَاروں کا نِظَام
مُضطَرِب ہَاتھ مِلَانے کے لِیے تھے جو عَوَام

سَازِ خَاموش تھے فَریَاد سے مَعمُور وَزِیر
قِصّۂ دَرد سُنَانے پَہ تھے مجبُور وَزِیر

(Jafery 1985: 87)

Eid prayers and that infinite crowd
When in Allah's presence were Ministers no doubt.
In the very first row they sat in their pride
Reserved their prayer mats—equality aside!

This is the state of prayers we can see today
From the same row for slave and master we've come a long way.

We too dipped the handkerchief in the scents full strong
We too brought the prayer mat proudly along
To the ministers from far off we too showed our face
We too did all the great men try to embrace.
Even now you say we are not really faithful.
With the courts of the monarchs though our heart is full!

In the sermon when the great were mentioned at all
We shouted and clapped; their praises did call
Our hearts indeed with idols were filled
The thoughts of God and HIS UNITY were killed.

And busy were the people in gossip; in sermon the *imam*
While the rich faced problems of waiting and walking calm,
And the people were eager to break all the bands
Do anything to shake, just once, the Ministers' hands.

(Translated from Urdu by Tariq Rahman)

In *Election kā sāqī nāma,* Jafery has parodied Iqbal's famous poem *Sāqī nāma* (To the Saqi).[4] In all the three parodies, Jafery has maintained a close resemblance to the original by an imitative use of the words, style, tone, and the subject-matter of the original. Its success depends on an untranslatable play upon the words. The contents of the original poems are alive, in the memory of the readers. The play upon the words presents a striking contrast between the sublime message of the original and the ridiculous behaviour of the characters in the parody. Humour develops within the context of empty rituals drawing their strength from the caricatured individuals and institutions. The same deep and abiding concern with political affairs and social issues is the main spring of Majeed Lahori's parodies.

Majeed Lahori was a Punjabi by birth and a working journalist by profession. During the last and more productive phase of his creative career, he edited the only humorous Urdu weekly of Pakistan entitled *Namakdān*. Most of his humorous verses of repute first appeared in this magazine. His poetry illuminates its readers on the main causes of politico-economic corruption and socio-moral decay. He was an exceptionally bold critic of men and matters in the ruling oligarchy of Pakistan. A comprehensive collection of his poetry was posthumously published in 1990, with the same title as his popular weekly newspaper, *Namakdān*.

Majeed has written excellent parodies of some of Iqbal's most popular *ġazals*. With his penetrating wit and unrestrained humour, Majeed changes a word here and an emphasis there and the whole *ġazal* falls down from the sublime heights of lofty ideals to the lowest depths of the harsh realities of the day. There is hardly an aspect of our political culture about which Majeed's parodies are not concerned. His humour reveals a great deal about the unwritten political history of the 1950s. His immediate but longlasting reactions in parodies to social, political and intellectual events are realistic and insightful specimens of social criticism. His poem *Amīr bacce kī du'ā* (Prayer of the Rich Child) brings Iqbal's simple and touching poem for children entitled *Bacce kī du'ā* (Prayer of the Child) into sharp focus. Let us first take a glance at the original:

لَب پہ آتی ہے دُعَا بَن کے تَمنّا میری
زِندَگی شَمَع کی صُورَت ہو خُدَایَا میری

دُور دُنیَا کَا میرے دَم سے اَندھیرَا ہو جَائے
ہَر جَگہ میرے چَمَکنے سے اُجَالَا ہو جَائے

ہو مِرے دَم سے یونہی میرے وَطَن کی زِینَت
جِس طَرَح پھُول سے ہوتی ہے چَمَن کی زِینَت

زِندگی ہو مِری پَروانے کی صُورَت یارَب
عِلم کی شَمع سے ہو مجھ کو مُحَبَّت یارَب

ہو مِرا کام غَریبوں کی حِمایَت کَرنا
دَردمَندوں سے، ضَعِیفوں سے مُحَبَّت کَرنا

مِرے اَللہ! بُرائِی سے بَچانا مجھ کو
نیک جو راہ ہو، اُس رَہ پہ چَلانا مجھ کو

(Iqbal 1990a: 65)

The desire of the heart comes as prayer to the lips
Let my life be like that of a candle O Lord!

Let the darkness of the world be removed by my self
Let bright light be radiant in the globe through my self.

Let my life in devotion be like that of the moth O Lord!
Let the torch of learning be the love of my heart O Lord!

Let my being be the decoration of my land my God
Like the flower is that of the garden my God.

Let me champion all life the cause of the poor
My task be to love them—the afflicted, the weak and the poor.

Save me from evil forever my God
And keep me ever constant on the path of virtue O God.

(Translated from Urdu by Tariq Rahman)

Now the parody:

لَب پہ آتِی ہَے دُعا بَن کے تَمَنّا میرِی
زِندَگی سیٹھ کی صُورَت ہو خُدایا میرِی
« لیارِی کوَاٹر » میں مِرے دَم سے اَندھیرا ہو جائے
میرے « چیمبَر » میں اُجالا ہِی اُجالا ہو جائے

ہو مِرے دَم سے یونہِی میرے کلَب کی زِینَت
جِس طَرَح چاند سے ہو جاتِی ہَے شَب کی زِینَت

زِندَگی ہو مِرِی «قَارُون» کی صُورَت یَارَب
«نیشَنَل بَنک» سے ہو مُجھ کو مُحَبَّت یَارَب
ہو مِرَا کَام اَمِیروں کی حِمَایَت کَرنَا
دَردمَندوں سے غَرِیبوں سے عَدَاوَت کَرنَا

میرے اَللہ! بھَلَائِی سے بَچَانَا مُجھ کو
جو بُرِی رَاہ ہو، بَس اُس پَہ چَلَانَا مُجھ کو

(Lahori 1990: 129)

The desire of the heart comes as prayer to the lips,
Let my life, O Lord, be like a tycoon of note.
Let the slums of the city be in darkness eternal plunged
Let my chamber with light be forever resplendent.

Let my presence thus illumine and beautify my club,
As the moon does that to the murkiest of nights.

Let my life be like the fabled Qarun O Lord!
May the National Bank be forever my Love O Lord!
Let me live forever supporting the wealthy
And hating, despising the underdog so earthy.

And save me from VIRTUE above all O Lord!
Keep me ever on the path of iniquity O Lord!

(Translated from Urdu by Tariq Rahman)

The parodies of Iqbal's poems are at once a tribute to the greatness of Iqbal as a poet-philosopher and a delightful protest against the evils and absurdities of contemporary life. The parodist is, thus, the comic guardian of the liberal, democratic and humanistic value system that lies dormant in the poetry and philosophy of Muhammad Iqbal.

NOTES

1. Syed Zamir Jafery is the most prolific contemporary humorous writer in Urdu. He has published about a dozen collections of humorous poetry and prose and three collections of serious poetry. He has served in the Pakistan Army. He lives in Islamabad and contributes humorous columns to more than one newspaper.
2. Mirza Mahmud Sarhadi used to earn his livelihood as a working journalist

in Peshawar. He has authored two collections of poetry namely: *Sangīne* and *Andeśa-i-śi'r.*

3. The quotation starts from the parody version of the following stanza of the original poem:

آ گیا عین لڑائی میں اگر وقتِ نماز
قبلہ رُو ہو کے زمیں بوس ہوئی قومِ حجاز
ایک ہی صف میں کھڑے ہو گئے محمود و ایاز
نہ کوئی بندہ رہا اور نہ کوئی بندہ نواز

بندہ و صاحب و محتاج و غنی ایک ہوئے
تیری سرکار میں پہنچے تو سبھی ایک ہوئے

(Iqbal 1990a: 192-3)

If the time for prayer came right in the midst of battle, the nation of Hijaz (the holy cities of Mekka and Madina in Arabia) turned towards Mecca and kissed the ground. In one and the same rank stood Mahmūd (the king) and Ayāz (the servant). No one was servant and no one was master. Slave and lord, poor and rich became one. When they arrived at your court, all were one. (Matthews 1993: 33)

4. For an excellent English version of Iqbal's *Śikvah* and *Sāqī Nāma,* see D.J. Matthews, 1993, *Iqbal: A Selection of the Urdu Verse.* London: SOAS, 1993.

REFERENCES

Gandhi, Rajmohan. 1988. *Eight Lives: A Study of the Hindu-Muslim Encounter.* Delhi: Roli Books.

Gay, Peter. 1968. *Weimar Culture.* New York: Harper and Row.

Iqbal, Muhammad. 1990a. *Kulliyāt (Urdu).* Lahore: Iqbal Academy.

———. 1990b. *Kulliyāt (Fārsī).* Lahore: Iqbal Academy.

Jafery, Syed Muhammad. 1985. *Śokhī-i-tahrīr.* Karachi: Maktaba-i-Daniyal.

Jafery, Syed Zamir. 1978. *Māfī'z-zamīr.* Lahore: Maktaba Urdu Dajjast.

Loeffler, Reinhold. 1988. *Islam in Practise.* New York: State University of New York.

Majeed Lahori. 1990. *Namakdān.* Lahore: Jang Pabl.

Matthews, David J. 1993. *Iqbal. A Selection of the Urdu Verse.* London: School of Oriental and African Studies.

Sarhadi, Mirza Mahmud. 1967. *Sangīne.* Lahore: Aina-i-adab

———. *Andeśa-i-śi'r.*

Singh, Iqbal. 1951. *Ardent Pilgrim.* Calcutta: Orient Longmans.

Smith, Wilfred Cantwell. 1957. *Islam in Modern History.* Princeton: Princeton University Press.

The Humour of Calcutta

WILLIAM RADICE

In his ambitious study of human imagination and creativity, *The Act of Creation* (1964), Arthur Koestler defines humour in terms of an unexpected connection between two hitherto unconnected frames of reference. He calls this process 'bisociation'. Whether or not Koestler's theory is strong enough to account for all varieties of humour in Calcutta or anywhere else, it certainly fits a type of humour that one recognizes as distinctively Calcuttan. Just as the culture that developed in nineteenth-century Calcutta was itself a rich blend of indigenous and Western traditions and influences, so the humour of the city's literature, drama and art exploited to the full the often ludicrous 'bisociation' of East and West, Bengali and English. The Calcutta *babu* became—throughout India—a comic stereotype that still lives on today. It would be wrong, however, to see the *babu* as merely or always comical. Originally the title was only applied to aristocrats (in his story *Ṭhākurdā*, 1895, Rabindranath Tagore writes of the wealth and *noblesse* that were required to qualify for it). In time it was given to the entire nineteenth-century English-educated class. Most modern Bengali writers have come from that class, and few have been prepared to reject completely the widening of horizons and enrichment of literary style and genre that English education gave and still gives to Bengal. So although Bengali writers have themselves often made fun of the *babu*, the term is not at all pejorative in ordinary Bengali usage. Added to the main (first) name, it is the normal, polite way to address and refer to a gentleman in Hindu Bengal. 'Satyajit Ray' would be 'Satyajit Babu' in Bengali.

The author of the first of the four examples of Calcutta humour that follow, Michael Madhusudan Datta (1824-73), was a far too proud and sophisticated beneficiary of Western education, and a far too ambitious and original writer, for any derogatory meaning in *babu* to be at all applicable. In any case, by converting to Christianity in 1843 (largely to escape an arranged Hindu marriage), he put himself beyond the Hindu pale. Remembered primarily for *Meghnādbadh-kābya*, an impressive literary epic based on the *Rāmāyaṇa* but influenced in structure, tone and its *amitrākṣar* (blank verse) by Homer, Virgil and Milton, Madhusudan was also a pioneering Bengali dramatist. The wit and ebullience that characterize his racy English letters (printed in all collected editions of his works) are also qualities to be found in his two farces, *Eke-i ki bale sabhyatā* and *Buṛa sāliker ghāṛe rõ*. These were written in 1859 at the request of Raja Isvarcandra Singh and Raja Pratapcandra Singh, who had commissioned Madhusudan's first play, *Śarmmiṣṭhā*, for performance in their Belgatchia Theatre. They wrote to him during the rehearsals for *Śarmmiṣṭhā*, asking him for 'some domestic farces to follow immediately after the first representation of the "Sharmistha" and before it is repeated, just to show the public that we can act the sublime and ridiculous both at the same time and with the same actors'.[1] A taste for farce had been created by a British fondness for amateur dramatics as strong in nineteenth-century Calcutta as it still is today anywhere where Britons congregate, and the Rajas had earlier planned to put on three English farces—'Prince for an Hour', 'Power and Principle', and 'Fast Train, High Pressure, Express'—until they decided to commission Madhusudan. In the event, his farces proved to be too near the bone of the *babus* who were likely to make up the audience for them. According to Kesabcandra Ganguli, one of the leading actors at the Belgatchia,

> A few of the 'Young Bengal' class, getting a scent of the farce *Eke-i ki bale sabhyatā* ('Is this called Civilization?') and feeling that the caricature made in it touched them too closely, raised a hue and cry, and choosing for their leader a gentleman of position and affluence who, they knew, had some influence with the Rajahs, deputed him to dissuade them from producing the farce on the boards of their Theatre. . . . Rajah Issur Chunder Singh was so disgusted at this affair that he resolved not only to give up the other farce too, but to have no more Bengali plays acted at Belgatchia Theatre. (Basu 1893: Appendix)

Eke-i ki bale sabhyatā was not, therefore, performed until 1865. It has proved to be much more popular and influential than its companion piece, *Buṛa sāliker ghāṛe rõ*, which exposes Hindu corruption and hypocrisy.[2] (This indicates, perhaps, that the Calcuttans find it easier to laugh at the 'English' aspect of their culture than at the Hindu.) The novelist Bankimchandra Chatterjee, writing in the *Calcutta Review*, assessed its impact as follows:

> The Bengali Press at the present day is very prolific . . . but perhaps no work has formed the model for so many imitators as *Is this Civilization*? It is a farce with a purpose, being intended chiefly to ridicule and so expose the vice of drunkenness and the other evils by which it is generally attended. The Burtolla Presses and shops actually overflow with little books, containing a dozen or twenty pages each, and selling for an anna or two, all directed against the vice of drunkenness. There are farces, too, of larger bulk, one of which, called *Bujhile ki-nā*, or *Do you understand*? is very popular, and often produced at private theatricals; and these, too, like the others, are mere copies of *Is this Civilization*? This little work, therefore, independently of its being in itself one of the two best farces in the language, gains additional importance from the large number of books written after its model.

To give any adequate idea of this clever little work by translated extracts would be entirely impossible, because half the fun lies in the absurd jargon interlarded with English words and the cant of debating clubs in which the characters speak. The scene is laid in the 'Gyan Tarangini Sabha'—a sort of scientific debating society which chiefly devotes itself to nautch girls and tippling. The types of life and character which it represents are sufficiently disgusting, and the important question is, whether the representation is correct.

To the shame of Bengal we must say that we fear the picture is a true one. The reformer who never gets beyond tipsy harangues full of English expressions, should not be confounded as he often is by Europeans with the really cultivated class. But it cannot be denied that he is a fair representative of that great horde of partly educated Babus, whose only claim to enlightenment lies in the fact that they drink, wear shabby trousers and stammer out barbarous English. . . .[3]

Bankim's Victorian pomposity is a little misleading, for the play is not a tract, but merrily partakes of the boistrous flamboyance of the characters it ridicules. Here is an extract from Act II Scene i—the centrepiece of the play—a hilarious satire on the debating clubs that were a notable feature of nineteenth-century Calcutta. The assembled members of the Jñānataraṅgiṇī Sabhā ('Wave of Knowledge Society'), together with two 'nautch-girls', have been waiting for their Chairman, Naba Babu, who eventually arrives late with his friend Kālī Babu to find the company well warmed up. As Bankim rightly says, translation (into English, at least) is impossible: all one can do is indicate the English words and phrases by inverted commas. It is, of course, much funnier to hear it in Bengali, even if one cannot follow the Bengali words mixed in with the English:

Naba and Kālī enter.

ALL (*rising to their feet*) 'Hip, hip, hooray!'

KĀLĪ (*drunkenly*) 'Hooray, hooray.'

NABA Sit down, friends, everyone sit down. (*they all sit*) Friends, you must 'excuse' us for being late—we were held up by some work we had to do.

ŚIBU (*drunkenly*) 'That's a lie.'

NABA (*angrily*) 'What?' Are you calling me a 'liar'? Do you want me to 'shoot' you?

CAITAN (*forcing Naba to sit down*) Oh leave it, leave it—why quarrel over such a 'trifling' matter?

NABA 'Trifling?' To call me a 'liar'—is that 'trifling'? Why didn't he speak to me in Bengali? Why didn't he call me a *mithyābādī*? No *śālā* would get angry at that. But 'liar'—that's intolerable.

CAITAN Oh let it go—don't go on about it. (*sitting down*)

CAITAN Ah, Payodharī, Nitambinī, are you well?

PAY. Yes, we're fine, but you don't look too good—you'd look better if you cooled down a bit.

NABA I'm perfectly cool, but now I think I'll warm myself up. Hey there, Balāi, give us a little 'brandy'.

ALL Hey, don't forget us. (*everyone drinks*)

NABA Kālī, you're very quiet.

KĀLĪ I was amazed at the way that Vaiṣṇava fellow behaved. There he was, rattling his holy beads, then the next minute he was taking a bribe and agreeing to tell lies. What a 'hypocrite'!

NABA To hell with him. Payodharī, let's have you both on your feet—give us a dance.

ALL No, no, your 'speech' first.

NABA (*rising*) All right. 'Gentlemen', turn your eyes to this wall for a moment: these few letters that you see, taken together read 'Jñānataraṅgiṇī Sabhā'.

ALL 'Hear hear.'

NABA 'Gentlemen', this Society is called the Jñānataraṅgiṇī Sabhā: we are all 'members' of it. We 'meet' so that knowledge may be born—'and we are jolly good fellows'.

ALL 'Hear hear, we are jolly good fellows.'

NABA 'Gentlemen', we are all Hindus by birth, but through education we have cut ourselves 'free' from the chains of 'superstition'. We don't bow down before idols; in us the darkness of ignorance has been dispelled by the light of knowledge. Now I pray that you all put your minds together to strive for the 'social reformation' of this country.

ALL 'Hear hear.'

NABA 'Gentlemen', 'educate' your daughters—give them liberty—break down caste barriers—let widows remarry: if you do this, and only if you do this, our beloved India will be able to compete with England and other civilized countries. Otherwise not.

ALL 'Hear hear.'

NABA But 'gentlemen', at present this country is an Immense gaol'; this room alone is our 'Liberty Hall', that is to say our House of Freedom. Here you may do as you please. 'Gentleman', in the name of freedom, let us enjoy ourselves.'
(*he sits*)

ALL 'Hear hear—hip, hip, hooray; Liberty Hall—be free—let us enjoy ourselves.'

NABA Balāi, give everyone some more.

BALĀI All right, here we are. (*they all drink*)

NABA Now let the dancing begin. 'Come, open the ball, my beauties.'
Payodharī and Nitambinī dance and sing.[4]

The two nautch-girls are appropriately named, for 'Payodharī' means 'big-breasted' and 'Nitambinī' means 'big-buttocked'. For a visual evocation of such girls and their admirers, one can do no better than turn to the 'Kalighat' paintings of the period.[5] Presumably the Babu in Figure 1 is holding a glass; in Figure 2 the lady is handing him some *pān,* perhaps, to go with his hookah. The Babu in Figure 3, with his pet dogs, has the mincing effeminacy that is another aspect, even today, of the Calcutta Babu stereotype:

We now move forward to the 1920s, to one of the immortal stories of 'Parasuram', who in real life was Rajsekhar Basu (1880-1960), a chemist and Director of Bengal Chemicals and Pharmaceuticals (which today belches out smoke over the 'Salt Lake' suburb of north Calcutta). His humorous stories have a rich cast of cranks, quacks, bogus holy men, and amiable eccentrics such as only Calcutta can produce. In the following extract, the bizarre contradictions in modern Bengali culture brought about by British colonial rule are widened to embrace the whole of India. Such has been the influence of Bengal on the formation of that culture, however, that one can safely regard *Ulaṭ Purāṇ,* the source of the extract, as an example of Calcutta humour *par excellence,* and not just because its author and language are Bengali. But are we actually in India?

JOCHNĀ Flappy, I can't cope with you any more. Is this how you want your hair? Your ears are sticking out. You're old enough to know better. See what a beautiful *khõpā* your sister has.

FLAPPY Let her! If my hair covers my ears I can't hear. I'll cut it short, like Miss Lanky Gosling next door.

JOCHNĀ What a girl you are! Mrs. Toady, I can't control your younger daughter.

MRS. TOADY Really, Flappy, you're getting worse everyday. Don't you realize how much trouble Jochnādi is taking over your education?

FLAPPY I don't want to learn anything. She can teach Fluffy.

JOCHNĀ 'Fluffy' again. Can't you remember to call her 'Didi'? And stop sucking your pencil. It's disgusting. All right, you can go now into that room and practise that Urdu gazal.

MRS. TOADY Jochnādi, would you have a *pān,* by any chance? Thank you.

JOCHNĀ Really, Mrs. Toady, you mustn't keep saying Thank you, Please, Sorry. It's a very bad habit. Your nation will never progress if you keep on saying so. It's false to express gratefulness or sorrow over such trivial things! . . . Fluffy, have you finished that Bengali novel?

Figure 1

Figure 2

Figure 3

FLUFFY It's very hard, I can't understand it at all.

JOCHNĀ There's no great need to understand it—just learn bits of it off by heart. I want people to think that you are acquainted with good Bengali books. But your pronunciation is terrible. If you want to go into polite society, you must acquire good Bengali pronunciation first, and learn a few Urdu songs. All right, let's hear you say *ek, dui, tin, cār.*

FLUFFY *ek, dui, tin, śār.*

JOCHNĀ Not *śār, CĀR.*

FLUFFY *Cār, pāic—*

JOCHNĀ Not *pāic, Pā̃c.*

FLUFFY *pā̃iś—*

JOCHNĀ *Pā̃—c.*

FLUFFY *phyā̃c.*

JOCHNĀ Hopeless! Mrs. Toady, don't let Fluffy eat so much chocolate—give her *cholābhājā,*[6] otherwise you'll never soften up her tongue.

[OFF-STAGE]: Deary!

MRS. TOADY Sweetheart! Where are you?

MR. TOADY In the bathroom. Give me a few more mangos.

JOCHNĀ Mangos in the bathroom?

MRS. TOADY What else can one do? Gabi says, that if one eats mangos one should eat them in the Indian way. But he's not skilled with his hands like you—the juice goes all over clothes, carpet and table-cloth. So I've told him to go and practise eating mangos in the bathroom. He holds the stones in both hands and sucks them and lets the juice run down. Horrid!

JOCHNĀ That's the right arrangement to make. But please, Mrs. Toady, it's not polite to call your husband 'Gabi'. Call him Gabi or Hābi in private if you must, but in front of others you must not utter his name. If necessary, refer to him as 'Uni'. And if you don't want to be so formal, call him '0'.

MRS. TOADY Really? Just a minute. I'd better give 'Oke' a mango.[7]

Like *Gulliver's Travels* or *Animal Farm, Ulaṭ Purāṇ* flows effortlessly from the gloriously witty strength of a basic idea. Deftly mixing dialogue, diaries, newspaper clippings, etc., it moves from the Toadys' efforts to give their children a good 'Bengali medium' education and upbringing, to Sir Tricksy Turncoat's speech to a crowd of rebellious subjects in Hyde Park, to the Universal British Women's League and their march from Regent's Park to Parliament, to the *Rājsūya Yajña* organized by the Indian Government to give the princes and princelings of Europe a chance to acknowledge its imperial supremacy, and finally to 'Prince Vom of Vomstadt' and his refusal—despite his sympathy for the cause—to preside over the Pan European meeting in the Hague, with *Mein Gott*! and *Gott im Himmel*! liberally peppering his elegant Bengali.

Colonial oppression and subservience, the alienation and affectation that arose from English education, the development of an elitist urban culture divorced from indigenous rural traditions, were of course the darker aspects of the Anglo-Bengali synthesis. They are memorably captured in the cartoons of Gaganendranath Tagore (1867-1938), that were until recently not as well-known as his 'straight' contributions to the modern 'Bengal school' of painting.[8] Gaganendranath was the grandson of the brother of Debendranath Tagore, Rabindranath's father, and his cartoons are but one of many products of the richly varied and original, powerfully intellectual Tagore family milieu. The Victoria and Albert Museum has a complete folio of them, *Adbhut Lok*, 'Realm of the Absurd',[9] published by Vichitra Press, Calcutta in 1917. They were exhibited at the Ashmolean Museum, Oxford, in 1986, but have not, so far as I know, been reproduced as a complete set before. By the kind permission of the Keeper of Indian Art at the Victoria and Albert Museum, here are all fifteen cartoons, plus the cover:

The cartoons are brilliant in conception and technique, but they are not exactly funny: several are savage, not jovial, in their satire. English and Bengali captions are given—the English sometimes expanding or contracting the Bengali, but not fundamentally diverging from it. The English captions are as follows:[10]

Fig. 5 Moral levitation
Fig. 6 Nuisance of a wife
Fig. 7 Purification by cow-dung
Fig. 8 By the sweat of my brow I tried to be mistaken for a Shaheb but still that man calls me Baboo.
Fig. 9 Horrifying news
'Two soldiers were caught fishing in the sacred river near Hardwar.'
Fig. 10 My love of my country is as big as I am.
Fig. 11 Profitable devotion
I will offer you two goats if I win this case.
Fig. 12 Metamorphosis
Don't disturb me now, I am about to become a Sab.
Fig. 13 Imperishable sacredness of a Brahman
Fig. 14 Confusion of ideas
Fig. 15 A wayside digression
Fig. 16 Vultures/Champagne party, evening party, etc. A noble man
Beggars/Sanitation, Education, Home Industries

Figure 4

Figure 5

Figure 6

Figure 7

Figure 8

Figure 9

Figure 10

Figure 11

Figure 12

Figure 13

Figure 14

Figure 15

Figure 16

Figure 17

Figure 18

Figure 19

Fig. 17 Millstone of caste
Fig. 18 Purification by muddy water
Fig. 19 Terribly sympathetic

The symbolism of the cover is striking: the Babu is smashing his own image in the mirror. The first cartoon (Figure 5) is enigmatic, but the labels on the buildings below—'Dancing', 'Singing', 'Tobacco'—will help viewers of the cartoon to make of it what they will. The expression on the cow's face in the third cartoon (Figure 7) is equally enigmatic. The fourth and eighth cartoons (Figures 8 and 12) take us into a world in which British rule has hardened into arrogant contempt for the Bengali Babus it has spawned. The fifth satirizes nationalist or neo-Hindu self-righteousness: the Babu who condemns the desecration of the holy river by fishing enjoys, of course, his *mācher jhol*.[11] The sixth (Figure 10) has a heading—with a question-mark—the word *Bāṅgokti*, which appears to be a pun on *byāṅgokti* ('taunt', 'quip') and *Baṅga-ukti* ('Bengal's utterance'). The seventh (Figure 11) reflects the enormous rôle that litigation played in the lives of nineteenth-century Babus. The ninth (Figure 13) is a more scathing version of the lampoon on Brahmanical behaviour that Michael Madhusudan Datta gave in the second of his farces, over fifty years earlier. The tenth (Figure 14) is the most famous of Gaganendranath's cartoons, and has been widely reproduced. Note the chicken poking out of the pocket of one Babu, and the cigarette in the hand of the other. The picture demonstrates Koestler's 'bisociation' theory perfectly. The eleventh (Figure 15) embodies a cliché of many late nineteenth-century Bengali novels—that of the suitor serenading a lady on her balcony from the street. The twelfth (Figure 16) excels even Aubrey Beardsley in the memorable vigour of its imagery and line. In the thirteenth (Figure 17) we detect, perhaps, the anguish of the high-minded nineteenth-century Bengali at the traditions his Westernized liberal values taught him to regard as iniquitous. In the fourteenth (Figure 18), the *Śānti jal* ('holy water') is being muddied by pinches from a bag labelled *Taṅkādebī*, the goddess of money. In the last picture (Figure 19), the man is an Englishman, presumably, but could he also be a *Kālo sāheb* ('brown saheb')?

After such dark visions, we need perhaps to return to the high spirits, the humanity, the love of language and poetry that characterize Calcutta culture at its best. So here is a poem from *Ābal-tābal*, a much-loved book of nonsense verse by Sukumar Ray (1887-1923), the father of Satyajit Ray. We do not find in it the East-West 'bisociation' that is so obviously present in my other three examples of Calcutta humour, though of course nonsense-verse depends for its effect on a riotous cavalcade of verbal and logical 'bisociations'. One can see in Sukumar Ray's verses the influence of Lewis Caroll and Edward Lear, and therefore a degree of support perhaps for the opinion of the well-known British radio and TV humorist Frank Muir in his introduction to his recent *Oxford Book of Humorous Prose* that 'the British invented humour'. But *Caṇḍīdāser Khuṛo*—'Chandidas's Uncle'—and the remarkable machine he has devised, represent a literary *cuisine* that is Calcuttan through and through, whatever the origin of its ingredients. Ray is lucky to have met his match in Sukanta Chaudhuri, one of Calcutta's finest English scholars, who himself manages to remain totally Calcuttan for all that he is an internationally renowned authority on European Renaissance pastoral literature. His delightful translation retains Sukumar Ray's own illustrations, as well as his rhythmic bounce and verbal virtuosity. The bubble of humour is generally pricked and extinguished by analysis, so let us give these three Calcuttans—Chandidas's Uncle, Sukumar Ray, and Sukanta Chaudhuri—the last, irrepressible word:[12]

The Inventor

Chandidas's Uncle has devised a grand machine:

> They've praised it in the highest terms wherever it's been seen.
> Indeed, they say this Uncle, at the tender age of one,
> Would burst out crying 'Goongaa' in a manner fit to stun.
> Now 'Mama', 'Gaga' and the like are all that kids can babble,
> So 'Goongaa' from this prodigy astounded all the rabble,
> And learned men would prophesy, 'Now should this child survive,
> We'll bet our beards he'll find a course to keep his name alive.'
> That infant grown to riper years has worked a fine invention
> To cover five hours' walk in one, without fatigue or tension.
> I've been to see the contrivance—it's quickly understood.
> Just handle it five hours or so, you'll get its hang for good.
> But words can scarce describe the work the learned world has praised:
> It's fixed upon your shoulder, with a rod in front upraised,
> And there you hang the kind of food you find the most enticing—
> A pie or pasty, fry or roll, or cake with almond icing.
> The mind aspires to reach the food, the lips move forth to swallow.
> The dainty flies before your gaze, and you perforce must follow.
> Thus spurred along by gluttony, you walk without a heed:
> The more you see the dangling bait, the more your turn of speed.
> A score of miles you quickly stride and never tire the least.
> With watering mouth and glinting eye agog to chase the feast.
> So now you know why man or boy who views this exhibition
> Returns amazed, and joins the ranks that hail the man of vision.

Figure 20: From *The Select Nonsense of Sukumar Ray*, Sukanta Chaudhuri (1987), Oxford University Press, Oxford.

NOTES

1. Letter quoted by Nagendranath Som (1916).
2. The title means literally 'Wool on the neck of an old *sālik*-bird', i.e. clothes worn by an old man that would suit a young man better.
3. *Calcutta Review*, No. 104, vol. 52, April 1871.
4. Translated from *Madhusūdan racanābalī* (Datta 1965: 250-1).
5. See W.G. Archer, *The Bazaar Paintings of Calcutta* (1953). Figures 1, 2 and 3 are, however, photographed directly from the holdings of the Victoria and Albert Museum, London, Nos. I.S. 23-1952, I.M. 137-1914, I.S. 43-1952 respectively.
6. Fried chick-peas.
7. Translated from *Ulaṭ Purāṇ* by 'Parasuram' (Rajsekhar Basu), from *Kajjalī*, a collection of stories (1928).
8. There is very little critical analysis of Gaganendranath's cartoons available in English. See O.C. Gangoly, *The Humorous Art of Ganganendranath Tagore*, an undated catalogue of an exhibition at the Birla Academy,

Calcutta, preserved in the Victoria and Albert Museum Library, and Nirad C. Chaudhuri's essay, reprinted in *Purabi: A Miscellany* on the fiftieth anniversary of Tagore's death.

9. No. I.S. 5-1987 (1).
10. Some of the captions fall outside the frame of the photos.
11. Fish curry.
12. *The Select Nonsense of Sukumar Ray* (1987: 7), illustrated with Sukumar's own drawings. For further demonstration of Professor Chaudhuri's devotion to Calcutta, see *Calcutta: the Living City* (1990), two huge richly illustrated volumes of essays on all aspects of the city, collected, edited and in many cases translated by him.

REFERENCES

Archer, W.G. 1953. *The Bazaar Paintings of Calcutta: the style of Kalighat.* London: HMSO.

Basu, Yogindranath. 1893. *Māikel madhusūdan datter jīban-carit.* Calcutta.

Datta, Krishna and Andrew Robinson (eds.). 1991. *Purabi: A Miscellany.* London: The Tagore Centre, U.K.

Datta, Michael Madhusudan. 1965. *Madhusūdan racanābalī.* Calcutta: Sahitya Samsad.

Gangoly, O.C. n.d. *The Humorous art of Gaganendranath Tagore.* Calcutta.

Koestler, Arthur. 1964. *The Act of Creation.* London.

'Parasuram' (Rajsekhar Basu). 1928. *Kajjalī.* Calcutta.

Som, Narendranath. 1916. *Madhu-smṛti.* Calcutta.

Tagore, Rabindranath. 1895. *Ṭhākurdā.* Translated by William Radice in *Selected Short Stories.* Harmondsworth: Penguin, rev. edn. 1994.

Thomas Mann's *Transposed Heads* and Girish Karnad's *Hayavadana*: An Indian Motif Re-imported

HEIDRUN BRÜCKNER

Introductory

In his story *Die Vertauschten Köpfe. Eine Indische Legende* (Stockholm 1940),[1] the German author Thomas Mann (1875-1955) drew inspiration from ancient Indian narrative literature, but added his own turn to these sources. Some thirty years later (1971), the Kannada playwright, actor and director, Girish Karnad (born 1938), based his play *Hayavadana* ('horse-face') on the same ancient Indian sources as well as on their treatment by Thomas Mann—again skilfully transforming the story in various ways. In this article, I want to examine these processes of what may be viewed as productive 'intercultural' reception. My focus is on the use of humour and irony in modern literary adaptations of oral or 'mythological' texts.

Neither of the two authors hesitates to piece together material from various sources and transpose it into different conceptual worlds. Thomas Mann and Girish Karnad are both highly intellectual authors who also have contributed to critical writing and consciously relate their own work to that of authors of earlier epochs. In the two compositions under discussion they employ seemingly simple forms to convey complex messages. Thomas Mann's 'Indian legend' may appear very 'Indian' to European readers unfamiliar with Indian culture. But a closer look under the layer of local colour and the ancient Indian core narrative reveals the European and especially 'Mannian' nature and treatment of the central theme. The elements of humour and irony vis-à-vis his characters, as well as their psychology—completely absent in the Indian source tales—point to process closely interlinked here one of 'literarization', i.e. transformation into a work of art, of modern written literature, and one of—in this case intercultural—reception and adaptation of 'myth' in the widest sense of the term. Especially, the concept of 'epic irony' is of central importance in Thomas Mann's understanding of art and of the role of the artist as mediator, Mann being the great ironist of twentieth-century German literature. Psychology for Mann is a means to recover myth and recognize it as 'lived life' (gelebte Vita Freud).[2]

For an author like Girish Karnad, equally familiar with European and Indian literary traditions, Mann's play with Indian material and the 'Europeanness' of his approach must have offered a special challenge. In a way—and again by means of humour and irony, Karnad does to Thomas Mann what Mann did to the ancient Indian tales. He uses and questions Mann's treatment at the same time, especially his psychology. He transposes the story into a new genre, drama—into a 'play' in the literal sense of the term. It combines sheer playfulness and an enchanting indulgence into the rich possibilities of Indian theatre(s) with self-consciousness, reflection and complexity. By drawing upon the epic traditions of Indian theatre it, at the same time, retains and integrates the frame structure of the original tales within the dramatic structure of the new genre. Moreover, the Sanskritic narrative content is complemented by—fictitious—regional folk narrative.

In blending traditional and modern, classical and folk forms of drama and theatre, Karnad not only re-contextualizes the story in an Indian setting, but also tries to come to terms with the diversity and multi-layeredness of Indian culture(s). Karnad's major device for questioning or rather re-questioning Mann's psychological problematic is a re-framing which reflects and subverts Thomas Mann's central theme—in a perspective entirely different from Mann's own ironization.

Thomas Mann's story and its Indian sources

Thomas Mann wrote *The Transposed Heads* in 1939/40, in his early sixties, while living in exile in the United States of America. The work was published from Stockholm in 1940. Just one year later, an English translation followed which led to a comparatively broad reception of the 'Indian Legend'.

Mann had no direct linguistic access to the Sanskrit sources that have been transmitted basically in three versions, forming part of three different collections. Firstly, the one in Somadeva's *Kathāsaritsāgara*, 'Ocean of Streams of Stories'; secondly, the one in Śivadāsa's *Vetālapañcaviṃśati*, 'Twenty-five Stories of the Graveyard Demon'; and, thirdly, a Jaina version, in Hemavijaya's *Kathāratnākara*, 'Jewel-mine of Stories'.[3] Mann did not use direct translations of Somadeva's and Śivadāsa's versions, but a rendering by Heinrich Zimmer[4] in which Zimmer blended the versions of Somadeva and Śivadāsa.[5] This account formed part of a talk about 'The Indian World-Mother' (Die Indische Weltmutter) Zimmer gave at Zurich in 1938 and which was printed in the ERANOS yearbook the same year. We know that in 1939 Zimmer sent an offprint to Thomas Mann. Besides this mixed version, slightly adapted by Zimmer, Thomas Mann also used Johannes Hertel's excellent German translations of Indian tales (Hertel 1921), which contained the late Jaina version of the story by Hemavijaya (1600/01). Hertel's carefully annotated translations must have conveyed to Mann some of the spirit of the original texts.

To retrace the processes of adaptation first by Heinrich Zimmer and then by Thomas Mann I shall briefly summarize the original stories:

In the *Kathāsaritsāgara*-version, a young washerman sees a girl taking a bath in a lake called Gaurītīrtha near the temple of the Goddess Gaurī during the latter's annual festival. The washerman falls in love with the girl. Through the mediation of his father he succeeds in marrying her. One day, the wife's brother arrives to convey to the couple his parents' invitation to a festival in honour of the Goddess Durgā. When, on their way, they pass by a temple of Durgā the young husband enters and is overwhelmed by the powerful presence of the Goddess. He takes a sword lying in front of the idol and decapitates himself in order to offer blood sacrifice to the goddess. When the brother-in-law finds the dead body he is so perturbed that he follows the example. Seeing both men lying dead the young wife desperately addresses the Goddess and then attempts to hang herself with a creeper. All of a sudden the voice of the Goddess is heard ordering her to put back the two severed heads on the bodies. In her confusion, the young woman places the heads on the wrong bodies. Then the three of them continue their journey. Only the wife seems to be aware of what has happened. In the frame story, the graveyard demon asks king Vikrama which of the two men should be considered the woman's husband. He replies that the one with the head of the husband is the lawful husband, because the head is the most important part of the body, the identity of the person depending on it.

In Śivadāsa's recension, the narrative differs in a few details. Firstly, the washerman watches the girl along with a friend. Secondly, he vows to Durgā that he will sacrifice himself to her if she helps him to marry the girl. Accordingly, his suicide in a temple of the Goddess is motivated by this vow, and is not a spontaneous act. Since the wife's brother is replaced in this version by the husband's friend the element of potential incest in the first version is also avoided (cp. Carbe 1970: 10-11). Apart from these differences, other variations are mainly stylistic. The king's judgement in the frame story is the same.

In the third, Jaina, version the hero is not a washerman, but a Brahman called Nārāyaṇa who has problems in obtaining his wife, promised to him since childhood, from his parents-in-law. When he goes to see them for the eighth time he makes a vow in a temple on his way. He is accompanied by his friend Keśava. The temple is not Durgā's but Śiva's and he promises a lotus to the god. Having finally obtained his wife, he decapitates himself on the way back, considering his head as the lotus to be offered. His friend then commits suicide, fearing he might be suspected of having killed his friend out of desire for his wife. In her bereavement the wife, too, tries to kill herself but is empowered by Śiva to bring the two men back to life. Here, too, she exchanges the heads. The two men start quarrelling over her.

The solution in the frame story is different from the other two versions, although the setting is similar, retaining the characters of the king and the Vetāla: Here, the king had heard of a princess challenging her suitors to tell her stories which would make her speak four times in one night. The unsuccessful candidates are humiliated by her. Incognito, the king, too, tries his luck and the Vetāla hides in a lamp. Addressing the lamp, the king tells the story of the transposed heads and asks the lamp who became the heroine's husband. In order to make the princess speak the Vetāla replies: 'The one with the husband's head.' Enraged by this reply considered wrong in this version the princess starts speaking, shouting at the lamp. The king then explains the correct solution to the lamp: The one with the body of the husband and the head of the friend is the husband, because the wedding is performed by the bridegroom taking the bride's hand with his own right hand which is part of the body.

Heinrich Zimmer contracts the first two versions by having two unnamed friends watch the girl at a bathing place of Kālī. He leaves out the vow. As in Somadeva's version the suicide is a spontaneous act, the husband being overwhelmed by the impact of the sight of the goddess' eighteen-armed image. For the rest, Zimmer's paraphrase follows Somadeva rather than Śivadāsa.

Zimmer adds a little comment of his own which might have been the starting point for Thomas Mann's treatment.[6] Commenting on the wife, who now possesses the friend's body under the husband's head, Zimmer wonders whether she may have been motivated by 'a secret wish' in exchanging the heads; whether the marriage might not have been happy and whether it was for that reason that the husband was 'so willing to die, so longing for salvation'. But Zimmer admits that the old tales themselves do not contain hints at any such motivation for 'this strange Freudian slip'. Thomas Mann himself acknowledged his indebtedness to Zimmer by dedicating the English edition of the *Transposed Heads* to him: 'To Heinrich Zimmer the Great Indian Scholar Returned with Thanks.'[7] On 28 June 1941 Mann wrote a letter to Zimmer in which he refers to his *Transposed Heads* as 'a little amplification of the product of your research'. Mann mentions that his contact with Indian material was very brief and occasional and that he had been prepared for it only metaphysically by Schopenhauer. He speaks of 'my very improvised India'(see Wilhelm 1970: 402) and draws a parallel to Goethe who also 'had picked up his *Paria* from somewhere'.[8]

In fact, Mann not only blends Zimmer's account with the Jaina version of the story but also with the 'Legende' (legend) of Goethe's poem-cycle *Paria* (see later). Out of set pieces from Hertel's collection of Indian tales and his notes, entries in a German lexicon and another similar unidentified source, Mann takes the elements that provide local colour to his 'Indian legend'. His technique is that of montage. He took most of the names as well as high-sounding epithets of deities from Heinrich Zimmer's book *Maya—Der Indische Mythos* (Maya, the Indian Myth) first published from Zurich in 1936.[9] Zimmer was in the habit of translating most Indian terms, including epithets and names, into German in his writings addressed to a wider audience. Although these translations are accurate they sometimes sound so strange or surprising in German that the impact is comic, e.g. the place-name 'Gedeihen der Kühe' ('welfare-of-cows') for *govardhana*. He also skilfully used the similar possibilities in the Sanskrit and German language to form compound words whilst translating Sanskrit compounds into German, e.g. 'Buntgipfel' for *citrakūṭa*; 'die Locke Glückskalb' for *śrīvatsa*, etc.[10]

Keeping in mind these sources and my introductory observations, we shall now take a closer look at Thomas Mann's text. In the German pocketbook edition, the twelve chapters of the 'Indian legend' fill 169 pages.[11] As compared to this, the Sanskrit tales would comprise just about three per cent of the volume of Mann's 'legend'. Most chapters are of roughly equal length, about 15 pages. The first (6 pages), fifth (10), sixth and seventh (each 7) chapters are considerably shorter, the last one is considerably longer (20 pages) there being a gradual increase in length after the two short chapters six and seven (eighth=13, ninth=15, tenth=16, eleventh=17, twelfth=20).

The first chapter starts with expository remarks by a narrator:

> The story of Sita of the beautiful hips, daughter of the cattle-breeder Sumantra of the warrior caste, and of her two husbands (if one may put it like that) is so sanguinary, so amazing to the senses, that it makes the greatest demands on the hearer's strength of mind and his power to resist the gruesome guiles of Maya. It would be well for the listener to take pattern from the fortitude of the teller, for it requires, if anything, more courage to tell such a tale than to hear it. But here it is, from first to last, just as it fell out.[12]

The narrator then establishes the time-frame, speaking in a ceremonious tone of ancient times when the cult of the Great Mother was in full swing. Next, he introduces the male protagonists, two youths living in the temple village 'Welfare-of-cows'. He speaks of their contrasting features and personalities, of their close friendship and their many philosophical and spiritual conversations. This is continued through the second chapter, in which the two friends set out on a journey and finally halt near the bathing place of a village temple situated on the banks of a little river. In chapter 3 they see the heroine, Sita, taking a ritual bath in the river. Here, Mann indulges in erotic descriptions interspersed with metaphysical and ethical reflections. Spiritual-minded Shridaman visualizes the girl as a divine image, whereas down-to-earth Nanda identifies her as a girl from a neighbouring village whom he had previously met at a fair. The impact of these contrasting perceptions is decidedly comic.

The first part of chapter 4 is devoted to Shridaman's subsequent suffering, which he himself interprets, in Kierkegaardian terms, as a 'sickness unto death' ('Krankheit zum Tode') until Nanda, with the approval of the narrator, provides the correct diagnosis, love, and suggests the appropriate remedy, marriage.

Chapter 5 sets in with a warning by the narrator:

> Here we warn the listener, perhaps misled by the so far pleasing course of the tale, not to fall prey to a misconception of its real character. For a little space there was silence, it turned its face away; when it turns back it is no more the same, but changed to a frightful mask, a face of horror, distracting, Medusalike, turning the beholder to stone, or maddening him to wild acts of abnegation—for so Shridaman, Nanda, and Sita saw it, on the journey which they—but everything in its turn. (40)[13]

Six months have elapsed. Sita is pregnant. The couple and their friend Nanda set out together to visit Sita's parents. While Nanda is driving the cart (drawn by a zebu and a dromedary!) the couple sits silently, lovely Sita glancing repeatedly at Nanda's shapely neck. When they finally lose their way, the narrator takes this as a spacial depiction of the protagonists' inner aberration and confusion. Landed up near a temple of the Goddess Durga, Shridaman goes alone to offer prayer. He is overwhelmed by the atmosphere of the secluded temple with its sculptures and peculiar architecture and by the gruesome image of the Goddess. With a sword lying in the shrine he finally decapitates himself in order to return into the womb of the Great Mother and get rid of his suffering ego. Absurdly, the narrator directs the 'listeners' not to consider such an act as usual or common but to show the proper 'nearly unbelieving amazement' (my transl.).

At the beginning of chapter 6 he takes us by the hand back to Sita and Nanda still waiting for Shridaman to return. When Nanda goes to look for him, the narrator exclaims 'And we, who know what a sight awaited him there! We must accompany him. . . .' Out of friendship as well as fear that he would be suspected of having killed his friend, Nanda, too, beheads himself. In chapter 7, Sita finds the two corpses. She first assumes the two friends killed each other because of her. But since there is only one sword she reconstructs the actual course of events and, being the only survivor, fears that she will be suspected of having killed both of them. She therefore decides to hang herself outside the temple. Chapter 8 opens with a loud shout by the Goddess, holding Sita back from her act of despair. The ensuing conversation, in part an argument, between the two females is one of the funniest passages in the book. The Goddess talks like a resolute mother scolding her naughty and silly daughter. Sita's attitude is self-centered and forward while, at the same time, she tries to show devotion and humility vis-à-vis the Goddess. Among other things, we are informed in detail about her feelings for her husband and Nanda. The Goddess decides to restore the two men to life and tells Sita to put back the heads on the bodies.

This is done in chapter 9. Seemingly overwhelmed by his concern for the protagonists, the narrator, directly addressing Sita, points out the mistake she has committed: 'Sita, what have you done. . .' We learn that she, in her 'flurry' (p. 67, German 'Huschlichkeit', p. 101) has exchanged the heads! Realizing her mistake she seeks the victims' forgiveness, but they rather enjoy the new situation. Weeping and laughing at the same time the three stand embracing. The person with Shridaman's head and Nanda's body, who speaks of himself as Shridaman, is particularly happy about the new state of affairs. And so is Sita, to whom the friend's body had always appeared more attractive than the husband's. She is only too willing to accept *this* composite figure as her husband. The other composite figure, the friend's head with the body of the husband, who identifies himself as Nanda, makes his claims, too, and insists on consulting a sage, Kamadamana.

Describing this hermit and the forest of ascetics (Büßerwald) in chapter 10, Mann blends details from Hindu, Buddhist and Jaina ascetic traditions and practices from the sources available to him. The Kamadamana chapter is one of the book's satirical highlights.

It opens:

> On the third day they reached the Dandaka forest, which was green with rains and thickly populated with holy men, though large enough to affòrd each one sufficient seclusion and his own grim little holding devoid of humankind. . . . All the hermits were one in wishing to know nothing of each other and each protested his conviction that he was alone in the wood, surrounded by his own unpeopled void. (78)[14]

The ascetic Kamadamana finally agrees to listen to the three of them;

> for my correction and to get rid of the idea that I am doing it for my own entertainment—the more one gets rid of, the better! (83)[15]

In the hermit's pretension, boasting and lustfulness, his wavering between asceticism and eroticism, Mann ridicules the very conflict between mind and body which is the theme of his story. Kamadamana is totally preoccupied with the temptations to which he enthusiastically exposes himself. At one point, he even breaks out into silly, lustful and vulgar verse describing the physical features and feasts he is resisting. Here is a sample:

> . . . the bliss-embrace of arms, the bloomy thighs, cool twin delight of hillocks that behind them lies—till all agog with lust at pitch they work at coupling play in hot and reekling dark, each urging other on more bliss to capture, they flute each other to a heaven of rapture—and this and that and here and there—I know it all, of all I am aware! (86)[16]

When they finally manage to get him to pronounce his judgement, he is so fickle that he first advocates the priority of the body and only then the priority of the head which—he stresses—is his 'last word'.

Sītā happily returns with Shridaman, while Nanda goes to spend the rest of his life in the forest. After a period of blissful married life of the 'married lovers' (eheliches Liebespaar)—described in Chapter 11—during which 'beautiful Sita' enjoys the best parts of both men, a gradual adaptation of the bodies to the heads is setting in. These biological changes and their psychological consequences are described in detail and are commented and reflected upon by the narrator. At the same time, Sita's secret longing is gradually re-directed again towards the 'other'. Chapter 12 reports the birth of a son. The transformations described in the previous chapter take place while the child is growing up. After four years, the heroine is so driven by desire and compassion for Nanda that she leaves home along with her little son to search for him in the forest when one time Shridaman is away on business. Again, she experiences a happy union with the object of her longing because, in the meantime, the gradual adaptation of body to head and *vice versa* has shown more favourable results with Nanda. When Shridaman arrives the three of them realize that there is no solution to live with. The two men kill each other in a kind of mutual suicide. Sītā commits *satī*. This second series of suicides is a completion of the first one in the temple—this time without divine intervention. The three protagonists leave behind Sita's little son, who, besides his mother's, has features of both men.

My first comment on the story concerns Mann's narrative technique, which can be viewed, at least in some respects, as a blend of Indian and European models. For example, Mann partly adopts the framing techniques of the original tale collections and re-creates a—fictitious—oral setting. He introduces the figure of a narrator who tells the story to an audience referred to as listeners, not readers. But, in contradistinction to the Indian frame stories, Mann's frame has no plot of its own such as the narrative of king Vikrama and the Vetāla. At the same time, his technique relates to traditions of nineteenth-century European prose fiction that use the figure of a narrator.

Especially the narrator's introduction of the story at the beginning of the first chapter serves to re-frame the tale and points to the didactic function which it shares with Indian narrative models. But, at the same time, the very first sentences reveal the author's underlying ironical attitude; this is conveyed through the figure of the narrator as well as through the narrative style. The narrator maintains an ostentatious distance vis-à-vis the characters. Not only the characters of the 'legend' are exposed to irony, but also some of the concepts and attitudes borrowed from Zimmer and Schopenhauer—or rather, from Schopenhauer as re-applied to Indian material by Zimmer in his Maya book (Zimmer 1936).

Thus, although the arena seems to be Indian, it is clearly an India of European projections, containing, for example, the typical European mix of Hindu and Buddhist concepts. It is another irony that Mann deconstructs some of these projections and not any underlying Indian notions as such. In spite of the very skilful use of local colour and scenery his European perspective surfaces even in descriptions of seemingly perfectly Indian settings. I want to give just one example which puzzled me for some time: When Shridaman and Nanda encounter Sita for the first time she is taking a bath in a river, at the bathing place of a village temple. The two friends secretly watch her. There is an Indian temple, an Indian bathing place with steps leading down into the river, Indian flora, a beautiful Indian girl with a body which could have served as a model for some of the descriptions in classical Indian *kāvya* literature. Why does one still feel that there is something strange about this scene, something definitely not 'Indian', to tentatively use a rather problematic category?

Ruben (1941: 12-13) appears to have had a similar feeling, but the explanation he gives is not fully convincing. He says that an Indian girl would never undress while taking a bath in the open and identifies Sita's nakedness as the reason for his feeling of 'unindianness'. As his frame of reference is contemporary social conventions, one could object that the story is situated in an unspecified past where such conventions may not have played a major role in many circles of society. One might point to god Krishna who watches the cowherd girls and hides their dresses while they are taking a bath naked; one might also point to Kālidāsa's descriptions in the *Raghuvaṃśa* where the women of the harem enjoy water sports with the king in a river. While to some extent contradicting Ruben, these examples also help us to specify at least one of the distinguishing features in Mann's description: It is, to my mind, the combination of female nakedness and of believing oneself to be *alone,* on the one hand, and the secret presence of two male observers, on the other. The gopis and the queens just mentioned are enjoying themselves innocently in a group playing in water. Krishna's concern is with the joke of hiding the clothes and having the girls beg for their return, not with secretly watching them naked. In the case of Kālidāsa's description there is no hidden observer present.[17] Mann's heroine, on the contrary, is aware of the fact that she is alone in a narcissistic way, and enjoys exposing her naked body to the sun. The one feature lacking in Mann's description which would have had us immediately identify, e.g. Tintoretto's sixteenth-century painting of 'Susanna taking a bath' (Susanna im Bade) as Mann's conscious or subconscious model is probably a mirror. The other important component of the scene is the pair of male observers. In most depictions of the biblical 'Susanna' motif so popular in European painting, the two lustful old men who watch the girl are more prominent, but Tintoretto's version, in all probability known to Mann, comes closest to his description.[18] The difference is that the two males are young and rather innocent. Finally, and this refers us back to the literary level, the two observers verbally reflect on the observed person and on the entire situation.

The scene also deviates from the Sanskrit narrative models, where a temple festival attended by many people forms the background of the encounter. In such a context, the two friends certainly could not have seen the girl all by herself and her nakedness is out of the question. But the temple festival had already been left out in Zimmer's account so that Mann's imagination could take another direction from the very beginning. We can observe here how a different field of associations from a different set of cultural images is nearly imperceptibly superimposed on a seemingly Indian scene like the famous 'veil of Maya' which so fascinated Mann. Stylistically, Mann's description expresses irony and sometimes humour by switching between an elevated and a lower level of speech.[19]

Such differences in detail apart, the central difference between the sources and Thomas Mann's treatment is that the problem really starts for Mann where the source stories end. Those tales had dealt with the juridical problem which of the two men would be the lawful husband of the young wife, a question set like a riddle in the frame stories. Thomas Mann takes the 'solution' as the starting point for a fresh investigation: If the head is the determining part of the body, will the body then not have to adjust to it? And what will be the psychological consequences of the change?

In a first step, Mann transforms the characters of the ancient stories into individuals with distinct and contrasting personalities. In this new setting, social factors like caste are not used in their social dimension but become means of personal characterization. The same applies to the physical features of the three protagonists, those of the two males not being mentioned at all in the ancient tales. Thus, Shridaman, the one of the two friends who later becomes the husband, is of Brahmanic descent, as in the Jaina version, although his father is a merchant once referred to as a 'Wanidja'. The other one, Nanda, is a smith and cowherd of lower caste but still supposed to be 'twice-born', wearing the sacred thread. The Brahman is a learned intellectual with a delicate face, spiritual inclinations, but a frail and somewhat flabby body. Nanda's body is dark, strong and full of vigour, but his face is plain and he has a goat's nose. The two become friends because of their opposite natures. This friendship is a central feature of Mann's story, whereas there is only a short reference to a friend in one of Mann's sources. Sita, the heroine, is provided by Mann with a Kshatriya ancestry. Her father Sumantra is a cattle breeder. She is an extremely beautiful and headstrong woman.

It is evident that Mann was not concerned with Indian social reality, past or present, such as ethnographic detail about caste and marriage practices. The way he means his protagonists and assigns certain castes and professions to them is not in accordance with Indian practices, such as the correlation between name and caste and the restriction of the use of certain names to particular social groups. Moreover, unlike Nanda, a perosn could never be a smith and a cowherd at the same time. Shridaman's 'inter-caste marriage' and his lower-caste friend becoming the mediator for the marriage would seem a bit out of a place as well. In fact the original Sanskrit tales stress the equal status of the two parties. Mann freely mixes literary and factual information. Thus he seems to have gathered information about the distribution of languages in Sanskrit drama and, on similar lines, utilizes this linguistic differentiation for his characterization of Nanda as 'folk' and Shridaman as 'refined' by having the former speak Prakrit and the latter Sanskrit. The contrasting physical descriptions should be viewed against the same background and not be mistaken as expressions of Mann's ethnic bias. In the first place, the contrast rather reproduces Indian perceptions of the typical Brahman and the lower castes. Secondly, in the *Transposed Heads*, the dark Nanda, who is repeatedly associated by Mann with the god Krishna, is an idealized representation of 'life', whereas in Mann's early novella *Tonio Kröger* the author had assigned a similar part to the fair-haired and blue-eyed Hans Hansen and Inge. By using the simple oppositions of a fairy tale Mann creates a polarity which underlines his psychological characterization and, on a higher plane, serves the discussion of a metaphysical query.

On this higher plane, Mann again relativizes the individuality and psychology of his characters and treats them and their problem as archetypal. His theme is the assumed dichotomy between mind and body, intellect and 'life', with which he had been preoccupied in much of his earlier writing. In this preoccupation he was influenced psychologically by Freud and Jung and philosophically by Schopenhauer.[20] As opposed to Mann's earlier treatment of the antinomies between art and intellect on the one hand and 'life' on the other, the two male protagonists of the *Transposed Heads* have to be viewed as ironic representations of 'intellect' and 'nature' respectively.[21] Alluding to the three protagonists in *Tonio Kröger*, Thomas Mann self-ironically commented in a letter to Agnes E. Mayer that now Tonio, Hans and Inge are united in a grave of flames (Carbe 1970: 24).

The tension between the poles just mentioned is also reflected in the tension between the form and content of Mann's story, i.e. the form of the legend and the psychological theme, to which he has repeatedly referred as a 'metaphysical joke' (metaphysischer Scherz).[22] This 'joke' is achieved by, among other things, a technique of alienation closely associated with Mann's understanding of humour and irony. From his mid-twentieth-century European perspective, both components addressed in the subtitle, the 'exotic' setting of the ancient Indian stories and the genre of the legend, serve the purpose of alienation on the one hand and generalization on the other. But, as Baum points out—Mann achieves alienation not primarily by creating a distance vis-à-vis the familiar, but by dealing with the unfamiliar or alien in a familiar way (Baum 1966: 450). The transposition of the heads through divine intervention which takes place in the old tales and which appears quite natural in that setting provides the precondition for Mann's investigation. And, once the otherwise impossible has happened, Mann can treat it in a matter-of-fact way: He is in a position to examine the biological and psychological consequences in a completely different conceptual framework.

The nearly scientific, experimental procedure recalls Goethe's approach in his novel *Wahlverwandtschaften* (Elective Affinities). In fact, in the figure of Sita's little son, Mann uses a motif from Goethe's *Elective Affinities*, but combines it with Zimmer's account of a *Mahābhārata*-motif. In both cases, the thoughts of a woman while conceiving have an impact on the features of the child. In Goethe's novel the child has the eyes of the wife's lover, whom she remembered in sexual union with her husband; in the *Mahābhārata*, the heroes' features are determined by their mothers' reactions to the sexual act with Vyāsa. Thus Pāṇḍu became so pale because his mother paled and Dhṛtarāṣṭra was born blind because his mother closed her eyes out of disgust. Mann shares Goethe's fascination with the concept of *Gedankensünde* (mental sin) developed in *Elective Affinities* and the idea of unknowingly becoming guilty ('schuldig, keiner Schuld bewußt') which Goethe elaborates in the 'Legend' of his *Paria* cycle.

Thus, in addition to the sources mentioned earlier, Mann's story is inspired by concepts and details of this poem cycle of 1823, consisting of the three poems 'Des Paria Gebet' (The Paria's prayer), 'Legende' (Legend), and 'Dank des Paria' (Thanks of the Paria).[23] The poem cycle is a treatment of the Reṇukā/Ellamma-story, in which the transposition of heads plays a central part as well, the head of an untouchable woman being placed on the body of the princess Reṇukā. The latter had been decapitated as punishment for a momentary deviation from service to her husband.[24] Mann borrowed the motif of the sword with which Sita is supposed to touch the wound before replacing the heads. In a more general way, too, Goethe's refined literarization and his use of the genre of 'legend' must have served Mann as a model for his own approach.[25]

Goethe also played an important role in Mann's understanding of the relationship between 'intellect' and 'life', which forms the central theme of the *Transposed Heads* as well. This theme had engaged Mann's thoughts throughout his oeuvre, one of the earliest treatments being his *Tonio Kröger.* At this early stage, he had always depicted the attraction between the representatives of art and intellect on the one hand and 'life' and 'beauty' on the other as one-sided. Intellect or art seeks life or beauty, but 'life' or 'beauty' do not seek intellect or art. It was Goethe who for Mann increasingly represented the union or synthesis between these poles. Just before starting to work on the *Transposed Heads*, Mann had elaborated his understanding of Goethe's personality in his novel *Lotte in Weimar.* There, it is the artist alone in whose consciousness the synthesis can be achieved—albeit on a plane 'where one secretly has in view art when practicing love'.[26] The 'Indian legend', which Mann first took up simply as an intermezzo before returning to his magnum opus *Joseph und seine Brüder*, a voluminous novel based on a story in Genesis of the Old Testament, is actually the first of Mann's works which thematizes the reciprocity of longing between the two poles mentioned above. But, the longing being fulfilled in such a surprisingly concrete manner in the ancient Indian tale, Mann was driven one step further, and the older formula of longing and harmony itself became suspicious to him.[27]

What is the result of the investigation he undertakes in the *Transposed Heads*? It is, in the first place, the recognition of the fact that the blissfulness of the experience of union can last only for a moment. Because as soon as the 'otherness' of the 'other' is appropriated, the other becomes the self and a union with oneself is a contradiction in terms. This union also precludes the element of longing so essential for the notion of fulfilment. When the other has become the self, the self's longing for union continues, and it has to start seeking another 'other'. Shridaman anticipates this development at two points in the story: Firstly, when he obtains Sita, the object of his longing, in marriage, he experiences a certain sadness that the alien has now become his own and can no longer be an object of longing (p. 71).[28] Secondly, when his head obtains Nanda's body he feels sad that now he himself is what he had been longing for.[29] On the next page the head is described as one that by owning the beautiful loses its love for the beautiful and thereby also more or less loses its own intellectual beauty.[30] Thus Mann's 'metaphysical joke' helps him to realize that a permanent union between intellect and life, even if possible, is not desirable, because longing itself is an important precondition for the possibility of experiencing the bliss of union.

Mann's attitude vis-à-vis this recognition is humorous and ironical, but also conciliatory and humane. In contradistinction to the one-sided longing described in earlier works his theme now is the reciprocity of longing and of eroticism. This is in accord with his concept of the artist as mediator between intellect and life, a function which requires a comprehensive perspective and also creates a distance vis-à-vis the phenomena the artist deals with. The distance is expressed in an ironic attitude. According to Baum (1996, *passim*), Mann's irony becomes a loving, humane irony through its association with his notion of mediatorship—in contradistinction to the attitude of Schopenhauer, for whom nature and intellect are absolutely separate. Baum quotes a statement by Mann which applies very well to his method in the *Transposed Heads*: 'The scientific, applied to the absolutely unscientific and fantastic, is pure irony.'[31]

Girish Karnad's play Hayavadana *('Horse-face')*

In spite of its 'tragic' plot, ending, like Mann's story, with the death of the three protagonists, *Hayavadana* is a very enjoyable play. This is due, on the one hand, to its overwhelming theatricality, and, on the other, to the elements of humour and irony which as with Thomas Mann convey the author's humanist attitude and reconcile us to the fate of the characters. In Girish Karnad's case *Hayavadana* is the first of his dramatic works in which humour plays such a prominent role. In yet another way, this line is continued in his *Nāgamaṇḍala* of 1988, which can be read both as a modern 'folk play' and as an ironic commentary on postmodernism. In *Taledaṇḍa* ('Capital punishment', 1990), he returns to the genre of historical drama started by *Tughlaq* in 1964. But both historical plots and mythological or legendary ones, always serve to tackle contemporary problems and convey contemporary messages. This holds true also for his very first play, *Yayāti* (1961), which takes its fable from an episode of the *Mahābhārata*, and for *Hiṭṭina huñja* ('The cock of dough', 1980), which uses a plot from medieval Kannaḍa literature.[32] Such a retrieval of myth for modern times also relates Karnad's work to Thomas Mann's literary programme. *Añjumallige* (1977) is the only play with an invented, modern plot and contemporary setting.

All of Karnad's dramatic oeuvre was originally written in his mother tongue, Kannaḍa. The author himself translated several of his plays into English. Most of them are also available in other Indian languages such as Hindi, Bengali and Marathi. Karnad's English translations or versions of his plays themselves document processes of 'intercultural' adaptation which form an interesting object of study. For the purposes of the present paper I confine my references to the author's English version of *Hayavadana*.[33]

One major difference between Mann's *Transposed Heads* and Karnad's *Hayavadana* is the change from narrative prose to drama. Within the drama, the common plot is embedded in a frame containing a subplot, the technique being in part adopted from south Indian folk theatre. Karnad takes over Mann's psychologization of the characters, but uses different devices to bring out the exemplary or general nature of the problem: He uses common or typifying names like Devadatta, Kapila and Padmini.[34] Devadatta's talents are even more fabulous than Shridaman's. Devadatta is not only well-versed in the scriptures but also a connoisseur of Sanskrit *kāvya* and a poet himself. Padmini is by no means the first girl he has fallen in love with, but the fifteenth! Kapila is only a smith, not also a cowherd as with Mann.

Karnad has the two male protagonists wear masks. This is, in the first instance, a theatrical device to show the transposition of the heads. According to the author (Karnad 1989: 103), the function of the masks is not to hide the faces, but to enlarge them, the head being the most important part. But there is also an element of irony in replacing the heads with masks, the heads being considered in the story the seats of the mind and of individuality, that part of the body which constitutes the person.

Whereas the psychology and inner motivation of the characters remain largely the same, Karnad takes up the metaphysical level of Mann's story only partly. Mann's preoccupation with the concept of *māyā*—as understood by Schopenhauer and Zimmer—is strongly reduced. Concerning the mind-body duality, Mann's irony is multiplied by the reflection of the main plot in the subplot of the frame story, embedding the dialogues of a modern drama in a sophisticated folk play. Song and music form yet another level of the work which—in a way—replaces Mann's Indo-German metaphysics. It is especially the lyrics that provide *Hayavadana* with a highly poetic dimension.[35]

In a way, the figure of the stage director, the Bhagavata (*bhāgavata*), corresponds to Thomas Mann's narrator and to the frame setting of the old stories. In contradistinction to the traditional function of the Bhagavata in folk theatre, Karnad's stage director not only appears in the frame plot but also interferes repeatedly in the action of the main plot. During a break in the play intended to have the audience think about the central problem, he has the Bhagavata have his tea-break on stage. The traditional Gaṇapati *pūjā*—worship of the God Gaṇapati, too, is made part of the theatrical performance. The figure of this elephant-headed god anticipates and reflects the central problem of the entire play, dealt with in both the main plot and the subplot. Thereby a kind of second ironical frame is created, because Gaṇapati's elephant head is in fact accidental and does not determine his nature in any way. At the same time, the theme of the transposed head is prefigured in Gaṇapati.[36] While the entire problem concerning the function of the head discussed in the main plot is questioned by the divine figure of Gaṇapati, the subplot seems to take it seriously, but drives the point to the absurd by a value inversion between the 'human' and the 'animalic'.

The subplot is brought about in the following way: After the worship of Gaṇapati and reflections about this god by the Bhagavata, the Bhagavata starts to introduce the characters of the play. In the manner of the old tales he names the place and its ruler and presents the two male protagonists Devadatta and Kapila. When he is just about to sing a song about them he is interrupted by an actor who rushes onto the stage, fleeing from a speaking horse he encountered along the way. Thus the subplot starts by interrupting the main plot.

Karnad combines here elements from three different traditions. The idea of a frame-plot, like the main plot itself, stems from ancient narrative literature. The irony of the frame-plot with respect to the main plot is a playful new way of using this pattern. The introduction of the play by a stage director and the setting in of the play as an apparent interruption of the introduction stems from classical Sanskrit drama. The special thing about Karnad's method is that the interruption does not lead into the main plot but only into another frame-plot viewed as a disturbance of the performance in spite of its being part of the script. The designation *bhāgavata* for the stage director is taken from the Yakṣagāna folk theatre of Karnataka, but the use Karnad makes of this figure is different and goes beyond his function in traditional theatre. Karnad seems to blend the 'epic' dimension of traditional Indian theatre with devices from the modern epic theatre of Brecht. But the didactic side, like the tea-break for contemplation, is always presented in a humorous or ironical manner.[37]

Like the beginning of the play the end also recalls classical Sanskrit drama: As in a Sanskrit *bharatavākya* the Bhagavata recites a verse to the gods and asks for blessings and also for some common sense for the ruling politicians,[38] but, again, the humour and irony contained in Karnad's version add a new dimension to the model he quotes.

The frame-plot anticipates the main plot by pointing out the consequences of the assumed priority of the head over the body. Whereas the overall function of the frame-plot is ironical it is full of humour in situations and dialogues. When the 'speaking horse' encountered by the actor finally arrives on stage, he turns out to be a human with the head of a horse. Taking his head for a mask the Bhagavata first tries to pull it off, but as in the case of Gaṇapati the horse's head is real. In this way, the concept of mask used in the main plot is also made fun of. It is after this horse-headed figure, *Hayavadana,* that the play is named.

Like the clownish intermezzos on the folk stage the frame-plot also provides space for more popular jokes and humour, including references to contemporary social reality. Thus the horse censures the actor when he tries to urinate by the wayside. Social and religious institutions like pilgrimages are made fun of when Hayavadana complains to the Bhagavata that neither his social commitment nor pious pilgrimages had helped him to acquire a normal human shape (see quote below). Finally the Bhagavata suggests approaching a certain goddess who always grants all wishes. Along with the actor Hayavadana sets out to visit her.

The sad biography of the horse-headed youth appears almost like a satire on themes and narrative structures of the ancient literature which served Mann and Karnad as a source. It is modelled on stories about princesses who chose their husband out of a number of eligible candidates in a ceremony termed *svayaṃvara,* self-choice. Very often, the candidates also had to perform acts of valour and the princess chose the winner. The frame story of the *Vetālapañcaviṃśatī* version of the 'Exchanged Heads', too, provides a similar context: The king has to fulfil a condition posed by the princess. He has to make her speak four times in one night. If he fails she will reject and humiliate him. In the guise of a regional folk narrative Karnad presents his own version of such a *svayaṃvara* held by a princess at least as headstrong as the one in the old tale and as his own heroine Padmini. Since the story provides another set of important variations of the central theme and is a good example of the author's sense of humour I shall quote the passage in full. Hayavadana tells the Bhagavata and the actor:

My mother was the Princess of Karnataka. She was a very beautiful girl. When she came of age, her father decided that she should choose her own husband. So princes of every kingdom in the world were invited—and they all came. From China, from Persia, from Africa. But she didn't like any of them. The last one to come was the Prince of Araby. My mother took one look at that handsome prince sitting on his great white stallion—and she fainted.

ACTOR. Ah!

HAYAVADANA. Her father at once decided that this was the man. All arrangements for the wedding were made. My mother woke up—and do you know what she said?

ACTOR. BHAGAVATA. What?

HAYAVADANA. She said she would only marry that horse!

ACTOR. What!

HAYAVADANA. Yes. She said she wouldn't listen to anyone. The Prince of Araby burst a blood-vessel.

ACTOR. Naturally.

HAYAVADANA. No one could dissuade her. So ultimately she was married off to the white stallion. She lived with him for fifteen years. One morning she wakes up—and no horse! In its place stood a beautiful Celestial Being, a *gandharva.* Apparently this Celestial Being had been cursed by the god Kuvera to be born a horse for some act of misbehaviour. After fifteen years of human love he had become his original self again.

BHAGAVATA. I must admit several such cases are on record.

HAYAVADANA. Released from his curse, he asked my mother to accompany him to his Heavenly Abode. But she wouldn't. She said she would come only if he became a horse again. So he cursed her. . . .

ACTOR. No!

HAYAVADANA. He cursed her to become a horse herself. So my mother became a horse and ran away happily. My father went back to his Heavenly Abode. Only I—the child of their marriage—was left behind.

BHAGAVATA. It's a sad story.

ACTOR. Very sad.

After this account, the dialogue moves on into a 'realistic' contemporary Indian setting providing ample opportunity to make fun of social, religious and political institutions, customs and clichés. The references to sadhus and so forth recall Mann's Kamadamana chapter (10), whereas Karnad makes no such references at the respective point in his main plot.

HAYAVADANA. What should I do now, Bhagavata Sir? What can I do to get rid of this head?

BHAGAVATA. Hayavadana, what's written on our foreheads cannot be altered.

HAYAVADANA. [*slapping himself on the forehead*]

But what a forehead! What a forehead! If it was a forehead like yours, I would have accepted anything. But this! . . . I have tried to accept my fate. My personal life has naturally been blameless. So I took interest in the social life of the Nation— Civics, Politics, Patriotism, Nationalism, Indianization, the Socialist Pattern of Society. . . . I have tried everything. But where's my society? Where? You must help me to become a complete man, Bhagavata Sir. But how? What can I do? [*Long silence. They think.*]

BHAGAVATA. Banaras?

HAYAVADANA. What?

BHAGAVATA. If you go to Banaras and make a vow in front of the god there . . . .

HAYAVADANA. I've tried that. Didn't work.

ACTOR. Rameshvar.

HAYAVADANA. Banaras, Rameshvar, Gokarn, Haridwar, Gaya, Kedarnath—not only those but the *Dargah* of Khwaja Yusuf Baba, the Grotto of Our Virgin Mary—I've tried them all. Magicians, mendicants, maharishis, fakirs, saints and sadhus—sadhus with short hair, sadhus with beards—sadhus in saffron, sadhus in the altogether—hanging, singing, rotating, gyrating—on the spikes, in the air, under water, under the ground. . . . I've covered them all. And what did I get out of all this? Everywhere I went I had to cover my head with a veil—and I started going bald. [*Pause. Shyly.*] You know, I hate this head—but I just can't help being fond of this lovely, long mane. [*Pause.*] So—I had to give the miss to Tirupati.[39]

[*Long silence.*]

BHAGAVATA. Come to think of it, Hayavadana, why don't you try the Kali of Mount Chitrakoot?

HAYAVADANA. Anything you say.

BHAGAVATA. It's a temple at the top of Mount Chitrakoot. The goddess there is famous for being ever-awake to the call of devotees. Thousands used to flock to her temple once. No one goes now, though.

HAYAVADANA. Why not?

BHAGAVATA. She used to give anything anyone asked for. As the people became aware of this they stopped going.

HAYAVADANA. Fools!

BHAGAVATA. Why don't you try her?

HAYAVADANA [*jumps up.*] Why not? I'll start at once. . . . (pp. 8-10)

While Hayavadana, accompanied by the actor, goes on the pilgrimage suggested by the Bhagavata, the main plot finally sets in. With Karnad, Devadatta encounters Padmini, the heroine, alone, without his friend Kapila, in the town and later gives a report to his friend. The friends make no journey at this point and there is no bathing scene. Whereas Devadatta hopes that his union with Padmini will further stimulate his creative genius, Kapila realizes, during his very first encounter with the girl, that his friend is no match for her:

KAPILA. Devadatta, my friend, I confess to you I'm feeling uneasy. You are a gentle soul. You can't bear a bitter word or an evil thought. But this one is fast as lightning—and as sharp. She is not for the likes of you. What she needs is a man of steel. But what can one do? You'll never listen to me. And I can't withdraw now. I'll have to talk to her family. . . .

The following events largely take the same course as with Thomas Mann. But Karnad combines the deities mentioned in the various versions and re-introduces the vow. Absurdly, Devadatta promises to give his head to Rudra and his arms to Kālī if he obtains the girl in marriage. Later, when he sacrifices his head to the goddess, she calls him a fool in front of Padmini. Karnad follows Mann in presenting the conversation between the goddess and the girl as a kind of deal between two women. With the possibilities of the stage and by means of reflection in the Hayavadana frame-plot, Karnad is able to further augment the impact of the scene. He has the goddess enter the stage behind a curtain with her image painted on it. When she appears to Padmini the curtain is taken away and, according to the stage instruction, one sees a terrifying figure, her arms stretched out, her mouth wide open with the tongue lolling out. But, shortly thereafter, it becomes clear that she was only yawning! She feels rather disturbed and wants to get rid of the whole problem as quickly as possible. When Padmini has placed the heads on the wrong bodies and the three protagonists, after the first few happy moments, start quarrelling about whose wife she is, the first act ends. Karnad has divided the play into two acts, significantly called 'halfs' in the Kannaḍa original (*pūrvārdha* and *uttarārdha*). At the end of the first act, we return to the level of the outer frame on which the Bhagavata comments on the protagonists' problem and requests the audience to think about it.

At the beginning of the second act, he refers to the frame story of the Sanskrit source tale *Vetālapañcaviṃśati*, wondering whether the decision of king Vikrama might appeal to the audience. He reports that the three friends consulted a rishi who came to the same conclusion as the king. Then, the protagonists themselves take over the stage again. The situation develops as with Mann and ultimately leads to the death of all three of them. As a special device, Karnad has introduced two dolls (enacted by children) who accompany the couple and comment on their lives; the dolls are even capable of seeing Padmini's dreams and can thus provide information about her secret wishes.

After the death of Devadatta, Kapila, and Padmini the play continues with the frame-plot. In a scene analogous to the encounter with the Goddess, in the main plot, the Goddess of Mount Chitrakoot immediately grants Hayavadana's wish to become complete, without even properly listening to what he says. As a result, he becomes a complete horse, only his human voice remains. He tries to get rid of it by constantly singing the national anthem and other patriotic songs. By having Hayavadana become a horse Karnad points to the logical consequence of the assumption that the head is the determining factor. This consequence appears absurd and thereby exposes and questions the solution of the main plot.[40]

Finally, the child of the main plot, the only survivor, is integrated into the frame-plot. Like the princess in the frame story of the old tale, the boy cannot be made to speak. Only when he hears the horse laugh, he, too, bursts into laughter, and wants to ride on the horse. He is even ready to sing a song: it is the lullaby that is associated with Padmini throughout the main plot as a kind of leitmotiv, speaking of a dead rider on a horse. Hayavadana finally manages to lose his human voice and starts braying. The child and the horse happily cross the stage: Life continues. The scene is highly poetic, pervaded equally by sadness and humour. Horse-headed Hayavadana, who by his laughter makes the child speak again, appears almost like an allegory of folk theatre itself, capable of re-invigorating modern problem-oriented psychological theatre. This is confirmed by Karnad, who is nevertheless well aware of the dangers of uncritical or unreflective usage of such theatre forms:

> It must be admitted that the popularity of traditional forms on the urban stage has much to do with the technical freedom they offer the director. Music, mime, and exotic imagery open up vast opportunities for colourful improvisation, which nevertheless can—and alas! all too often does—degenerate into self-indulgence. So far, however, the benefits have far outweighed the shortcomings, and our past—or, if you prefer, our parallel if ignored present—has provided a source of energy that will keep at least some of us going for quite a while. (Karnad 1989: 105)

It is important to note that when adapting elements from various theatre forms Girish Karnad always blends their original function with his own concepts and thereby imparts new meanings to these elements. The half curtain, for example, is taken from folk theatre forms like Yakṣagāna. But Karnad, first of all, alters its function and secondly, uses different types of curtains in his play. The Yakṣagāna curtain is not painted and serves the characters for their individual entries, since there is no front curtain on the stage. Karnad's use of a curtain for the entry of the Goddess comes closest to this. But his curtain is painted with an image of the Goddess. Secondly, he uses a white curtain, behind which the protagonists 'freeze' at certain points in the play. Thirdly, he uses a curtain with flames painted on it to allude to Padmini's committing *satī*. The painted curtains recall the painted backdrops of earlier European theatre as well as of the Parsee theatre.

The Bhagavata, too, switches between traditional and new functions in Karnad's play. He moves on all planes and takes part even in the main plot, the 'modern' play, giving information to the protagonists, discussing with them, answering a question in their stead, providing assistance to them and making comments to the audience.

It is not only the theatrical devices that help to re-contextualize the story in an Indian setting. New sets of textual, literary references, too, fulfil the same purpose. Thus, the three protagonists are once compared to Rāma, Sītā and Lakṣmaṇa. At the end, before the men kill each other, they discuss with Padmini the possibility of living together like Draupadī and the Pāṇḍavas and dismiss it. The scene in which Kapila goes to fetch a flower for Padmini and returns with a whole armful recalls the *Kalyāṇasaugandhika* episode from the *Mahābhārata*, so popular in all traditional south Indian theatre forms, in which Bhīma goes to fetch flowers for Draupadī. When Padmini commits *satī*, she complains that she cannot even wish to obtain the same husband in her next life—an irony possible only against an Indian background.[41]

With *Hayavadana* Karnad has succeeded in creating a meaningful synthesis of elements from classical drama, Indian folk theatre and modern psychological and problem-oriented theatre. On the level of the plot he achieves a similar integration of elements from ancient Indian narrative literature and a twentieth-century European psychologizing treatment of these sources by Thomas Mann. Whereas Karnad treats Mann's theme psychologically in his main plot, he carries it to the absurd in his frame-plot. On a third level, represented by the God Gaṇapati, the problem does not seem to exist at all. But the Gaṇapati scene of the play is not really a religious ritual and therefore does not seriously offer an alternative. It is as much a part of the theatrical performance as the rest of the play. Still, playing with plays is not all we are left with.

The tale from ancient India has turned out to be equally helpful to the European author Thomas Mann and to the Indian author Girish Karnad for overcoming earlier formal and conceptual limitations imposed by their respective cultural backgrounds. On both, the matter-of-fact way of handling the grotesque and fantastic, examplified in the old tale, appears to have had a liberating impact. Mann is enabled to rethink his old problem of the mind-body-polarity under new premises. Karnad is encouraged by the tale as well as by Thomas Mann's version of it to bring together for the first time the various strands of Indian theatre and drama and to try out new modes of mediation between the narrative and the theatrical. For both authors, humour and irony are indispensable in approaching and handling the old material in a new cultural context, and make a meaningful intercultural reception possible. But humour and irony not only help to maintain a critical cultural distance, they also help to bridge it.

NOTES

1. English edition: *The Transposed Heads: A Legend of India*, New York 1941.
2. Compare Baum 1966: 449.
3. Pandit Jagadisa Lal Sastri (ed). 1970. *Kathāsaritsāgara* (Sanskrit). Delhi, Patna, Varanasi: Motilal Banarsidass, 419-21; English translation: *The*

Ocean of Story, being C.H. Tawney's translation of Somadeva's *Kathāsaritsāgara*, ed. by N.M. Penzer in 10 volumes, London 1926. See vol. vi, 204-8 for a translation of the present story. H. Uhle (ed.). 1881. *Vetālapañcaviṃśati* (Sanskrit). Leipzig, story VI, pp. 22-4 (reprint Nendeln 1966). Cp. also Jambhaladatta's Version of the *Vetālapañcaviṃśati*, ed. and transl. by M.B. Emeneau, New Haven 1934, 58-63. The Sanskrit text of the *Kathāratnākara* is available to me only as a bound xerox copy of Hiralal Hamsaraja's edition, Jamnagar 1911, kept in the Tübingen University library and comprising 699 leaves; German transl. in Hertel 1921: 173-6.

4. Zimmer (1890-1943), professor of Indology at the University of Heidelberg, was suspended from this position by the racist Nazi rulers in 1939 because his wife, Christiane von Hofmannsthal, a daughter of the poet and writer Hugo von Hofmannsthal, was of partly Jewish origin. The couple first went to Oxford and then emigrated to the United States in 1940. Zimmer became a visiting professor at Columbia University, New York (see Stache-Rosen 1981: 229-31).
5. Thomas Mann's use of the various sources has been studied most elaborately by Monika Carbe in her Marburg Ph.D. thesis of 1970 to which I owe most of the following information. Among other things, Carbe has examined 36 pages of handwritten notes and excerpts Thomas Mann prepared for writing the *Transposed Heads*. This material is available at the Thomas Mann archive in Zurich, Switzerland.
6. Zimmer 1938, reprinted in Wilhelm 1980: 20.
7. The dedication is reproduced in the Vintage Books edition, New York 1959, which is a pocket book reprint of the 1941 edition.
8. The letter is quoted in full in the original German in Wilhelm 1970: 399 and in English translation (parts) in Wilhelm 1977/78: 412.
9. Heinrich Zimmer. 1936. *Maya: Der Indische Mythos*. Zurich; reprinted as vol. 2 of Zimmer's Collected Works, Zürich 1952. Mann's copy in the Thomas Mann archive contains a dedication by Zimmer. See Carbe 1970: 72.
10. See Wilhelm 1970: 401 for more examples. Cp. Ruben 1941: 13.
11. In the English reprint edition, they fill 115 pages—mainly due to a different layout with less space between lines, but also due to the translation which sometimes slightly abbreviates the original.
12. The original reads: 'Die Geschichte der schönhüftigen Sita, Tochter des aus Kriegerblut stammenden Kuhzüchters Sumantra, und ihrer beiden Gatten (wenn man so sagen darf) stellt, blutig und sinnverwirrend wie sie ist, die höchsten Anforderungen an die Seelenkräfte des Lauschenden und an sein Vermögen, den grausamen Gaukeleien der Maya des Geistes Spitze zu bieten. Es wäre zu wünschen, daß die Zuhörer sich an der Festigkeit des Überliefernden ein Beispiel nähmen, denn fast mehr Mut noch gehört dazu, eine solche Geschichte zu erzählen, als sie zu vernehmen. Von Anfang bis Ende trug sie sich aber zu, wie folgt.'
13. This is one of the passages where the English translation considerably reduces the powerful, solemn and very ironic tone of the original German, which reads: 'Möchten doch nur die Lauschenden nicht,

verführt durch den bisher so freundlichen Gang dieser Geschichte, der Fanggrube der Täuschung anheimgefallen sein über ihren wahren Charakter! Während wir schwiegen, hat sie einen Augenblick ihr Gesicht abgewandt, und wie sie es euch wieder zuwendet, ist es dasselbe nicht mehr: es ist zu einer gräßlichen Maske verzerrt, einem verstörenden, versteinernden oder zu wilden Opfertaten hinreißenden Schreckensantlitz, wie Schridaman, Nanda und Sita es auf der Reise erblickten, welche sie . . . Aber eins nach dem anderen.' (p. 61)

14. The German reads: 'Der regengrüne Dandakawald, zu dem unsere Freunde am dritten Tage gelangten, war stark bevölkert mit Heiligen; doch war er groß genug, um einem jeden hinlängliche Abgeschiedenheit und ein Stück grausiger Menschenleere zu bieten. Es wurde den Wallfahrern nicht leicht, sich von Einsamkeit zu Einsamkeit zu Kamadamana, dem Bezwinger der Wünsche, durchzufragen. Denn die Einsiedler rings wollten einer vom anderen nichts wissen, und jeder beharrte auf seinem Eindruck, daß er allein sei im weiten Walde und vollkommene Menschenleere ihn umgebe. Es waren Heilige verschiedenen Grades, welche die *Einsamkeiten* bewohnten . . .' (116). Especially the German plural *Einsamkeiten* (solitudes, lonelinesses, tr. 'unpeopled voids') in the last sentence is a contradiction in itself. The scene has also been taken as alluding to the situation of the German intellectuals living in exile in the United States at the same time as Mann.
15. Much more graphic in German: '. . . zu meiner Kasteiung will ich euch anhören und dabei die Einflüsterung ertöten, ich täte es zu meiner Unterhaltung—es kann gar nicht genug zu ertöten geben!' (123).
16. More explicit and more comic in German, e.g. words invented by Mann like 'Doppellust' and 'Zeugezeug': '. . . der Arme Wonnedruck, der Schenkel Blust,—des Hinterfleisches kühle Doppellust,—und, von dem allen gierig aufgebracht,—das Zeugezeug in schwül unflätiger Nacht,—das man sich voll Entsetzen zeigt,—einand' damit zum siebenten Himmel geigt—und dies und das und hier und da,—ich weiß es ja! Ich weiß es ja . . .' (128). Thomas Mann reports that everyone, including himself, burst into laughter when he first read out the chapter from his manuscript to a small group of friends.
17. The element of voyeurism in erotic poetry is a different question not to be discussed here.
18. Ruben, too, recalls 'Susanna' but does not give any reason for it. He also mentions the Greek motif of the nymph, mostly associated with springs and lakes, and fawns watching her.
19. A last observation concerning this scene is that Mann stresses the unity and harmony between head/face and body in the case of his heroine, anticipating—by way of contrast—the central theme of his story.
20. Cf. Carbe 1970: 44ff.
21. Cf. also Baum 1966: 454.
22. For example in a letter to Hermann Hesse, dated 2 January 1941.
23. See Goethe, *Works*. Hamburg edition, vol. 1, poems and epics 1, München 1988, 361-6. An English translation of the 'prayer' is quoted in Wilhelm 1977/78: 411.

24. Goethe's source was a travelogue by P. Sonnerat, first published in French in 1782 and in German translation in 1783: P. Sonnerat. 1782. *Voyage aux Indes orientales et China.* Paris. *Reise nach Ostindien und China.* Zürich 1783. This source of Goethe's was first identified by Th. Zachariae in his article 'Zu Goethes Parialegende', reprinted in *Kleine Schriften,* Bonn/Leipzig 1920: 118-25. See also Wilhelm 1977/78: 410-11 and Carbe 1970: 5-6, 30-1 and passim.
25. Carbe points out a possible connection between the 'Paria' motif and the bathing scene (see above), since Sita once compares Nanda to the Gandharva king Citraratha, whose sight as reflected in the water of the river had diverted Reṇukā's thoughts (1970: 37).
26. '. . . wo man heimlich Kunst meint, wenn man Liebe betreibt. . . .' (cf. Hamburger 1965: 50).
27. See Hamburger 1965: 26.
28. In German: ' . . . gewisse Traurigkeit, daβ das Fremde nun mein geworden . . .' (106).
29. In German: '[Traurigkeit . . .,] daβ er nun selber war, wonach ihn verlangt hatte.' (146).
30. In German: '[Haupt . . .,] das durch den Besitz des Schönen der Liebe zu diesem und damit der geistigen Schönheit mehr oder weniger verlustig geht.' (147). Carbe 1970: 25 sqq. draws attention to the fact that Mann makes a similar statement in his *Betrachtungen eines Unpolitischen.* There, Thomas Mann states that a permanent union between intellect and life is not possible; only a short, intoxicating illusion of union, an eternal tension without solution. It is in the light of this statement that Carbe views the two short periods of bliss Sita experiences with each of the two composite heroes.
31. 'Denn das Wissenschaftliche, angewandt auf das ganz Unwissenschaftliche und Märchenhafte, ist pure Ironie' (quoted according to Baum 1966: 451).
32. Janna's *Yaśodhara carite,* composed in AD 1209. See now: TRS Sharma, (tr.). 1994. Janna, *Tale of the Glory-Bearer* and *The Episode of Candaśāsana.* Delhi: Penguin India.
33. I am presently preparing German translations of three of Girish Karnad's plays (*Hayavadana, Nāgamaṇḍala, Taledaṇḍa*), accompanied by introductory studies which also address problems of translation, comparing the author's English versions with the original Kannaḍa (see Brückner, under preparation).
34. Especially Mann's choice of the name Sita for his heroine would have been problematic in an Indian context, where this name stands for a particular concept of ideal womanhood. *Padminī,* as Karnad explains (1989: 103), is the classificatory name of one of six types of woman mentioned in the *Kāmaśāstra.*
35. Karnad comments that song and music are intended to again remove the plot into a mythical and elemental sphere (Karnad 1989: 103). A more detailed discussion of the songs would have to go back to the Kannaḍa version of the play.

36. The God Śiva had, by mistake, decapitated his own son and ordered his attendants to quickly fetch another head and place it on the body. They first came across an elephant and brought back its head.
37. Karnad acknowledges that Brecht made him more sensitive to the potential of non-naturalistic techniques in traditional Indian theatre.
38. 'Bhagavata. . . . Unfathomable indeed is the mercy of the Elephant-headed Ganesa. He fulfils the desires of all—a grandson to a grandfather, a smile to a child, a neigh to a horse. How indeed can one describe his glory in our poor, disabled words?
Come, Hayavadana, come. Enough of this dancing. Our play is over and it's time we all prayed and thanked the Lord for having ensured the completion and success of our play.
[*Hayavadana comes and stands by the Bhagavata. The Bhagavata helps the child down. At this point the curtain, with the fire painted on it,—which has been there all the time—is dropped and Padmini, Kapila and Devadatta step forward and join the Bhagavata in prayer.*]
Grant us, O Lord, good rains, good crop,
Prosperity in poetry, science, industry and other affairs.
Give the rulers of our country success in all endeavours,
and along with it, a little bit of sense.'
39. Because people give their hair as an offering at the famous temple there. [H.B.]
40. Cf. Karnad 1989: 104 'The central logic of the tale remains intact, while its basic premise is denied.'
41. 'PADMINI. . . . Kali, Mother of all Nature, you must have your joke even now. Other women can die praying that they should get the same husband in all lives to come. You haven't left me even that little consolation. . . .'

REFERENCES

Primary Literature (texts and editions used)

Goethe, Johann Wolfgang von. 1988. 'Paria' (Trilogie, 1823). In: *Werke.* Hamburger Ausgabe, Band 1, Gedichte und Epen 1, 361-6, München. (References to other works of Goethe's are based on the same Hamburg edition of his works in 13 volumes).

Hemavijaya, see *Kathāratnākara.*

Hertel, Johannes. 1920. *Kathāratnākara. Das Märchenmeer.* Eine Sammlung indischer Erzählungen von Hemavijaya. Deutsch von Johannes Hertel. Two volumes. Munique (the translations are not based on the edition quoted, but on the copy of a manuscript).

Hertel, Johannes. 1921. *Indische Märchen.* Jena: Eugen Diederichs (contains a German translations of Hemavijaya's version of the 'Transposed Heads', pp. 173-6).

Works of Girish Karnad and Thomas Mann

Añjumallige (Kannaḍa). [2]1989. Dharavada: Manohara Granthamala.
Hayavadana (Kannaḍa). [2]1972. Dharavada: Manohara Granthamala.
Hayavadana (English), transl. by the author. 1981. Madras etc.: OUP.
Hiṭṭina Huñja (Kannaḍa). 1980. Dharavada: Manohara Granthamala.
Nāgamaṇḍala (Kannaḍa), rev. edn. 1993. Dharavada: Manohara Granthamala.
Nāga-Mandala. Play with a Cobra (English). 1990. Delhi etc.: OUP.
Taledaṇḍa, (Kannaḍa). [2]1991. Dharavada: Manohara Granthamala.
Tughlak (Kannaḍa).[5]1987. Dharavada: Manohara Granthamala.
Tughlaq (English). 1972. Delhi etc.: OUP.
Yayāti (Kannaḍa), reprint 1971. Dharavada: Manohara Granthamala.

Other Original Sources

Kathāsaritsāgara (Sanskrit). ed. by Pandit Jagadisa Lal Sastri. 1970. Delhi, Patna, Varanasi: Motilal Banarsidass, 419-21.

The Ocean of Story, being C.H. Tawney's Translation of Somadeva's *Kathāsaritsāgara,* ed. by N.M. Penzer in 10 volumes. 1926. London. See vol. vi, 204-8, for a translation of the present story.

Kathāratnākara (Skt.), ed. by Hiralal Hamsaraj. 1911. Jamnagar (xerox copy in the Tübingen University library).

Mann, Thomas. 1988. *Die Vertauschten Köpfe. Eine Indische Legende.* Frankfurt: Fischer (first published from Stockholm in 1940).

Mann, Thomas. 1941. *The Transposed Heads: A Legend of India.* Translated from the German by H.T. Lowe-Porter. New York: Alfred Knopf. Reprint, New York: Vintage Books, 1959.

All other references to works of Thomas Mann are based on the German edition of his Collected Works in 13 volumes, 1990, Frankfurt am Main: Fischer.

Somadeva, see *Kathāsaritsāgara* (Sanskrit and English)

Śivadāsa, see *Vetālapañcaviṃśati*

Vetalapañcaviṃśati (Sanskrit), ed. by H. Uhle. 1881. Leipzig, story VI, pp. 22-4 (rpt Nendeln 1966).

Cp. also Jambhaladatta's Version of the *Vetālapañcaviṃśati,* ed. and transl. by M.B. Emeneau, 58-63. New Haven 1934.

Secondary Literature

Baum, Georgina. 1966. 'Ironie und Thomas Manns Erzählung "Die Vertauschten Köpfe" '. *Weimarer Beiträge. Zeitschrift für Literaturwissenschaft* XII: 446-459.

Brückner, Heidrun (under preparation). 'Pferdegesicht', 'Schlan-genspiel' und 'Todesstrafe'—Drei Stücke von Girish Karnad. Übersetzung und Studie.

Carbe, Monika. 1970. Thomas Mann: Die Vertauschten Köpfe. Eine Interpretation der Erzählung. Dissertation Marburg.

Hamburger, Käte. 1965. *Der Humor bei Thomas Mann. Zum Joseph-Roman.* München: Nymphenburger Verlagshandlung.

Karnad, Girish. 1989. 'In Search of a New Theatre.' In: *Contemporary Indian Tradition. Voices on Culture, Nature and the Challenge of Change,* ed. Carla Borden, 93-105. Washington and London: Smithsonian Institution Press.

Kerényi, Karl. 1963. *Tessiner Schreibtisch. Mythologisches Un-mythologisches.* Stuttgart: Steingrüben.

Ruben, Walter. 'Ein indisches Motiv bei Goethe und Thomas Mann.' Ankara 22.4.1941 (Typoscript, 17 pages).

Stache-Rosen, Valentina. 1981. *German Indologists Biographies of Scholars in Indian Studies Writing in German.* With a summary of Indology in German Speaking Countries (= Dialogue 80/81). New Delhi: Max Mueller Bhavan.

Wilhelm, Friedrich. 1970. 'Thomas Mann über seine indische Le-gende.' *Euphorion* 64:399-403.

Wilhelm, Friedrich. 1977-8. 'The Transposed Heads: The Migration of an Indian Motif.' *Annals of the Bhaṇḍarkar Oriental Research Institute* (Diamond Jubilee Volume), 407-12. Poona.

Zachariae, Theodor. 1920. 'Zu Goethes Parialegende.' *Kleine Schriften,* 118-25. Bonn und Leipzig: Kurt Schroeder.

Zimmer, Heinrich. 1936. *Maya—Der Indische Mythos.* Zürich. Reprinted as vol. 2 of Zimmer's Collected Works, Zürich 1952.

Zimmer, Heinrich. 1938. *Die Indische Weltmutter.* (Eranos-Jahrbuch 1938, Zürich 1939) Reprinted in: Zimmer, Heinrich. 1980. *Die Indische Weltmutter.* Aufsätze, ed. Friedrich Wilhelm, 17-56. Frankfurt am Main: Insel 1980.

Zimmer, Heinrich. 1966. 'Der König mit dem Leichnam.' *Vetalapantschavinsati. Die Fünfundzwanzig Erzählungen eines Dämons.* Übersetzt von Heinrich Uhle. Eingeleitet durch: 'Der König mit dem Leichnam', von Heinrich Zimmer, 9-42. Darmstadt: Wissenschaftliche Buchgesellschaft

Joking and Laughing in Modern Tamil Literature

GABRIELLA EICHINGER FERRO-LUZZI

Introduction

People all over the world joke and laugh though the degree to which they do so varies greatly. Whether and to what extent they joke and laugh about the same things in different cultures has long been debated among laymen and scholars. Obviously there are many cross-cultural similarities in humour, but it is equally clear that an alien people's humour may, at times, fall flat or be incomprehensible to members of another culture.

Works of literature are useful as a means to assess whether their sense of humour is the same, in that they are largely free from contingent facts like the joker's performative skill and the stimulating or restraining effect of the audience. Besides, by examining what Tamil authors consider funny, one would be relying on knowledgeable informants who are usually keen and thoughtful observers of their culture and fellow-countrymen's behaviour. Theoretically a comparison of Tamil and Western humour in literature would require that the literatures of both cultures be examined, but since I am addressing myself to a Western audience the knowledge of Western humour may be taken for granted and I shall concentrate only on the largely unknown Tamil humour. Since the cultural differences between Western countries are relatively minor compared to the differences between the West and India I shall speak generically of Western humour.

Before proceeding to compare Tamil and Western humour I shall examine humour in modern Tamil literature under two headings: humour and irony on the part of the narrator, on the one hand and the characters' joking and laughing on the other. In doing so I wish to make an ethnographic contribution to a little known aspect of Tamil culture.

I. *Humour in Modern Tamil Literature*

1. HONOUR AND IRONY ON THE PART OF THE NARRATOR

In an earlier study on the culture-specific themes of Tamil short stories (1983) I noticed that many of these stories, according to our modern

Western taste, are excessively sentimental. Not infrequently, however, their sentimentality or lacrimosity is mitigated by joking and ironic remarks on the part of the narrator. It was this observation that prompted me to take up the study of Tamil humour. In speaking of the narrator's humour *and* irony I seemingly adopt a distinction that has long been current in the West. According to this view, irony is a rhetoric technique distinct from humour. Irony is also thought to have its essence in insincerity. Recently, Sperber and Wilson (1988) have rightly pointed out that insincerity cannot define irony because there exist exceptions to it, but their proposal to consider 'echoic mention' the essence of irony runs into the same difficulty in that it does not apply to all cases. In my opinion, irony can be as little defined in an essentialist sense as humour itself. Both are polythetic-prototype concepts (Eichinger Ferro-Luzzi 1990), i.e. they have elements recurring with great frequency but none that run through the whole concept. It is easy to show that irony and humour overlap at several points. Insincerity, which would be called its most prototypical feature, for instance, also applies to gross exaggeration, which is normally classified as a factor of humour. In my usage, therefore, irony is a special subcategory of the wider concept of humour.

Humorous or ironic comments by the narrator occur in Tamil novels and short stories from their very beginning. Vedanayaham Pillai, the author of the first Tamil novel, for instance, states, tongue in cheek: 'We have heard that, during a lawsuit lawyers frequently ask for fees like some deities frequently ask for blood sacrifice' (1984/1879: 294). Rajam Aiyar in his famous novel (Kamalāmpāl's Life Story) pursues a serious religious-philosophical intent, but despite his youth (he was only twenty-one when he wrote the novel) he is able to look at life with detached amusement. For instance, speaking of the music accompanying a religious ceremony he writes: 'The drummer begun to simultaneously pierce the by-standers' ears and the skin of his drum' (literally, he bored holes into them as if they had been sieves). In a postscript Rajam Aiyar thanks his readers for having patiently put up with his invented story (1972/1896: 137, 265).

Self-directed irony or mockery also occurs in contemporary serious prose. In an autobiographical work Ramamirtham tells us that he shuns quarrels but also does not keep silent in front of injustice. In saying so, he writes, 'I stick out my head a little from my rat hole' (note the Tamil equivalent of the Western ivory tower). Having voiced his opinion, Ramamirtham adds with self-directed irony: 'then I courageously pull in my head again' (1984: 140-1). In one of the same author's tragic tales the narrator is capable of self-directed mockery. After a boisterous youth he has calmed down and become like ordinary decent people. 'My grandchildren climb up and down on me playfully like rats and bandicoots jump over the presiding deity of a dilapidated temple', he tells us (1972: 30).

Putumaippittan, a critical and innovatory writer, likes to intersperse his serious tales with humorous remarks. For instance, in a tragic story about parents who become involuntarily guilty of their child's death he calls the father's unwashed hair an apt place for an all-India lice congress (1977: 8). Occasionally Putumaippittan writes wholly comic stories. In his parodic 'The New Skanda Purana' (1968) he seemingly upgrades the banal life story of an ordinary man by equating it with well-known episodes from the life of god Murukan. For instance, though Kantapiḷḷai was not suckled by the Kārtika sisters he nevertheless thrives fed by a metal Kāmadhenu. Her milk-nectar called Millins Glaxo had come from a region west of Jambudvipa.

Sankaranarayanan, a Tamil writer of the younger generation, tends to describe the darker side of life sometimes in comic terms. In a tale about temptation to commit adultery which has been resisted he speaks of a wife who adores her husband beyond socially expected limits. She is said to be proud of her husband even when he blows his nose (1985: 162).

Bhaskaran's 'The Earth around the Roots' (1974) is a wholly humorous story that has a surprise ending involving the outwitting of one matron by another. But the superbly comic character of the tale owes much to the narrator's metaphoric language and his self-directed irony. He starts with the alliterative saying 'Madness makes all sorts of things (literally, madness makes ten things). My madness made a marriage.' Then he explains: 'I do not mean the marriage I contracted twenty years ago, that was not my madness but that of the woman who married me. I refer myself to my daughter's marriage that I arranged two months ago.'

2. CHARACTERS WHO JOKE AND LAUGH

The humour of the narrators' words in the above instances may have been understood, especially when taking into account facts and premises of Tamil and Indian culture in general. But humorous remarks, especially ironic remarks, are also easily mistaken for serious assertions. For instance, in a comment that appeared in *Current Anthropology* (1978: 412-13) I once made fun of scholars who continue to believe that menstruating women make flowers wither; but my irony was not clearly recognized (Neumann 1978: 413-15). Therefore, the fictional characters' reaction to joking, especially their laughter, would seem to be particularly valuable for a study of Tamil humour.

Not surprisingly, joking characters are common in humorous stories and comedies. In addition to the humorous plots mostly based on the reversal of the normal or accepted situation, Marina's comedies derive much of their fun from the characters' way of speaking. They have the gift of the gab and prefer colourful expressions to matter-of-fact statements. In several comedies inveterate jokers appear who may amuse but sometimes get on people's nerves. The joking of the characters in comedies and other works of literature relies on all the standard techniques—incongruity, surprise, exaggeration, paradox, absurdity, etc.—that have been identified in jokes by Western students of humour which are also found in Tamil jokes published in magazines and jest books. By standard techniques I mean frequently occurring or prototypical techniques, but not essential ones, since none of them applies to all jokes.

Puns are one of the Tamil humorist's staples both in jokes independent of context and in humorous literature. In Rajam Aiyar's earlier-mentioned novel a husband jokingly conversing with his wife asks her for some water (*tīrttam*). She pretends to understand the Sanskrit word as holy water, the meaning given to it by all but the most orthodox Brahmans, and replies that in her house no holy water is offered (1972: 2).

Play on words has lost nothing of its attraction for the Tamils. It may have even increased since the widespread use of English permits the humorist to include English in his interlingual repertoire. In one of Marina's comedies (1980: 20) an uncle, by mistake, breaks his brother's shampoo bottle. He ruefully asks where he can buy another one. Mockingly, his brother replies: 'It is shampoo, isn't it; so try a flower shop (*pūkkaṭai*).' He pretends to incongruously understand the last syllable of the English-Hindi word as if it were the Tamil word for flower and thus creates an interlingual pun.

Hyperbole is just as much a staple of humour in context-free jokes as in humorous literature. In Vijayaraghavachariar's (known as S.V.V.) novel *Leisure Time* (1986: 32) two characters engage in a comic quarrel about the size of mosquitoes in their respective localities. Vellore mosquitoes are said to sting like scorpions, they would be able to swallow a hundred Kumbakonan mosquitoes and then belch with satisfaction. The champion of Kumbakonan mosquitoes denying this replies that Vellore mosquitoes, on seeing Kumbakonan mosquitoes at a mile's distance, would run away their tails drawn in between their legs.

The modification of standard sayings is another fertile source of humour. In another comedy by Marina (1982: 77) the female protagonist Ammākkaṇṇu's girl friend marries the latter's elder brother. When the girl friend reminds Ammākkaṇṇu, who is a few years older than herself, that she is now her social superior, Ammākkaṇṇu in comic deference asks to be forgiven addressing her as 'O mother who has not brought me up. . . .' Her words, which amount to a cultural absurdity, playfully invert a standard funeral lament of grown-up children at the death of their mother.

Received metaphoric wisdom may also be reinterpreted in a funny way. In Marina's comedy *Marriage Market* (1987: 24) a young man had boasted to his girlfriend that he would courageously speak to his father about his intention to marry her but hides when he sees his father come. The girlfriend mockingly asks him why he hides himself. Before taking to his heels he has time to answer: 'Don't you know that the tiger hides before jumping at his victims?' His patent self-contradiction is funny to the audience though not to the prospective bride.

II. *Peculiarities of Tamil Humour*

Not all the aforementioned instances of joking and laughing in modern Tamil literature may have seemed very funny. Some may even have sounded a little silly. This impression, however, is not due to any defective reasoning on the part of the Tamil humorist—all major mental processes of Western humour are also found in Tamil humour—but to the subject matter that may have no counterpart in the West or may have lost its attraction. Since we do not attach much importance to the hierarchy of age, especially when the difference in age is small, the conversation between the two girl friends in Marina's comedy will not be as funny as it is to the Tamils. Since young men afraid of speaking to their parents about their marriage plans have become anachronistic in the West, jokes about it have lost much of their humorous potential.

The Tamil authors' wordplays are also likely to be judged as unamusing by Westerners. Differences in the subject-matter of humour due to the presence or absence of cultural facts would stand to reason, but the lower rating of linguistic humour in the modern West compared to Tamilnadu is a purely arbitrary fashion. Wordplay based on rhyme, alliteration and double meaning was common in Western humour until recently. Besides it has not really disappeared but has simply been shifted from jokes as such to publicity slogans and newspaper headings in which rhyme, alliteration and double meaning are used to add salience and sometimes a comic note.

1. THE ECHO

Apart from the Tamil humorists' love of linguistic humour that quantitatively distinguishes Tamil humour from Western humour there exists one Tamil form of linguistic humour that has no equivalent in the West. I have called this form 'echo' joke (1986) giving the term echo a rather wide and metaphoric meaning. 'Echo' jokes seem to be inspired by the echo-word construction. The echo-word construction is clearly not Indo-European, but occurs in all four branches of Indian languages, i.e. it is an areal feature. If 'echo' jokes were found in non-Indian languages having the echo-word construction, such as Turkish, this would confirm my conjecture about the linguistic origin of 'echo' jokes. It would be one of the few instances in which a people's language does influence thought. It would not, of course, support the existence of a language-dependent logic, but it would show that language can cultivate a certain taste, in this case a taste for redundance. In the echo-word construction any noun can be repeated by an echo-word changing the first syllable of the first word usually to *kī.* The *ad hoc* created echo-word adds the meaning 'and the like' or simply stresses what is said. For instance: I do not want persons like holy men (*cāmiyār kīmiyār*) in my house. In the 'echo' joke, conversely, the so-called 'echo' is an existing word joined to the first word echo-like through rhyme or alliteration. The combination may be pure nonsense only determined by sound or it may be partly motivated by meaning disregarding similarity of sound. It may also exploit a double meaning. In rare cases the two words may be joined not by similarity of meaning but by contrast or opposition. 'Echo' jokes are absent from my corpus of jokes published in magazines and jest books but fairly common in humorous literature.

Cītāppāṭṭi, grandmother Sītā, the heroine of a series of comic stories by Bhagyam Ramaswamy, trying to get rid of an importune beggar wants to give him an old shirt of her husband Appūcami. He, however, disagrees and tells the beggar: 'You will get neither a *caṭṭai* (shirt) nor a *maṭṭai* (palmyra stem)' (1977: 165). He thus devises a purely nonsensical rhymed echo. In one of Marina's comedies a mother-in-law is accused of ingratiating herself with her daughter-in-law by flattering her. Flattering is expressed by a curious idiomatic expression that literally means 'to catch crows'. The mother-in-law denies this saying that she neither caught crows nor little birds. Her alliterative 'echo' *kuruvi* (little bird) of crow (*kākkay*) (Marina 1974: 95) is motivated by a zoological correspondence but extends a saying in a nonsensical way. The love for 'echo' jokes is such that even English words may be used in it. A character in another of Marina's comedies does not believe a certain tale and calls it a 'cock and bull story' (1978: 14) in English. The accused counters that he knows nothing about cock and bull or hen and cow stories but told the truth. His repetition echoic in an extended sense is based only on similarity of meaning without similarity of sound.

Ramamirtham (1988: 47) devises a more complicated 'echo'. His protagonist explicitly states that he does so because he is in a jocular mood. He thus disperses possible doubts about the comic intention of this joke technique. A Kerala girl talks to the protagonist and narrator in Malayalam mixed with Tamil. Hearing his offer to travel with him to Madras she incredulously asks whether he is joking. Since the verb she uses *kaḷipaṟaiyaṟatā* sounds funny to him he replies: 'Neither flour soup (*kaḷi*) nor rice gruel (*kañci*). I am serious.' His alliterative 'echo' is based on the polysemy of the word *kaḷi* meaning both to joke and flour soup. He comically pretends to understand it in the culinary sense and then stresses this sense through a second preparation.

A still more complicated 'echo' is also based on a double meaning, this time an interlingual one, but it joins the two words by opposition rather than similarity. In the comic novel *A [Hindu] Wedding in Washington* by Cavi a fictional Mrs Rockefeller wanting to see a Hindu wedding has the whole wedding party come to Washington at her expense. One passenger in the chartered plane hearing the name of the river Potomac which he sees below him understands it as *pōṭāmakku* (in the Tamil pronunciation foreign words may become almost incomprehensible through a change of stress). A more knowledgeable friend corrects him saying: 'Neither go, you fool, nor come, you wizard, say Potomac correctly' (n.d.: 30). The first passenger understands the name of the river as if it consisted of the two Tamil words 'go' (*pōṭā*) and 'fool' (*makku*) the friend then comically stresses this fanciful sense by a verb and a noun with opposite meanings.

2. SENSE OF HUMOUR

Apart from this peculiar technique of Tamil linguistic jokes other differences between Tamil and Western humour appreciation and expression of mirth are only of degree and not of kind. There cannot even exist any clear-cut distinction because of the wide individual variations within each culture. The following remarks, therefore, have to be taken as tentative suggestions. It seems to me that the Tamils are more inclined than the Westerners to consider funny the blunt expression of truth. The marriage broker in one of Marina's comedies claims that, according to the sacred law books, if one wants to know all about a family, it is enough to ask the servant and the family doctor. If the family is very rich one has also to make enquiries with the cook and the driver (1978: 17-18). The attribution of common sense wisdom to the Hindu sacred lawbooks would probably be comic also to the Western Indianist but hardly the common sense wisdom itself. To the Tamils both aspects of the discourse are comic.

Unlike children anywhere in the world who may laugh at a person falling and rolling down a staircase, in well educated Western adults compassion tends to override a potential laughter stimulus. This is much less so with the Tamils both in real life and in fiction. In a novel by Ramamirtham (1987: 39) a woman is happy to meet again her former boss whom she has not seen for years. Though she has great respect and affection for him she doubles up with laughter when he shows her his empty pockets telling her that he has been pickpocketed. The boss does not seem to resent her insensibility.

Also in a more general sense the adult Tamils' reaction to unusual or unforeseen things is closer to that of children everywhere, who tend to laugh at anything new, than to that of the blasé Western adult. A Western chemist who was shown a laundry bill rather than the medical prescription might smilingly return it to the customer. In one of Marina's comedies[1] the chemist laughs so heartily that his denture drops from his mouth, which causes the distracted customer to burst out laughing too.

3. EXPRESSION OF MIRTH

Homeric characters roared with laughter but nowadays boisterous laughter is somewhat discredited in the West. The Tamils have a separate term for noisy laughter, *cirippāṇi* and may behave accordingly on culturally prescribed and other occasions.

Institutionalized humour occurs sporadically in various communities all over the world, but is nearly unknown in the West. Institutionalized funeral humour, in particular, has no parallel in the West to my knowledge. Rajanarayanan describes a Tamil instance set in a village of Tirunelveli district. In his story 'The Departure' (1975: 91) the funeral of a man whose longevity seems to have defied the laws of nature is transformed into a farce. A man riding a dummy horse pretends to beat his breast in despair. A woman ironically advises him not to beat too hard otherwise blood will come. These words make the whole funeral party roar with laughter.

Joking and laughing during the wedding ceremony has a wider distribution than funeral humour and also occurs in the West. Several modern Tamil authors speak about institutionalized joking at weddings. In one case there is a hint at a possible social distinction in the expression of mirth. The Brahman protagonist and narrator in a story by Ramamirtham (1972: 149) marries a widow. His non-Brahman office friends appreciate his courageous step and noisily express their joy during the wedding ceremony. The narrator who prefers peace and quiet comments on their loud laughter: 'This is a nuisance in their caste.' Such a social distinction is not, of course, absolute. Brahman characters may laugh loudly too, but apart from individual reactions, also in India loud laughter seems to be less acceptable to the highly educated than to the little educated and the illiterate.

The Brahman writer S.V.V.'s *Leisure Time* does speak of loud and uncontrollable laughter on the part of Brahman characters and thus seemingly contradicts Ramamirtham's observation on a social difference in the expression of mirth. A judge, his illiterate wife, their four adolescent children and a friend of the family gather every evening on their roof terrace to engage in pleasant mostly joking conversation that sometimes provokes their uncontrollable laughter. I said that S.V.V.'s novel seemingly contradicts Ramamirtham's statement. It must be born in mind, in fact, that the novel was written fifty years ago, that the laughter occurs in the intimacy of the family and that it is mostly the adolescent children who laugh noisily. If their father does likewise one might postulate the well-known contagiousness of laughter. Nevertheless, the stress on laughter in S.V.V.'s novel is striking.

For instance, when the judge's illiterate wife proposes that the law should punish the husbands who do not teach their wives how to read and write, the judge laughs so much that he falls to the ground. The Tamil equivalent for doubling up with laughter, it is true, literally means 'to laugh falling' and the expression has certainly been coined because of people's habit to do so, but in this case S.V.V. explicitly states that his character rolled on the ground (1986: 125-6). Incidentally, this as well as other fictional episodes of uncontrollable laughter contradict M. Douglas' claim (1975: 83-9) that the bodily expression of joy is determined by the social structure. The looser the social structure, the more contortions; the more rigid the social structure, the more restrained the laughter. The caste system, by general agreement, is more rigid than the social systems of Western countries and yet it is the Tamils who are more likely to roll on the ground than we are. In the light of the Tamil material, therefore, I claim that no particular social structure but culture in its widest most diffuse sense may influence the bodily expression of our feelings. This applies not only to laughter but, amongst other things, also to weeping. In Schubert's songs, tears are constantly in the eyes of male characters; now most men north of the Alps would not be able to cry even if they wanted to.

I should like to end this overview of joking and laughing in modern Tamil literature with a story by Sundara Ramaswamy (1977: 9-29) that combines loud laughter and a sense of humour which is somewhat different from what we might expect.

A policeman is in dire need of five rupees which his wife had asked him for to celebrate the birthday of their little daughter. On a ridiculous pretext he arrests a priest and tries to extort the money from him. When the priest claims not to carry any money the policeman loses interest in him. Hearing the policeman tell a shopkeeper of his money problems a little later the priest suddenly understands the reason for his arrest. Still a little afraid, because beating suspects is accepted practice in Tamil police stations, he starts to laugh aloud. His laughter infects the policeman and soon both laugh to their heart's content at the absurdity of the situation. They part as good friends.

It seems to me that a Westerner seeing through a trick to extort money from him might make some sarcastic remarks but would not burst out laughing and that a Western extortioner realizing that his foul trick had been discovered would not join in the laughter.

Conclusive Remarks

Joking and laughing in modern Tamil literature should enable one to correct two stereotypes about the Indians held by Western laymen but sometimes also by students of Indian culture. One stereotype holds that the Indians' joy in life is reduced because of their social inequality and economic problems. According to another stereotype the Indians' spirituality, their other-worldly aims, makes them less interested in life in this world than the materialistic Westerner. The great number of humorous works of modern Tamil literature and the boisterous expression of mirth in them shows that the Tamils enjoy life at least as much, if not more, than the average Westerner.

NOTE

1. The scene appears on the Columbia record of the comedy *Ta<u>n</u>ik kuṭittaṉam* (Separate Household) but not in the written version of it.

REFERENCES

Bhagyam Ramaswamy. 1977. *Appucāmi kataikaḷ* (Stories about Appuswamy). Madras: Pumpukar Press.

Bhaskaran, R. 'Vēraṭi maṇ' (The Earth around the Roots). *Ananda Vikatan* 10.11. (1974): 34-40.

Cavi. n.d. *Vāṣiṇtaṉil tirumaṇam* [A (Hindu) Wedding in Washington]. Madras: Mona Publications, 4th Impression.

Douglas, Mary. 1975. *Implicit Meanings: Essays in Anthropology*. London: Routledge and Kegan Paul.

Eichinger Ferro-Luzzi, G. 1978. Comment on Neumann, T.W. 'A Bio-cultural Approach to Salt Taboos: The Case of the Southeastern United States.' *Current Anthropology* 19: 412-13.

———.1983. *Cool Fire: Culture-specific Themes in Tamil Short Stories*. Aachen: Edition Herodot/Rader Verlag.

———. 1986. 'Language, Thought, and Tamil Verbal Humor.' *Current Anthropology* 27: 265-72.

———. 1987. *The Self-milking Cow and the Bleeding Liṅgam: Criss-cross of Motifs in Indian Temple Legends*. Wiesbaden: Otto Harrassowitz.

———. 1990. 'Tamil Jokes and the Polythetic-prototype Approach to Humor.' *Humor* 3: 147-158.

Marina. 1974. *Taṉik kuṭittaṉam* (Separate Household). Madras: Vikatan Press.

———. 1978. *Kālkaṭṭu* (Wedlock). Madras: Puram Publications.

———. 1980. *Skailāp campanti* (The Skylab Father-in-law). Madras: Puram Publications.

———. 1982. *Aṭāvāṭi Ammākkaṇṇu* (Quarrelsome Ammākkaṇṇu). Madras: Puram Publications.

———. 1987. *Kalyāṇa mārkkeṭ* (Marriage Market). Madras: Puram Publications.

Neumann, T. W. 1978. 'Reply to Eichinger Ferro-Luzzi 1978'. *Current Anthropology* 19: 413-15.

Putumaippittan. 1968. 'Putiya kantap purāṇam' (The New Skanda Purāṇa). In his: *Āṇmai* (Virility). Madras: Star Publications: 59-63.

———. 1977. *Ciṟṟaṉṉai* (Stepmother). Madurai: Meenakshi Puthaka Nilayam.

Rajam Aiyar. 1972. *Āpattukkiṭamāṉa apavātam allatu Kamalāmpāḷ carittiram* (Dangerous Slander or Kamalāmpāḷ's Life Story). Madras: Tingal Press.

Rajanarayanan, K. 1975. 'Puṟappāṭu' (The Departure). In his *Kaṉṉimai* (Virginity). Madurai: P.K. Books: 79-94.

Ramamirtham, L.S. 1972. 'Apūrva rākam' (An Extraordinary Rāga) and 'Cāṭci' (The Testimony). In his: *Paccaik kaṉavu* (The Green Dream). Madras: Kalainyan Pathippagam: 25-51, 149-73.

———. 1984. *Pārkaṭal* (The Milk Sea). Madras: Ainthinaip Pathippagam.

———. 1987. *Kal cirikkiṟatu* (The Smile of the Stone [Statue]). Madras: Ainthinaip Pathippagam.

———. 1988. *Kēraḷattil eṅkō* . . . (Somewhere in Kerala). Madras: Ainthinaip Pathippagam.

Sankaranarayanan, S. 1985. 'Pūkampam' (The Earthquake). In his: *Aṭcarēkai tīrkkarēkai* (Latitude and Longitude). Madras: Ainthinaip Pathippagam: 159-1973.

Sperber, Dan, and Deirdre Wilson. 1988. 'Irony and the Use-Mention Distinction'. In *Radical Pragmatics*, ed. P. Cole, 295-318. New York: Academic Press.

Sundara Ramaswamy. 1977. 'Piracāṭam' (The Gift of God). In his homonymous book. Madras: Tamil Puthakalayam: 9-29.

Vedanayaham Pillai. 1984. *Piratāpa mutaliyār carittiram* (Piratāpa Mutaliyār's Life Story). Madras: Vanavil Press.

Vijayaraghavachariar (S.V.V.) 1986. *Ullāca vēḷai* (Leisure Time). Madras: Alliance Company.

Powers of the Timid: Aspects of Humour in the Rājasthānī Oral Epic of Devnārāyaṇ

ADITYA MALIK[1]

Introductory

The epic of Devnārāyaṇ is one of the longest and most popular religious oral narratives of Rajasthan.[2] It is performed by pairs of itinerant singers (*Bhopās*) belonging to the Gūjar, Kumahār or Bābhī communities in front of an elaborately painted scroll (*paṛ*). The performance, called *paṛ vā̃cṇo* (reading the *pāṛ*) includes reciting episodes from the epic, dancing and playing a stringed instrument (*bīṇ* or *jantar*) while pointing to scenes and characters on the scroll related to sections of the narrative being recited. Performances usually takes place during all night vigils (*jāgraṇ*)[3] in front of an audience comprised the devotees of Devnārāyaṇ, the chief deity of the Gūjar community.[4] The recitation of the epic alternates between song (*gāv*) and declamatory chant (*arthāv*). Thus relatively compact verses (*kaṛī*) that are sung are followed by longer prose sequences which actually 'explain' the short, terse verse sections while at the same time extending the narrative further.

The narrative can be classified under the category of 'martial' epics. 'Martial' epics revolve around themes such as 'revenge, regaining lost land, or restoring lost rights . . . (they) celebrate external—often military or political—conflict and a warrior ethic' (Blackburn *et al.* 1989: 5). Often the conflict is between groups related to one another either through marriage or ancestry. Thus, a central concern of the epic of Devnārāyaṇ is the simultaneous kinship and rivalry between the Gūjar and Rajput communities.[5] The epic has two main parts, from which various other sub-narratives branch off. The first part called the *Bagaṛāvat* or sometimes *Bagaṛāvat Bhārat,* deals with the short but heroic lives of twenty-four Gūjar brothers who are collectively called the Bagaṛāvats.[6] According to Bhopās the general tone of this part of the epic is one of suffering and pain (*dukh*), perhaps one could even call it tragedy. Thus, although characterized by valour and courage, the story's ultimate outcome is death, defeat and the loss of honour for its heroes. The second part called the *Devnārāyaṇ Kathā* (or *Gāthā*) is concerned with the birth and deeds of Lord Devnārāyaṇ, an incarnation of Bhagavān, who took birth after the twenty-four Bagaṛāvats died in battle against a Rajput chieftain (*Rāṇā*).[7] The overall tone of this part of the epic is said to be one of miracles and wonders or testimony (*parcyo*). Thus, although about vengeance,[8] it is simultaneously characterized by healing and reunion. Here the narrative offers an explanation for the establishment of the deity's cult, i.e. the founding of various temples and shrines, the manner of worship and the creation of a lineage of priests (*Bhopās*), who thereafter serve Devnārāyaṇ, either through the performance of the epic or in temples. In many ways the second part entails a completion of unfinished events of the first part.[9]

Notwithstanding the martial character of the first part, which is followed by the almost detached and serene activity of Lord Devnārāyaṇ in the second part, there are many humorous episodes and characters in the epic. In the following preliminary examination of the theme of humour in the epic, I shall be concentrating on three short episodes from the second part of the epic.[10] While using the term 'humour' I have two overlapping descriptions in mind. Both are taken from encyclopaedias, and are therefore general in nature. At the same time they provide, in my opinion, sound 'working definitions' of the term:

(1) the perception of the incongruous and the inconsistent is the cause or source of humour. It is invariably associated with alertness and breadth of mind, a keen sense of proportion, and faculties of quick observation and comparison. . . . Not infrequently the contrast involves a moral incongruity. It is this fact that places humour as a weapon in the hands of the reformer. . . . It is a protection against excess; it fosters humility, and yet lessens the bitterness of failure and blundering. . . . (*Encyclopaedia of Religion and Ethics*, vol. 6: 872)

(2) humour and satire are aimed at the comic victor/victim, at once the image of dignity and the epitome of hopeless frailty. For the believer humour and satire are expressions of faith that the grossly human and grandly sublime are magnificently and dialectically mixed. (*Encyclopaedia of Religion*, vol. 6: 526)

The question that I will be raising here is about the ways through which humour, in the senses outlined above, is expressed in the narrative: how much of it is expressed through particular characters, how much is situational, and how much is expressed through particular kinds of speech or language forms. Lastly, I will be looking at the underlying purpose of humour in these episodes within the context of the epic and cult of Devnārāyaṇ as a whole.

Episode 1

Devnārāyaṇ first appears riding on a jet of water that rises from the underworld while his mother performs asceticism on the Mālāsarī Hill.[11] After the Rāṇā tries twice to have him killed, Sāḍū Mātā,

Devnārāyaṇ's mother, flees to her maternal home in Malwa, where Devnārāyaṇ spends his childhood. One day when Devnārāyaṇ is about ten or twelve years old, their peaceful and untroubled existence is disturbed by Chochū Bhāṭ, the Bagaṛāvat's family genealogist. Chochū Bhāṭ has come to inform Devnārāyaṇ of his ancestors' deaths and of his real purpose in life, which is to avenge their deaths by defeating the Rāṇā and regaining the territory and property lost in the battle. Sāḍū Mātā, who naturally is against her son taking up arms, proposes that the confrontation with the Rāṇā be postponed till Devnārāyaṇ and his four cousins have met.[12] The most treacherous and difficult task in this mission is that of locating Bhūṇo or Khaṇḍerāv,[13] who has been adopted by the Rāṇā and has grown up in the Rāṇā's court. The following episode which is called the '*hero*' ('search') of Bhūṇo, deals with Devnārāyaṇ's attempt at locating Bhūṇo. As in many sections of the narrative, here too Devnārāyaṇ is not directly involved in the 'action'. Rather it is his 'assistants' Kālā and Gorā Bhairū and Chochū Bhāṭ who function as his active counterparts. Chochū Bhāṭ volunteers to find Bhūṇo. This is an extremely risky task, since Chochū has to enter the enemy city, where he is well known.[14] In order that he can undertake this search without arousing the suspicion of the enemy, Devnārāyaṇ alters Chochū's age and physical appearance by transforming him into a young man of twenty-five, and giving him his own features. Before leaving for the Rāṇā's city, the Bhāṭ visits his old mother, Ḍelū Mātā, in order to see whether she recognizes him or not. Since she does not recognize him, he is assured of his safety and proceeds to the enemy's city.[15]

After the Bhāṭ had spent a couple of nights in the city, one morning he went to the bazar (*aṛadū kā bazār*). He tethered his horse inside an old, broken-down shop, hung his *bīṇ*[16] and waterbottle on a nail, and went down to the middle of the street. There he collected piles of sand in his shield and started throwing the sand into the wind like one does with chaff. Now just at that time the king's younger brother, Nīmde, was passing through with his entourage. The leading Sirdār[17] said to the Bhāṭ: 'Hey, Dholīyo[18] move over! Can't you see that King Nīmde's entourage is passing through?' But the Bhāṭ replied: 'Hey, Sirdārs, I don't care whether Nīmā or Pīmā lives here in this city. I've lost something that belongs to me in this bazar and I'm not moving till I've found it.' He continued throwing up the sand. The horsemen shook their clothes free of the sand and said: 'Oh, let him be, let's move on!' Just then King Nīmde's entourage arrived. So, what did King Nīmde say to the Bhāṭ? 'O brother Dholīyo, you have costly shoes and your clothes are white, why do you fling up sand in my bazar?' Now who said this? King Nīmde said this upon arriving in the bazar.

The Bhāṭ thought to himself: 'Let me find out whether Nīmde is clever or if he is just a 'broken drum' (*phūṭīyo ḍhol*). So, what did the Bhāṭ say to King Nīmde: 'Yes the shoes on my feet are expensive and the clothes I wear are white.

O Nīmā, I've lost twenty-four rubies and one diamond and I'm looking for them here.' Now King Nīmde was not that clever that he could understand what the Bhāṭ had said. The Bhāṭ hadn't even told the smallest lie: he'd made the twenty-four Bagaṛāvats into rubies and Bhūṇojī into the diamond. But King Nīmde didn't understand anything. The Bhāṭ thought to himself: 'The enemy doesn't understand, he's a broken drum. I'll finish him off right now.' So what did the Bhāṭ say: 'O Nīmājī, it's true that my shoes are studded with diamonds and pearls, but it's time for my opium now. If only I could find some gold coins belonging to the Bagaṛāvats. O King Nīmde, I've heard that in some bygone age the Bagaṛāvats lived here. They used to string necklaces together of gold coins weighing five *tolas* each, which they'd tie around their horses' necks. Then they'd gallop down this road and the necklaces would break, scattering the coins everywhere. If only I could find one coin I'd be able to buy enough opium for today's supply.' King Nīmde said: 'Hey, Muṅgtā, which country are you from?' 'I come from across the seven seas.' 'What's your profession?' 'I'm the Bhāṭ of Kings'. 'Name?' 'People call me Jagīśyo.' 'Listen Jagīśyo, do you know how many years ago that was? There are no such coins here today, idiot!'

The Bhāṭ thought to himself: 'If I can find some coins here, then I'll be able to put him in his place.' So he prayed to Lord Devnārāyaṇ for some coins: 'O Lord, put five gold coins into my shield, so I can teach the enemy a lesson.' He took Devnārāyaṇ's name and put his shield down on the ground. The Lord of the Three Worlds (*tīn tilokī ko nāth*) was present in Causle Kheḍā. He laughed aloud (*bak bak hãsiyā*). The *pheph*-blossoms[19] came into bloom. Bhairūnāth asked him: 'O Lord, why do you laugh?' [Devnārāyaṇ said:] 'Look, the Bhāṭ wants gold coins to appear in the dust!' Bhairūnāth said: 'Lord, we should grant the old man his wish.' The Bhāṭ took Devnārāyaṇ's name and pulled out a string of gold coins. He showed them to Nīmde: 'Look carefully, Nīmde. Are these the gold coins which the Bagaṛāvats scattered here?' Nīmde stuck his finger into his mouth and said: 'Sirdārs, give the poor man whatever he wants and let's move on.' King Nīmde did not understand anything.

As Nīmde was about to leave he saw the Bhāṭ's *bīṇ*. He said: 'Dholīyo!' 'Yes, Lord?' ' Who does the *bīṇ* belong to? Is it yours?' 'Yes, Lord, it belongs to me.' King Nīmde said 'It's been so long since I heard someone playing the *bīṇ*. Long ago the Bagaṛāvats' Bhāṭ used to play the *bīṇ* when he accompanied them. Play me a little [tune]!' 'Yes, certainly Lord.' King Nīmde said: 'You play the *bīṇ* very beautifully. O Brother, tell me, where do you come from? I haven't followed!' The Bhāṭ thought to himself: 'He's a broken drum anyway. Just tell him anything you like, he won't understand.' So the Bhāṭ said: 'Well, I have places to live in all four corners of the world. I'm King Harcand's Bhāṭ. My residence is in Mathura.' Now the Bhāṭ didn't tell even the smallest lie: he made Savāī Bhoj[20] into King Harcand and Ṭhākur[21] Devmahārāj's residence into Mathura. Now King Nīmde wasn't that clever that he could follow this. He asked his horsemen: 'Where does this King Harcand live?' They replied: 'O Lord, the country is long and wide, there are so many places, who knows where he lives? Who should keep a watch?'' King Nīmde said: 'Sirdārs, let's move on.'

The Bhāṭ thought to himself: 'The enemy's moving on without my having put him to shame. Let me sing a song of praise (*āsakā*) to the entourage.' What song of praise did he sing for King Nīmde? 'The Rāṇā's army is full of princes and kings from other lands. There are many Mughals and Paṭhāns. Accept the blessings of Jagiśyā Bhāṭ, they will bring you fame!' The leading Sirdār listened carefully to the Bhāṭ. He said to King Nīmde: 'O Lord, the song was really wonderful, but he gestured with his left hand.' King Nīmde gave the Bhāṭ a shove: 'Hey, Muṅgtā, why did you gesture with your left hand? Am I not a king?' The Bhāṭ said: 'Forgive me, Lord, but that right arm, you know, it doesn't belong to me!' 'Then who does it belong to?' 'I pawned it off to someone.' 'Hey, Dholīyo, you pawned off your own arm? What do you take?' The Bhāṭ said: 'I eat opium don't I?' 'How much? A *pāv* or so?' 'More than that!' 'A *ser* or two?' 'Oh, no, more than that!' 'Then what five or ten *ser* ?' 'No, no, more than that!' 'Listen Jagiśyā, you had better tell me how much you consume.' The Bhāṭ said: 'Well, you see, Lord, people don't ask me how much I consume. If they do and I tell them then they have to supply me with all that I need. I don't let the person move ahead till he fulfils my demands! I'll tell you if you can fulfil my wishes, otherwise just move on down the road.'

King Nīmde said: 'Listen, Dholīyo, I'm King Nīmde. That's no small thing, is it? I'm the Rāṇā's younger brother. I'll get you what you need, just tell me now! You can't be consuming a *maṇ* or two, could you?' 'No Lord, much more than that!' 'Tell me, how much?' What did the Bhāṭ tell King Nīmde? ' At dawn I swallow one-and-a-half *maṇ* of opium, after that seven baskets full. I eat that much to begin with. Later on there's no limit to bits and pieces. So, when I wake up it's one-and-a-half *maṇ*. Then I go to the sons of kings and they throw me bits and pieces. There is no measure of those!' King Nīmde said: 'Sirdārs, we've found a great opium-eater (*amaḷdār*). Is there anything you eat along with the opium?' he asked. 'Yes, I do. I chew up two-and-a-half *maṇ* of roasted chick-peas (*bhūṅgaṛā*). Then I consume one-and-a-half *maṇ* of *bhāṅg*. And if I'm still not intoxicated then I order a couple of portions of poison.' 'What sort of poison?' 'Oh things like *ākaṛā, nīmaṛā,* and *dhaturā*. I mix them all up.' King Nīmde said: 'Sirdārs, we've found a great opium-eater!' King Nīmde gave the command. In no time they brought one-and-a-half *maṇ* of opium, two-and-a-half *maṇ* of chick-peas, one-and-a-half *maṇ* of *bhāṅg*. They churned the *ākaṛā* and *nīmaṛā* together and got two *tablas* full ready. 'There you are Dholīyo.' The Bhāṭ said: 'You may be a great king, but you don't have a spot of sense. Yes, you're a broken drum. You brought all these huge chunks of opium and have thrown them in front of me, how am I supposed to eat them? Cut them up into smaller pieces.' The Rajpūt's son had a knife, so it didn't take long cutting up the large chunks into smaller pieces. 'There you are, Jagīśyā. The opium is ready.' The Bhāṭ said: 'Nīmde, you don't have a spot of sense.' 'Now what's the matter?' The Bhāṭ said: 'Look how I'm surrounded by your horsemen. If I eat the opium in front of them, I'll explode and die. Yes, I'll explode and die like the pod of a chick pea explodes. Set up a tent. I'll only eat the opium in a tent.' It took no time for a tent to be set up. King Nīmde said: 'There you are, brother Dholīyo,' and pushed him inside the tent. 'Call out when you're finished.'

Now the Bhāṭ had never even touched opium, not even when he had been offered some. He thought to himself: 'If I eat even a *pāv* of this poison I'll die inside here. But if I go outside without eating it then King Nīmde is sure to kill me straight away. If there's anything like death calling, then this must be it.' The Bhāṭ thought: 'Let me try some of it at least, is it sweet or bitter?' He put some of it on his tongue. Damn, was it bitter! Oh, was it bitter, bitter, bitter! He spat it out! Then he thought to himself: 'God has sent you here, hasn't he, think of him, he'll help you.' So, the Bhāṭ prayed to Devnārāyaṇ: 'Listen to my plea. The Bhāṭ of the Bagaṛāvats is about to die here!' Lord Devnārāyaṇ laughed aloud. Bhairūnāth asked him: 'O Lord, why are you laughing?' Devnārāyaṇ said: 'Look, Bhairūnāth, Bābā Bhāṭ's calling.' Bhairūnāth said: 'Lord, we should fulfil the old man's wishes.' Devnārāyaṇ said: 'Bhairūnāth, go over there and take whatever offerings are being made. Let the Bhāṭ be victorious!' So the fifty-two Bhairū, sixty-four Joginī and seventy-eight Khetrapāl[22] quietly entered the tent and asked the Bhāṭ: 'O Bhāṭjī, why did you call us?' The Bhāṭ said: 'I'm in bad trouble!' 'What trouble?' The Bhāṭ took some opium in his hands and offered it to Kālā and Gorā Bhairū. The fifty-two Bhairū and sixty-four Joginī swooped down on all the opium, *bhāṅg*, and chick-peas. Gorā Bhairū drank up all the poison. And then he said: 'Any other wish?' The Bhāṭ thanked them and said he would now manage on his own.

He waited awhile in the tent and then ripped it open on the side and came out yawning: 'Hey Nīmde' he said, 'That was useless stuff, where did you get it from! It didn't intoxicate me at all.' Nīmde turned around to his horsemen and said: 'Sirdārs, the man's consumed the harvest from seven villages and says he's still not intoxicated.' The Bhāṭ said: 'Oh that doesn't matter, I'll have some more when we go to the fort.' Nīmde said: 'You hear that, he's eaten away the harvest from seven villages and now he wants to eat the rest of the reserves we have in the fort! If he stays here a day or two he'll finish off everything we have. Give him a lakh [of rupees] and tell him to leave.' Just then one of the horsemen said: 'Shouldn't we check whether he's really eaten the opium?' The Sirdār went inside the tent and saw that even the sand had been eaten away in the tent not even a pebble remained. That was what Ṭhākur Devmahārāj did when he heard the Bhāṭ calling for him. . . .

In the episode related above (as in many other episodes in the epic) the Bhāṭ functions as Devnārāyaṇ's *alter ego.* While the god continues to dwell at his residence in Causle Kheḍā, he sends the Bhāṭ out to locate Bhūṇo. The Bhāṭ, both boastful and timid at the same time, not quite knowing how far to go, always falls back on Devnārāyaṇ's divine abilities. The Bhāṭ's sole intention in this episode is to ridicule the Rāṇā's younger brother, King Nīmde. He tests the king's cleverness through riddles such as the one about the diamond and the twenty-four rubies. Gradually he becomes more and more insolent till he openly calls the king a fool and a 'broken drum'.[23] Once the Bhāṭ finds the gold coins created by Devnārāyaṇ, he begins to boast about the quantities of opium he consumes. He improvises all along, only in order to humiliate the powerful king. The claim about his daily consumption of opium and *bhāṅg* reaches unimaginable dimensions: tens of kilos at a single session along with a mixture of poisonous herbs and plants (*ākaḍā, nīmaḍā, dhaturā*).[24] The king is both mistrustful and wonderstruck at the Bhāṭ's tall claim, repeatedly turning to his soldiers with the phrase: 'Sirdārs, we've found a great opium-eater.' Ultimately, however, there is no escape for the Bhāṭ, except to prove that his assertion is true or to die. In all these situations he has been relying on Devnārāyaṇ's powers to rescue him. In the final scene, Devnārāyaṇ dispatches his assistants Kālā and Gorā Bhairū along with the sixty-four Joginīs and the seventy-eight Khetrapāls to enter the Bhāṭ's tent and receive all the 'offerings' of opium, etc. After they have eaten the kilos of opium and *bhāṅg*, the Bhāṭ makes it a point to come out of the tent in a most bored and disinterested manner, indicating that the produce of the king's lands is useless. The astounded king turns down the Bhāṭ's suggestion to take him to the fort and supply him with the opium stored there.

The episode is thus marked by the Bhāṭ's foolhardiness, boasting and ultimately his steadfast trust in Devnārāyaṇ's powers. The social intention certainly is one of ridicule of the Rajput community symbolized by the Rāṇā and his younger brother Nīmde. But beyond this, and equally importantly, the humour expressed through the character of the Bhāṭ and the dangerous circumstances he finds himself in, is closely interwoven with the issue of 'testimony'. It is about 'divine proof' that comes to light each time the Bhāṭ is rescued and helped by Devnārāyaṇ. King Nīmde, however, is too dull to realize that the events occurring in front of him are the result of divine intervention. In the episode related below, this issue is taken up again, resulting in the transformation of Bhūṇo's faith in Devnārāyaṇ.

Episode 2

The following episode occurs soon after Chochū Bhāṭ has met Bhūṇo. They arrive in the famous pilgrimage town of Puṣkara. In the same manner in which the Bhāṭ has earlier provoked Nīmde, he begins to provoke Bhūṇo. He chides Bhūṇo for not taking up arms against the Rāṇā's generals, who also happen to be camping outside Pushkar. Bhūṇo remains even-tempered, until out of exasperation he confronts the Bhāṭ, demanding 'proof' (*parcyo*) about Devnārāyaṇ's divine nature.

[The Bhāṭ begins the dialogue:]

'When Dharmarājā[25] Devji left on account of Sītā, O Bhūṇo, how large was the army he took along with him on that day? When he left on account of Sītājī how large an army did he take along with him on that day?' Bhūṇoji said: 'Hey, Muṅgtā, is the one who left on account of Sītā your master?' [Chochū] said: 'He is one and the same.' [Bhūṇo] said: 'Muṅgtā, how long have you been about?' He caught hold of [the Bhāṭ's] arm and took him down the steps[26] in Puṣkar. 'Just you wait, Bhāṭ,' [he] said. '[You say] your master left on account of Sītā. I'll find out now!' Bhūṇoji placed Dūḍa's sword, which had been given to him, on the steps. The bow and arrow(s) [he also placed on the steps]. 'Listen, Bhāṭ, he is your master, isn't he! [If] the sword leaves its sheath on it's own, and the arrow strings itself on the bow, [only then] is your master the one who left on account of Sītā! If not, then Muṅgtā, I'll drown you in the water, after I cut off your head. The Bagaṛāvat's Bhāṭ spat on his hands without removing his shoes he jumped into Puṣkar and went under. What did he cry out to Bhagavān, as he came up? Let us see.

By God's grace, [the Bhāṭ] said the following: '. . . If you listen to my call here, then I'll return alive and bring Bhūṇo with me! If not, watch the Bagaṛāvat's scroll drown!' He took a second dive. 'I'll stay in the water now!' Devmahārāj was present in Causle Kheḍā. Kālā and Gorā Bhairavānāth . . .[27] Devmahārāj laughed out aloud (*bak bak hāsiyā*). The *pheph*-blossoms [bloomed]. Bhairavānāth asked: 'Śrī Mahārāj, what's the reason for your laughter?' [Devjī] said: 'Bābā Bhāṭ's asking for a miracle now on the steps.' [Bhairavānāth] said: 'Śrī Mahārāj, you should do what the old man wants you to do!' 'Bhairavānāth, get the Bhāṭ out quickly, otherwise the Bagaṛāvat's scroll will drown! Go swiftly!' By God's grace, Bhairavānāth went and caught hold of the Bhāṭ's arms. He pulled the Bhāṭ out: 'Why are you drowning?' [The Bhāṭ] said: 'Bad times have befallen me, that's why!' [Bhairavānāth] said: 'What bad [times]? If you say so, I'll turn everything in the Mela[28] upside down.' [Chochū] said: 'No, No, No, No. By God's grace, that arrow should string itself onto the bow, and that sword should leave its sheath on its own. Do these two things. And then sit on Bhūṇo's right arm for a while.' . . . Gorāji Mahārāj strung the arrow onto the bow. By God's grace, Kālājī Mahārāj drew out the sword from its sheath. This came to Bhūṇo's attention. Bhūṇoji said: 'Bābā Bhāṭ, come out of Puṣkar, come out of the water. Hey, some *goyalā* animal might devour you! Come out! I consent! Your master is the one who brought Sītā [back]. I agree, brother. Now I'll fight (?) anyone you say in the Mela.' By God's grace, Bhūṇoji said: 'Bābā Bhāṭ, don't wait any more!' [This is how] the Lord of the Three Worlds, Bhagavān Dev, created a miracle. [And] Bhairavānāth sat on Bhūṇo's arm. . . .

As in the previous episode, the Bhāṭ manages to create a situation that poses a threat to his own life. The courage and fear that he simultaneously expresses, makes the situation comic. Even the scene in which he is about to drown in the lake of Pushkar has an element of comic. As always the Bhāṭ cries out to Devnārāyaṇ for help. As always Devnārāyaṇ laughs his radiant laugh and sends Kālā and Gorā Bhairū rescue the Bhāṭ. Kālā and Gorā Bhairū, succesfully perform the test Bhūṇo has set up for the Bhāṭ, proving the divinity of the Bhāṭ's master. The humour in this situation is not the result of ridicule directed toward the Rajputs. Rather it is connected to the figure of the Bhāṭ and the dire circumstances he has involved himself in. The underlying purpose of the episode is, again, to provide 'proof' of Devnārāyaṇ's powers.

Episode 3

In the third and last episode to be related, we encounter two of the Rāṇā's generals: Kālū Mīr and Dīyājī Jodhkā. They often function as the Rāṇā's advisors and usually appear in the epic in conjunction with one another. Kālū Mīr is a Paṭhān, and Dīyājī Jodhkā, a Rajput. The lines spoken by Kālū Mīr are in Hindustānī and not in Mārvāṛī like the rest of the narrative. This in itself has a comic effect. Kālū Mīr's and Dīyājī Jodhkā's plans and schemes invariably go awry. In the following episode both generals are at the mercy of Bhūṇo, who has turned his back on the Rāṇā after realizing that the Rāṇā has been responsible for his ancestors' deaths. Bhūṇo arrives at a well that has been dug by the Bagaṛāvats. The Rāṇā's generals have camped nearby with their soldiers. It is summer and very, very warm. Bhūṇo forbids the soldiers to draw water from the well. Soon they are in dire need of water. The Mīr and Dīyājī decide to ask Bhūṇo, whom they have known since he was a child, for permission to drink there.

Both Amarāvs[29] went to Bhūṇo's camp and said: 'Kāwar Sāhab, [we] salute [you].' 'Welcome, Mīr, [welcome].' [Mīr] said: 'Why are you doing this, just after you have arrived? Won't my army die of thirst?' [he] said. [Bhūṇo] said: 'Hey Mīr, brother, the well belongs to my father. If you want to drink water, then come down into the well and drink it here![30] There will be no taking water out!' 'Well, brother Dīyā, at least we'll stay alive. Put the tent up nearby, what else can I do?' Mīr gave the command: 'It's Kāwar's wish, come here if you want to drink water.' The entire army entered the well. Bhūṇojī stood above on the steps. [As] each Sirdār drank water and returned, Bhūṇo cut off one side of [his] moustache, and cut off a piece of one ear! When Mīr's turn came, by the grace of God, [Bhūṇo] cut off one moustache and one ear. Mīr said: 'Don't worry, come along, Sirdārs. There is no threat to life! This is a moustache, it is like grass in the month of Sāvan, it'll grow back tomorrow. The ear can be pressed under the turban. There's no harmful intention.' When the Rāv's[31] Amarāv came out after drinking water, Bhūṇoji made a mark on all of them. . . .

No doubt, the comedy of the situation has something to do with Bhūṇo's somewhat cruel and humiliating act of cutting off half of the soldiers' moustaches and a piece of their ears. But equally significant is the fact that the Mīr and Dīyājī are more concerned about their physical survival than they are about their honour. In fact, the Mīr pacifies his soldiers by comparing the cut moustache to grass that will grow back, and by advising them to hide the ear from which a piece has been cut off, by tucking it under their turbans. Their lack of concern for the humiliation involved adds further to their negative image as warriors.

Conclusion

The epic of the Bagaṛāvats and Devnārāyaṇ is, on the one hand, about the life and death of Gūjar heroes. On the other hand, it is about the incarnation of the Gūjars' chief deity, who nevertheless transcends a narrow caste identity, being worshipped by followers from different communities. Humour in the episodes related earlier is closely linked to two important themes of the epic, viz., the 'class-conflict' between Gūjars and Rajputs, and the establishment of the deity's cult through the miracles he performs. Thus, the first and third episodes are aimed directly at humiliating the Rajputs. The first and second episodes are also about providing 'proof' of Devnārāyaṇ's divine powers. In the first two episodes, Chochū Bhāṭ, genealogist and bard, plays a pivotal role. Often called '*nāradī Bhāṭ*', he matches his Purāṇic counterpart Nārada's ability to disrupt and provoke. In his role as trickster he is able to involve himself in potentially volatile circumstances while always managing to remain unharmed. His survival, however, depends on Devnārāyaṇ's intervention. He is both *alter ego* and clown to Devnārāyaṇ in the latter's dual capacity as deity and king. Timid and fearful as a human bard, he continually draws power from his divine patron, to fulfil the latter's mission of avenging the deaths of his ancestors and of confirming his divinity as an incarnation of Bhagavān. The definitions of humour provided at the beginning of this paper are thus substantiated in many ways: The bard continuously exhibits 'alertness and breadth of mind, a keen sense of proportion, and faculties of quick observation and comparison'. Although he is rather frail, appearing again and again to be the victim, he ultimately succeeds in baffling and humiliating the would be victors of the narrative.

NOTES

1. The author would like to acknowledge the support of the German Research Council for funding research between 1991-4 on the oral epic of Devnārāyaṇ.
2. The length of the epic ranges from anywhere between fifty to one hundred hours.
3. It is considered inauspicious to unroll the scroll during the day.
4. Although devotees by and large belong to the Gūjar community, there are no caste restrictions regarding who may and who may not attend a *jāgraṇ*. Three places are considered auspicious for performing the epic: (a) the courtyard of the house of a devotee, (b) the place in front of a temple of Devnārāyaṇ, Sāvāī Bhoj or Bhuṇojī, and (c) the area in front of the place where community meets (*hathāī*).
5. Conflict between inter-related groups or families, is, of course, a theme that also occurs widely in the Purāṇas and Sanskrit epics.
6. Although the Gūjars are pastoralists and farmers, their self-image, however, is one of a martial or warrior (*kṣatriya*) caste. For a summary of the main sections of the narrative, see for example, Joshi (1976).
7. For an analysis of Devnārāyaṇ's '*byāvlo*', a narrative dealing with the deity's birth, childhood and marriages, see Malik (1993).

8. In the end the Rajput chieftain is hunted down and killed by Devnārāyaṇ and his four brothers.
9. Cp. Blackburn's notion of the 'intergenerational' character of Indian epics (Blackburn *et al.* 1989: 31f.).
10. I shall not be discussing the question of humour and jokes in connection with the *performance* of the epic. For details on this, see Miller (1980) and Singh (1980).
11. The hill is located near the town of Āsīnd in Bhilwara Dist., Rajasthan, and is the location of one of the cult's main shrines.
12. Having grown up with foster parents, Devnārāyaṇ's cousins are also unware of their family history. Their names are Bhāṅgi, Medū, Madno, and Bhūṇo.
13. This is the name that has been given to Bhūṇo by the Rāṇā. Bhūṇojī is perhaps the most important of the five brothers next to Devnārāyaṇ. He occupies a central position in the iconography of Devnārāyaṇ, and in the pilgrimage town of Pushkar, there is a temple dedicated solely to him.
14. Chochū Bhāṭ is known to the Rāṇā and his generals from the time when the Bagaṛāvats fraternized with the Rāṇā. The Bagaṛāvats and the Rāṇā are 'turban brothers' (*pagaḍ bhāī*), i.e. they have exchanged turbans.
15. The recitation of the narrative consists of a dialogue which alternates between lines sung or spoken by the lead singer and those sung or spoken by his partner. The second singer's 'text' is called *hũkāro.* The *hũkāro* usually entails a completion or repetition of the lead singer's lines. In the following translation I have combined the lead and second singer's lines into continuous single sentences.
16. Name of a double-gourd, string instrument used by Bhopās during recitations of the epic.
17. A term used for Rajput warriors.
18. *Dholīyo* means 'white one'.
19. Name of a mythical flower.
20. Savāī Bhoj is the most courageous and revered of the twenty-four Bagaṛāvats.
21. Title used for Rajput landowners as well as for addressing God in general. Cp. German: '*Herr*'; or Spanish: '*Señor*'.
22. Bhairū, (Bhairūnāth), Joginī and Khetrapāl are names for three lower ranked folk deities that appear in many folk religious narratives in Rajasthan and north India.
23. Later on in the narrative he poses the same riddle to Bhūṇo, who instantly understands that the rubies and diamonds refer to people the Bhāṭ has known.
24. Cp. Vijay Dan Detha's Rajasthani short story *Mapīṇau* (1984: 172-6).
25. Dharmarājā is one of Devnārāyaṇ's epithets.
26. Ghāṭs.
27. The text is unclear here.
28. Melā refers to the annual fair held in Pushkar during the month of Kārttika.
29. Generals.

30. The well has steps leading down to the water.
31. Title referring to the Rāṇā.

REFERENCES

Blackburn, S.H. *et al.* (eds.) 1989. *Oral Epics in India.* Berkeley: University of California Press.

Brückner, Heidrun, Lothar Lutze and Aditya Malik (eds.) 1993. *Flags of Fame: Studies in South Asian Folk Culture.* New Delhi: Manohar.

Callewaert, W.M. (ed.) 1980. *Early Hindi Devotional Literature in Current Research.* Leuven: Departement Orientalistiek Katholieke Universiteit.

Detha, Vijay Dan. 1984. 'Mapīṇau'. In: *Alekhū Hiṭlar.* New Delhi/Patna: Rajkamal Prakashan.

———.1993. 'Jedem sein Maβ.' Tr. into German by Lothar Lutze and Bahadur Singh. In: *Südasien-Anthologie,* ed. Günther-Dietz Sontheimer, 204-10. Stuttgart: Franz Steiner Verlag.

Eliade, Mircea (ed.) 1987. *Encyclopaedia of Religion.* New York: Macmillan.

Hastings, James (ed.) 1967. *Encyclopaedia of Religion and Ethics.* Edinburgh: T. and T. Clark.

Joshi, O.P. 1976. *Painted Folklore and Folklore Painters of India.* Delhi: Concept Publishing Company.

Malik, Aditya. 1993. 'Avatāra, avenger, and king: Narrative themes in the Rājasthānī oral epic of Devnārāyaṇ.' In Brückner *et al.* (eds:), 375-409.

Miller, Joseph. 1980. 'Current investigations in the genre of Rājasthānī *paṛ* painting recitations.' In: W.M. Callewaert (ed.), 116-25.

Singh, Bahadur. 1980. 'The Bagaṛāvat: A popular heroic narrative of Rājasthān.' W.M. Callewaert (ed.), 162-7.

'My Mother an Apsarā, the Father a Kṣatriya, my Uncle the Son of a Gandharva': Humour in the Oral Poetry of the Himalaya

CLAUS PETER ZOLLER

The title of this paper should not lead to the misconception that the inhabitants of the Indian Himalaya would burst into laughter if one were to tell them one's mother is a nymph. I have borrowed the quote from a song sung at marriage ceremonies in order to suggest how the topic humour is to be limited in this paper. To this particular song I will return later. I do not want to deal with genres and forms of humour of which one can say that, despite disparities in external form, they have in common a certain innocuous entertainment value, that they are a kind of pastime. Such stories—say, comic tales, fables, and jokes—are very much alive in large numbers in the Indian Himalaya: for example, how the farmer outwits death, or how the partridge makes the fox laugh, or about the jackal and the tiger. Bachtin (1990: 30) probably would call this type of humour 'das unterhaltende Lachen' (entertaining laughter), which he distinguishes from the 'rein satirische Lachen' [purely satirical laughter (ibid.)]. He believes that these were the two culturally sanctioned forms of humour among the bourgeois of the nineteenth century. It would perhaps be worthwhile to investigate how far these two forms of humour have spread in the course of worldwide modernization since then, and how far they have edged out other cultural forms of humour, especially its carnivalesque forms.

I neither want to elaborate upon entertaining forms of humour nor do I intend to deal with satire, that serious and aggressive variety of humour. Instead, I first want to present some forms of humour which are not easily recognizable as such, which do not stare one in the face, so to speak. And second I will present some more obvious forms (indicated in the title above) which nevertheless also call for reflection as to why they are humorous. On an abstract level, all these examples of humour are based on the principle of incongruity, ranging from mild metaphorical or metonymical forms of 'Verfremdung'[1] to crass paradoxical contrasts. It appears to me, however, that not all incongruities are understood by the people of the central Himalaya as distortions, as something wrong. There seems to exist a knowledge that reality cannot be something perfectly rounded and well-balanced, but that its basic features comprise disturbances of symmetry, dissonances, and ambiguities, which sometimes appear like small holes and cracks in a perfect façade, through which a deeper reality may be felt.

In humour theory an important distinction is made between referential and verbal jokes (Attardo 1994: 95f.) The former are based only on the meaning of the text, and thus can be translated without problem, whereas the latter also make use of the phonological realization, and thus are difficult to be translated. Much of the humour I am going to present can also not be translated without difficulty. Here, however, the problem is not the phonology but the foreignness of the culture. The humour I will describe evokes laughter among native speakers, but it will hardly evoke any laughter among the readers.

Before I start off with the examples, however, I must say a few words about the sense in which I would like humour to be understood. For the word is surely not unambiguous in itself. First of all, humour is a human competence and thus cannot be defined (Raskin 1985: 3, Attardo 1994: 3). Its innumerable forms of expression are nevertheless culturally bound (Apte 1985), and what people find humorous changes historically (Attardo 1994: 7). Thus, all proposed definitions of humour are culturally and historically conditioned and tend to be circular. It is, however, a universally valid assertion that all humour is based on the principle of incongruity (Attardo 1994). A rather narrow definition, which, in fact, turns the principle of incongruity upside down, is found in the *Brockhaus* Encyclopaedia, where humour is defined as an attitude which recognizes sense and amiability even in the meaningless and the adverse, and which is oriented towards reconciliation, wisdom, and love. *Brockhaus* moreover observes that humour as an expression of a forbearing sensibility is rare in the literatures of Antiquity and the Middle Ages.[2]

To come back to the oral poetry of the Indian Himalaya if the *Brockhaus* definition were absolutely valid, then there would be very little verbal art which could be categorized under it. This in no way means that the people of the Indian Himalaya lack a sense of humour; in fact, the opposite is true. But let me say it very pointedly one cannot expect much reconciliatory poetry from a region where martial and heroic traditions have always been of central importance. Humour, especially in religious and ritual contexts, neither is reconciliatory nor is it simple, banal laughter. It is joyful, creative, and liberating, sometimes indecent and obscene, but never pedantic.

There are, for instance, low-caste bards who at certain festivals mimic the powers that be. The funny effect results from their playing parts (e.g. acting as office-bearers) in a way which simultaneously suggests and discards an identification with real persons. Or put in other words, the acting suggests the simultaneous association of several different images with the same person. At festivals like *Buṛi Divāli* or *Ḍaknatsaṇ*, members of low castes use mimicry to ridicule members of high castes. It is never the other way round, because it is the powers that be which represent official society and culture.

Outside festivals, humour is found in institutionalized joking relationships or in serious oral poetry with a humorous undercurrent. Before I turn to the latter, a few remarks about joking relationships are in order. In western Garhwal joking relationships exist, besides those involving certain categories of relatives, also between different villages, between the deity *Pauvasi-Mahāsu* and *Kauilāth* (who is his subordinate guardian-deity), or between husbands and wives in case the wives are in their parental village together with their husbands. Although Apte says (1985: 61) that the common explanations for meaning and function of joking relationships 'are educated guesses at best', we can say with certainty that the examples from Garhwal have something to do with incongruity and ambiguity. I do not yet know why the relations between certain villages are humorous, but the other examples are quite clear. The relation between *Pauvasi* and *Kauilāth* is funny because *Kauilāth* is simultaneously a subordinate of *Pauvasi*, who is an independent village deity in a number of places, and he is leader of the fairies. The fairies are, on the other hand, kept under control by *Pauvasi*. And there is a funny feeling between husbands and their wives when they are in the wife's parental village, because married women traditionally behave in their parental home in many ways as if they were not married. Thus, there is a bisociation, because their husbands simultaneously perceive them, in a way, as both married and unmarried.[3]

Parallel to the earlier-mentioned case of the low-caste bard, in the examples given here the active funmakers are always only on one particular side, namely, on the socially lower one: thus it is the women who crack the jokes when they are in their parental villages, and it is *Kauilath* whose shamans make funny remarks, and the same probably holds even for the joking relationships between particular villages.

To come to the examples from oral poetry: those to be described here are from an otherwise completely martial heroic ballad, and from a collection of sad lyrics from the Bangan (*bauṅgāṇ*) region.[4] Both the ballad and the lyrics deal with the tragic tale of the hero Jitu Jaṛiaṇ (*dzitu dzauṛiaṇ*), his father Dalu (*daulu*), and his mother Joṭṛi (*joṭṛi*). I taped the ballad, which is locally called a *chaṛi* in 1989. The lyrics, locally called *tshoṛa*, were taped during field excursions during the last couple of years. Whereas *chaṛis* alter between songs and highly dramatized and rhythmical prose, the *tshoṛas* are quatrains in alternate rhyme. *Tshoṛas* are sung by Rajput men and women as responsories. They express inner states rather than telling whole stories. Therefore, they are very elliptic, full of allusions, and thus for outsiders extremely difficult to understand.

Chaṛis are sung by low-caste bards. They are called *Devāḷ*. The word has its origins in the Sanskrit term *devapāla* 'god defender'. Its original Bangani sense, however, seems to be 'controller of gods', an indication of the bards' once important religious status. *Chaṛis* are sung by the *Devāḷs* in the month of *Māgh* (January-February). The *Devāḷs* are invited by the Rajputs to their houses, where such performances are generally given. *Chaṛis* are supposed to arouse a strong collective feeling of courage and pride among the audience. This comes about not only as a result of the martial content but also as a result of the dramatic quality of the performance. Even the portrayal of the comic scenes is kept very dramatic, like the rest of the song.

In the *chaṛi* called Jitu Jaṛiaṇ it is not the deeds of Jitu that constitute the focal point but instead several episodes from the life of his father Dalu. Dalu was a shepherd, hero, and head-hunter. At the instigation of a vizier (legal representative) of the powerful god *Mahāsu*, he captured and carried off the heads of two enemies. The enemy clan then took their revenge by beheading nine men from Dalu's village. The song ends with the malicious killing of Jitu and Dalu by men from the adjacent region Śiktūr. Jitu was killed when he was still a young boy and before he himself had killed any enemy. My question as to why the song was called Jitu Jaṛiaṇ and not Dalu Jaṛiaṇ brought forth an interesting reply from the locals: 'Because Jitu would have been an even greater hero than his father, had he not been treacherously murdered.'

The *tshoṛas* too deal but little with Jitu's deeds. Whereas the *chaṛi* describes Dalu's deeds until his and his son's killing, the *tshoṛas* deal with the subsequent events, namely the way Joṭṛi undertakes revenge. I will return to this later on. There is no doubt, that Jitu, Joṭṛi, and Dalu are historical figures and that the events described in the songs really happened. The Jaṛiaṇs probably lived nine generations ago in the second half of the eighteenth century.[5]

Jean-Claude Galey has shown the existence of two types of power or legitimacy in Garhwal, which are complementary to each other in many ways. The first type he describes as 'chiefdom' or 'chieftainship' (1992: 193); and he associates it with 'local origin' (ibid., 196), 'kinship ties' (1992: 193), and 'clan cults' (1992: 196). The second type relates to the notion of 'lordship'. Lordship is associated with the whole caste hierarchy, with hierarchized pantheons and with a multiplicity of official functions. Representatives of the principle of lordship in Bangan include the dominant god *Mahāsu*,[6] his two Rajput viziers (who represent the god's legal force), his Brahmans, treasurers, oracles, bards, and so on. Other representatives of this principle would be the former *Thokdārs* (Galey 1992: 193f.) and kings, and today's mayors, village councillors and similar other officeholders. Representatives of the principle of chiefdom include warriors of the *Khūnd* lineages (a segment of the Rajputs) and *dzagas*. The *dzagas* are a kind of 'female tutelary spirit' pertaining mainly to Rajput lineages. They reside in parallelepiped village sanctuaries made of stones. In the middle of these constructions are holes into which the heads of slain hostile warriors were placed in former times. A *Khūnd* warrior can experience a *dzaga* as a driving and stimulating force, which makes him free from fear. Additionally, *dzagas* are responsible for the fertility of their villages. In contrast to the hierarchized pantheon of *Mahāsu*, which symbolizes centrality and dominance, *dzagas* do not have religious specialists of their own. The *dzagas* symbolize equality and dissipation.[7] I have shown elsewhere (Zoller 1997) that the story of Jitu Jaṛiaṇ is built on a conflict between the principles of chiefdom and lordship, and that it seems to give evidence for a slow historical shift from the once dominating warrior culture of western Garhwal to the presently dominant cultural form of 'Hindu folk religion'. With regard to our present subject, I want to demonstrate that the humour found in the heroic and melancholic songs of Jitu Jaṛiaṇ arises out of several patterns of incongruity, one being the incongruity between the two politico-religious principles of chiefdom and lordship.

At one point in the *chaṛi* the following takes place. There is a vizier of god *Mahāsu* by the name Bidi Goicaṇ (*bidi goitsaṇ*). Apart from 'vizier' he is also called *Rāwat*, which has its origin in the Sanskrit term *rājaputra*. The vizier is thus a Rajput or a Kṣatriya just like Dalu. But Dalu is, as we have seen, a Khūnd. Besides administering law, one of the vizier's tasks was (and still is) to collect taxes for his god, in the form of natural produce.

Now Bidi Goitsaṇ has gone too far and has exploited the people too much. So Dalu decides to kill him. He does not simply do it but goes to Bidi's house instead, and then the following events take place. They are given now in translation:

Then Bidi, this Rāwat, came down with his hookah (called) *Tiladei* in hand. He shows great respect for Dalu.[9] Dalu first fastened the hookah to himself. Then he tied up Bidi, 'the umbrella of the ten times hundred'.[10] Bidi walks half on his own, half goaded along by Dalu. The Khūnd is strong, the Rāwat is weak. Bidi was a Rāwat, Dalu is a Khūnd. Dalu brought him over to (his village) Sarās. Dalu's wife, Joṭṛi, saw the two of them. She thinks: 'Had this one[11] been a Khūnd, he would have been a proud and strong fellow. He is surely a Rāwat, (for) he (looks) soft.' As they come nearer and nearer, Joṭṛi realizes: 'Oh, that's the vizier, "the umbrella of the ten times hundred".' So saying she jumps down from the balcony (into the courtyard to save the vizier) and says to her husband: 'I shall burn your beard, singe your head. You should have fought with a Khūnd.[12] You want to fight with him, with a Rāwat?' She gave Dalu a kick and took Bidi into the house with her. She prepared 'cold things and warm things' for him.[13] She let him have a bath and said to him: 'My dear brother, did Dalu want to kill you?' He answers: 'No dear sister, he did not want to kill me.[14] He brought me here in all love. He did not beat me up, nor has he played any mischief. I have just been tied up (a little bit) and brought here by him.'

Now what is so funny about this scene? For the Banganis two things: first the relationship between husband and wife, Dalu and Joṭṛi, and second, the relation between the two Rajputs, Dalu and Bidi. One of the reasons why the Banganis say that the bride and groom should be from the same caste is because they believe that the members of different castes differ also with regard to the amount of *bīrya* 'virility' or 'seed'. *Bīrya* as 'seed' is ascribed to both men and women. And it is important that the marital partners are on an equal level regarding their *bīrya.* In the view of the Banganis, heroism and sexuality are closely related.[15] Though it is not possible to go into details, it must be said here that a hero as outstanding as Dalu must also have an above average amount of *bīrya.* But simultaneously Dalu has to bear in mind a rule, which all the heroes in this part of the Himalayas have to follow, if he and his wife are to live together: *bare ka phaspas, bitre ka madudās.* Exact translation is impossible but the meaning is something like: 'A hero should show his teeth outside, but at home he ought to be a (servile) slave.' That the wife has the say at home and the husband behaves a bit foolishly is surely funny for the locals; but it is, according to their understanding, also necessary in order that the marital relationship remain balanced. On a more basic level, however, the humour of this scene is based on bisociations (i.e. in congruities, according to Attardo 1994: 175): a Bangani hero has a very close and intimate relation with his sacred *dzaga,* and he is simultaneously married to a human woman. Moreover, his wife is believed to contain within her the invisible presence of the *dzaga* of her parental village (see Zoller forthcoming). An incongruous and multilayered affair! Very funny for the Banganis, but hard to understand for us.

Similarly, the relationship between the Khūnd (the hero) and the vizier is incongruous, and consequently their relation acquires comic tones. Not only becuase they represent two rival forms of power, which means that each one regards the other as somehow inferior, but also because the ways in which they are related to these powers are so different. The vizier as a visible representative of the deity Mahāsu is on par with the god. This relation is expressed in a refrain which is repeated in the song: *adi kau deu, adi kau mautiāṇ.*[16] Translated, the refrain would mean 'one half for the god, the other half for the vizier'. This means two things: (1) half of the tax collection goes to the god and the other half to the vizier, and (2) that the vizier commands the same degree of respect as the god. The vizier is not a tool in the hands of the god; in fact, he possesses a certain power over him, can control him, for the song also says *ulṭi bolela, sulṭi śune*, which means '(even if the vizier utters) a lie (or something false, the God Mahāsu) hears it as the truth (or the right thing)'. On the other hand, a Khūnd is neither representative of his *dzaga* nor can he control her. At the time of a fight her energy puts him into a frenzy and battle intoxication. In a sense it is she who acts through him. The principle of lordship tends to smell somewhat of cool calculation and sometimes even corruption, whereas that of chieftainship is marked by emotion and ecstasy.

The earlier-quoted sentence, 'The Khūnd is strong, the Rāwat is weak', reflects the sense of the Bangani sentence *Khūndɛ kau maroṛa, Rautu kau luṇmunauĩ*, but it is not a literal translation, which would be: 'The Khūnd is a killer, the Rāwat is a weakling.' The oppressive Rāwat is a person worthy of being killed. But Dalu does not kill Bidi; he only abducts him. After Joṭri has taken the vizier under her wing, the story goes on: The next day Dalu goes from his village to Hanōl. Hanōl is the place where Mahāsu's most important temple is located. From there he sends two men to fetch Bidi. But Joṭri hides Bidi away and the men return empty-handed. Dalu takes a sword from the temple which represents the god. The sword is brought to his village and his wife says, 'Oh, now the god himself is here.' Then Bidi is compelled to go to Hanōl where he and Dalu have a massive argument. Everyone expects that Dalu will now kill Bidi. But then comes a surprise: once again Dalu lets Bidi get away.

The question now arises what this has to do with humour as such. A great deal, in fact. In 1990, when I worked on the translation of this song, I had made the following note in the margin in the text: 'The Banganis seem to find it funny that Dalu does not kill Bidi.' While making the tape-recording I had noticed that the audience found this scene funny.

I think that for the insider the humour again lies in the coincidence and combination of several incongruous relations and perspectives. When Dalu approaches the vizier with the intention of abducting him, the vizier says to his bodyguards, 'He is my Khūnd; he hasn't got it in for me.' In this way he expresses his feeling of superiority. However, that contradicts the statement 'the Khūnd is a killer, the Rāwat is a weakling'. On the other hand, the vizier appears almost stronger than the actual deity in his functions as a representative of the mightiest god of the region. Nevertheless, the Khūnd forces Mahāsu to force his own vizier back to his temple. But Dalu *cannot* kill the vizier—a ridiculous fact, as we have seen—because had Dalu killed the vizier, he would not only have damaged his relationship with his wife but would also have jeopardized his fame as a great hero.

There is a theory about the phylogenetic origin of humour which says that it originated in olden times from the triumphant laughter of the winner over the conquered or the vanquished enemy. Seen in this light, the humour of the Banganis, who find it funny that someone is *not* killed, is anything but old-fashioned. More important, however, is the fact that the humorous undercurrent in this heroic story is not simply made up of a linear ordering of incongruity and resolution (see Attardo 1994: 143-5), but consists, in fact, of a whole web of incongruities and incompatible perspectives. These, however, seem to be essential to the plot, as if they were necessary for its progression.

The same holds true for the *tshoṛas,* the lyrics which deal with Joṭṛi's reaction after the death of her husband and son. Joṭṛi wants—and gets—revenge, although only after great difficulties. So let me list just a few humorous situations: When Joṭṛi rightly expects of her affinal and parental families that they undertake revenge, they, the members of warrior families, turn out to be cowards who shirk the danger. When they hear of the cruel incident,

> they sit, o brother, on the walls of the threshing floor as if they had had their lunch.

Joṭṛi then asks Baṅguaṇ, the second vizier of Mahāsu to do the job. Amazingly, he is ready to pursue the revenge—however, only against a substantial remuneration: a deer-skin knapsack full of silver coins! A ludicrous situation: it is not a real relative, but only a fictional one, who is ready to help, and then only against a cash return. He is furthermore not a warrior, but the 'colleague' of the vizier who is responsible for the whole mess. And in the course of the punitive campaign conducted by a family member of Baṅguaṇ, not only the actual culprits are killed but, ironically, also the son of the first vizier, Bidi Goicaṇ. And so it goes. In this way, the viziers of Mahāsu appear to temporarily assume the role of the Khūnd.

Incongruity is also evident in the ceremonial song sung at marriages, one verse of which I have used as the title of this essay. It originates from a so-called *māṅgal* song from Garhwal. It can be found in a collection of songs published in 1956. *Māṅgal* corresponds to the Hindi *maṅgal, māṅgalik* 'auspicious, propitious'. These māṅgal songs are sung at weddings and they comment in their own way upon the various stages of the marriage.

The last stage before the *kanyādāna* rite is called *gotroccār* '*gotra*-recital'. The pundits have to announce in a loud voice the *gotra* and *pravara,* that is the subdivision of the caste and the lineage of the bride and the groom (Pandey 1976: 214). The māṅgal song sung at this point in Garhwal goes:

> Daughter, O daughter, I want to color you with saffron
> I want to perfume you with musk and massage you with sandalwood.

Name, O daughter, your *gotra.*
(Bride): 'My mother is *Parvatī* and father *Mahādeva*
and my maternal uncle[17] is the son of sages.'[18]
That is precisely the descent of a virgin.

Son, O son, I want to colour you with saffron
Want to perfume you with musk
Name, O son, your *gotra*
(Groom): 'My mother is an Apsarā, the father a Kṣatriya,[19]
and my maternal uncle is the son of Gandharvas.'
Such is the descent of the groom.

That is the song. Now, it is clear what gives rise to humour here. Not because it would sound comic to say that one's mother is a nymph (Apsarā) but because the bride and the groom are portrayed as belonging to different and incongruous classes or castes: the bride from an upper-caste family and the groom from a lower, rather dubious one. Similar tones are set in other humorous māṅgal songs. For example: the bride is fair, the groom dark; or she comes from an upper-caste family (*sukul*), whereas he is the son of an ironsmith or a cobbler, etc. (see also Pandey 1975: 123, 358; Joshi 1971: 141ff.)

Without going into a comprehensive analysis of affinal relations, so much is clear about this song: first, it mockingly suggests a hypogamous *pratiloma* ('unnatural') marriage; second, the naming of the two gotras and pravaras in the song is nothing but the description of two so-called atoms of relationships that stand opposed to each other. Lévi Strauss says that the real elementary relationship structure, the relationship atom, consists of a husband, a wife, a child, and a representative of the group from which the one (husband) has received the other (wife) (see Oppitz 1975: 109f.). The relationship atom thus consists of four elements, and the representative whom Lévi Strauss speaks of is, of course, the maternal uncle, *māmā* in north India. Precisely this atom is found in the māṅgal song.

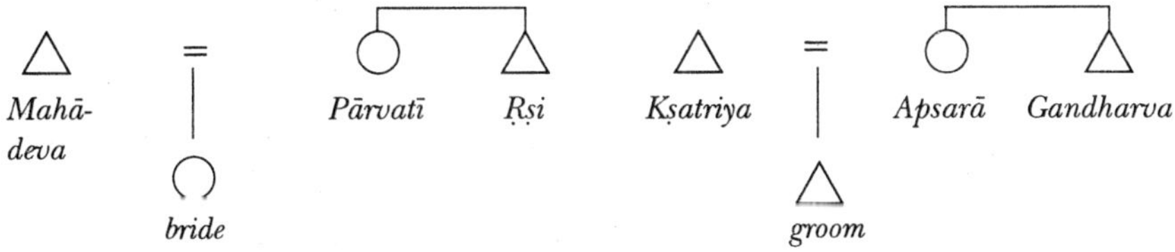

The first incongruity results from the mimicry of the serious announcement of the family backgrounds of bride and groom. But there are two more incongruities. The first is an inversion of the normal situation, in which the wife-giving family is lower ranked than the wife-taking family. Even if the song does not appear transparent to the reader, there are many other passages in the māṅgal songs which provide ample evidence for the (sometimes literal) denigration of the groom and his family. The second incongruity is a shift away from the highly ethical divine couple Sītā and Rāma, who appear in many other wedding songs sung before and after this ceremony. This leads to a split into the opposing 'couples' Mahādeva and Pārvatī, and Kṣatriya and nymph. Neither of the two represents a paradigmatic husband and wife, although I have to emphasize that Mahādeva and Pārvatī are more venerated and esteemed in the Garhwal hills than Sītā and Rāma are. On the other hand, there is a touch of indecent sex inherent in both the 'funny' couples. However, whereas the atom of the bride's family is unambiguously marked as positive, the atom of the groom's family is ambiguous in several ways.

Let us first of all consider the word Kṣatriya. One might perhaps wonder why Kṣatriya should be ambiguous. Before I explain, I must point out that the verse which I have cited earlier does not exactly represent the Garhwali original. As regards the words Apsarā and Gandharva, they are not Garhwali but borrowed words. Nevertheless, it is clear that Apsarā implies on the one hand the divine dancers at Indra's court in heaven and on the other hand lower-caste professional dancers who at times even sell their bodies and who wander in the hills together with their male accompanists. Gandharva has a similar double meaning. They are the divine musicians who live with the Apsarās; but the word is also a euphemism for wandering percussionists (drummers) of a lower caste.

Additionally, the word Kṣatriya is nowhere to be found in the text; the word Khatri appears instead. Khatri does originate from the word Kṣatriya, but apart from 'warrior' it can also mean 'trader'. So also this word is ambiguous. I have taken the liberty of using Kṣatriya because Khatri is not widely understood, unlike the words Apsarā and Gandharva, which are. Khatri means not only Kṣatriya but also denotes a caste of traders and officials (clerks), found mainly in the Punjab (Crooke 1980: 109f.). In many areas it is actually a respected caste; all or almost all the Sikh gurus were Khatris. On the other hand, it is interesting that in jokes and sayings the Khatris are always described as cowards.

Thus one sees that the relationship atom of the groom is ambiguous as opposed to the unambiguously positive one of the bride. For one thing, this is related to the fact that in the part of Garhwal which the song originates from, Khatri traders or Baniyās are frequently looked down upon. Hence if we were to interpret Khatri as trader then the negative relationship atom would 'read' thus: the father of the groom is a trader and the mother his concubine/mistress, and as a result the groom an illegitimate child. But that is not all. Normally female professional dancers and their accompanists form a married couple;

therefore, they cannot be consanguine. But that is exactly what is said in the verse: the uncle of the groom is the pimp of the mother.

This is one semantic level of the verse. On another level we have the heavenly nymph, her heavenly accompanist, and the earthly Kṣatriya. The incongruity of this second group must be explained differently. Namely: it is not the Khatri himself who is viewed negatively, but the relationship between the earthly, mortal Kṣatriya and the divine, immortal nymph. For this, too, is a kind of *pratiloma*-relation like the earlier one between the low-caste groom and the high-caste bride. And this entire configuration reminds one of an old, famous Indian myth, the story of Urvaśī and Purūravas. Purūravas was a mortal Kṣatriya king, Urvaśī an immortal divine nymph. As is well known, their relationship was unstable and of a short duration; eventually the Gandharvas managed to smuggle her back into heaven and, according to the version in *Śatapatha-brāhmaṇa* xi.5.1.1ff., Purūravas pleaded with the Gandharvas to transform him into one of them. In this way he could change an 'unnatural' hypogamous relationship into an 'endogamous' one.

It is difficult to say how this story from ancient India should have left its traces in the wedding song. The basic pattern of the story, however, reappears in Garhwali oral tales which tell of unhappy love stories between shepherds and *ăchari*-fairies.[20] Thus it surely looks as if such hypogamous relationships are somehow illegal and unstable and sometimes even comic and ephemeral. The vedic hymns about Purūravas and Urvaśī abound in frivolous and flippant remarks. At the same time, the relationship between such persons also seems to inherently possess a distinct generative potential. Purūravas and Urvaśī are identified, in the *Śatapatha-brāhmaṇa* iii.4.1, 22 in the context of *soma* sacrifice, with the two components of the fire-beater: he with the beating rod and she with the beating block. And lighting a fire with a beater is compared with the process of biological creation (Winternitz 1981: 156). This may be a widespread concept in South Asia.[21]

I have heard people say in the Himalaya that Brahman girls are crazy after Kṣatriya boys very often. And the belief about illegitimate children of parents from different castes is that they are much healthier and stronger than the legitimate ones. In the light of the stories and songs presented earlier, many of which have something of the obscene and not quite right in it (a sign of healthiness?), and since it is an essential feature of humour as such, according to Funk and Wagnalls, to have 'something of the obscene and not quite right in it' (1972: 608), the finicky and academic *Brockhaus* definition of humour quoted at the beginning of this essay is perhaps not as stupid as it sounds. Perhaps it is even funny?

NOTES

1. There is no exact English counterpart to this German word. Russian *ostranenie* seems to convey a similar meaning, but not the English *alienation.*
2. 'In der Literatur ist reiner Humor als Ausfluβ eines duldsamen Lebensgefühls . . . im Altertum und Mittelalter selten.'
3. My notion of bisociation slightly deviates here from the concept in the bisociation theory of Koestler mentioned in the introduction. According to Koestler, bisociation is 'the perceiving of a situation or idea . . . in two self-consistent but habitually incompatible frames of reference' (1964: 35). However, I understand bisociation here as a simultaneous association of someone or something with two different complexes of ideas.
4. North-west Garhwal Himalaya between the valleys of the rivers Tons and Pabar.
5. For a detailed account of the historical background, see Zoller 1997.
6. The name *Mahāsu* in fact designates four brother deities who rule over a vast stretch of land in western Garhwal and eastern Himachal Pradesh.
7. A detailed treatment of the two types of power is given in Zoller 1996 and forthcoming.
8. The refrains have been omitted.
9. The continual alternation between past and present tense, which may appear somewhat strange to the reader, is not the expression of an imperfect control over the language by the singers. Its basic function is actually a change of focus, with the present tense intensifying the plot.
10. An epithet meaning roughly 'Lord of countless people'.
11. She means Bidi.
12. Namely, with his archenemy Phandaṭo who killed nine men from Dalu's village.
13. An idiomatic expression meanig brandy and a hot bath.
14. Women in Bangan address representatives of the lordship, for instance, a king or the viziers of a deity, as if they were members of their parental family.
15. Both are connected with *tāp* 'heat', and the 'psycho-physiological' processes which lead to sexual excitement and to fighting intoxication are supposed to be very similar. See Zoller forthcoming.
16. This last word means the same as Goitsaṇ, i.e. the vizier.
17. *Māmā.*
18. *Ṛṣis.*
19. *Khatri.*
20. The word *āchari* is a derivation from Sanskrit *apsarā.*
21. Note that important persons of the *Mahābhārata* have similar couples as parents, i.e. the father either a king or a belligerent ascetic, and the mother either a river goddess or a nymph: Kṛpī, daughter of Jālapadī and Gautama Śaradvat; Droṇa, son of Ghṛtācī and Bharadvāja, Bhīṣma, son of Śantanu and Gaṅgā, etc.

REFERENCES

Apte, M.L. 1985. *Humor and Laughter. An Anthropological Approach.* London: Cornell University Press.

Attardo, S. 1994. *Linguistic Theories of Humor.* Berlin: Mouton de Gruyter.

Bachtin, M.M. 1990. *Literatur und Karneval. Zur Romantheorie und Lachkultur.* Frankfurt: Fischer.

Crooke, W. 1980 (1907). *Natives of Northern India.* Delhi: Royal Reprints.

Galey, J.-C. 1992. 'Hindu Kingship in its Ritual Realm: The Garhwali Configuration.' In: M.P. Joshi, A.C. Fanger and Ch. W. Brown (eds.) 1992. *Himalaya: Past and Present,* vol. II (1991-2). Shree Almora Book Depot, Almora [ASH (Association of Studies on Himalayas) Publication Series, 3]: 173-237.

Joshi, K. 1971. *Kumāũṁ kā Lok Sāhitya (Paricayātmak Saṃgrah).* Bareilly: Prakash Book Depot.

Koestler, A. 1964. *The Act of Creation.* London: Hutchinson.

Leach, M. (ed.) and J. Fried (ass. ed.) 1972 (1949-50). *Funk and Wagnalls Standard Dictionary of Folklore, Mythology, and Legend.* Reissue of the 1949-50 ed. with minor corrections.

Pandey, R.B. 1976 (1969). *Hindu Saṁskāras. Socio-Religious Study of the Hindu Sacraments.* Delhi: Motilal Banarsidass.

Pandey, T. 1975 (1962). *Kumāũṁ kā Lok Sāhitya.* Almora: Sri Almora Book Depot.

Winternitz, M. 1981. *A History of Indian Literature.* Delhi: Motilal Barnasidass.

Zoller, C.P. 1997. Heroic Ballads and the Biography of a Woman. On Coping with Conflicts in the Western Garhwal Himalayas. In: *Contributions to Comparative High Mountain Research: Pakistan-India-Nepal* (Cultural Area Karakorum, Scientific Papers, 3). Hamburg: Wezler.

———. Forthcoming. *Himalayan Heroes.*

